AVP
ALIENS VS. PREDATOR
THREE WORLD WAR

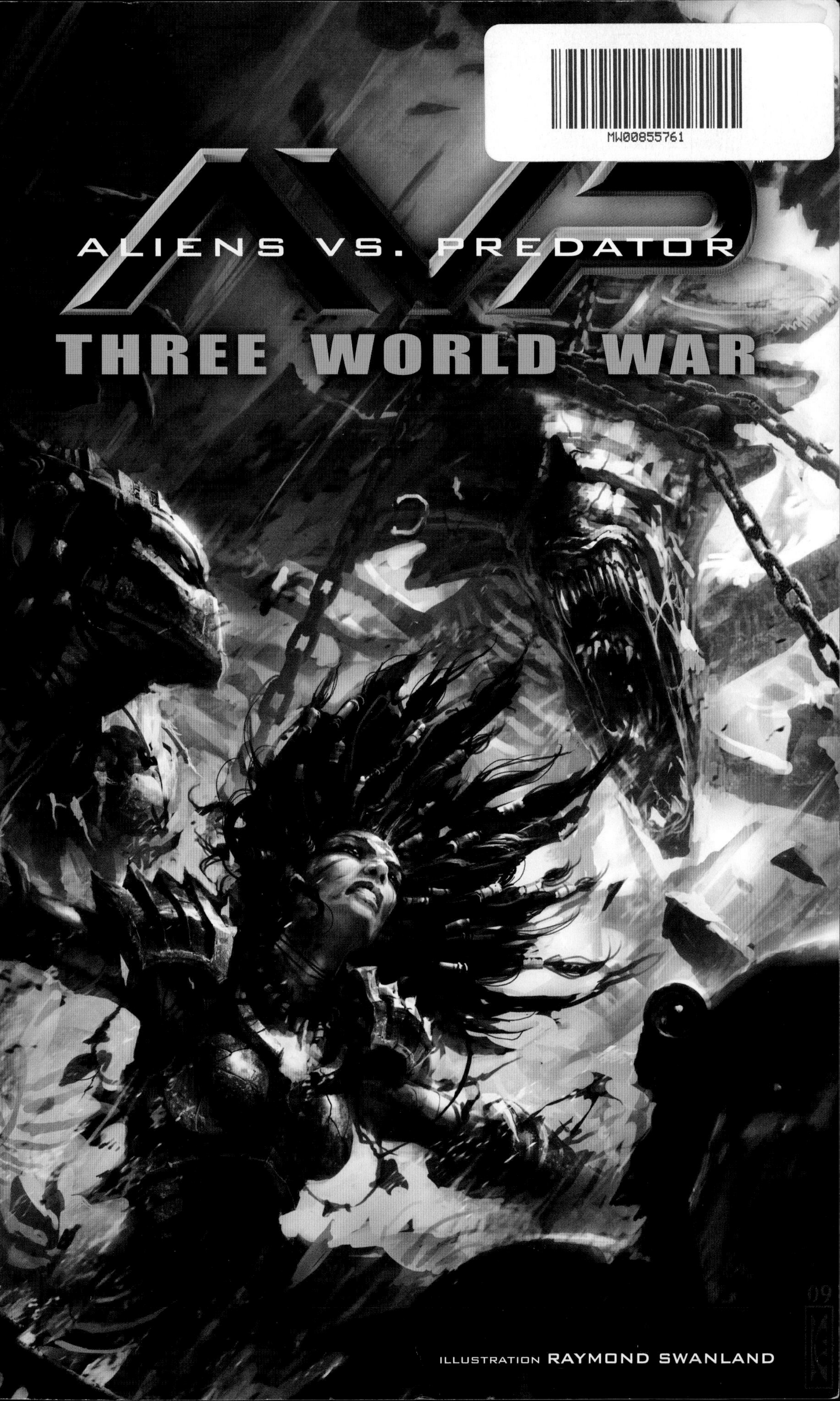

ILLUSTRATION RAYMOND SWANLAND

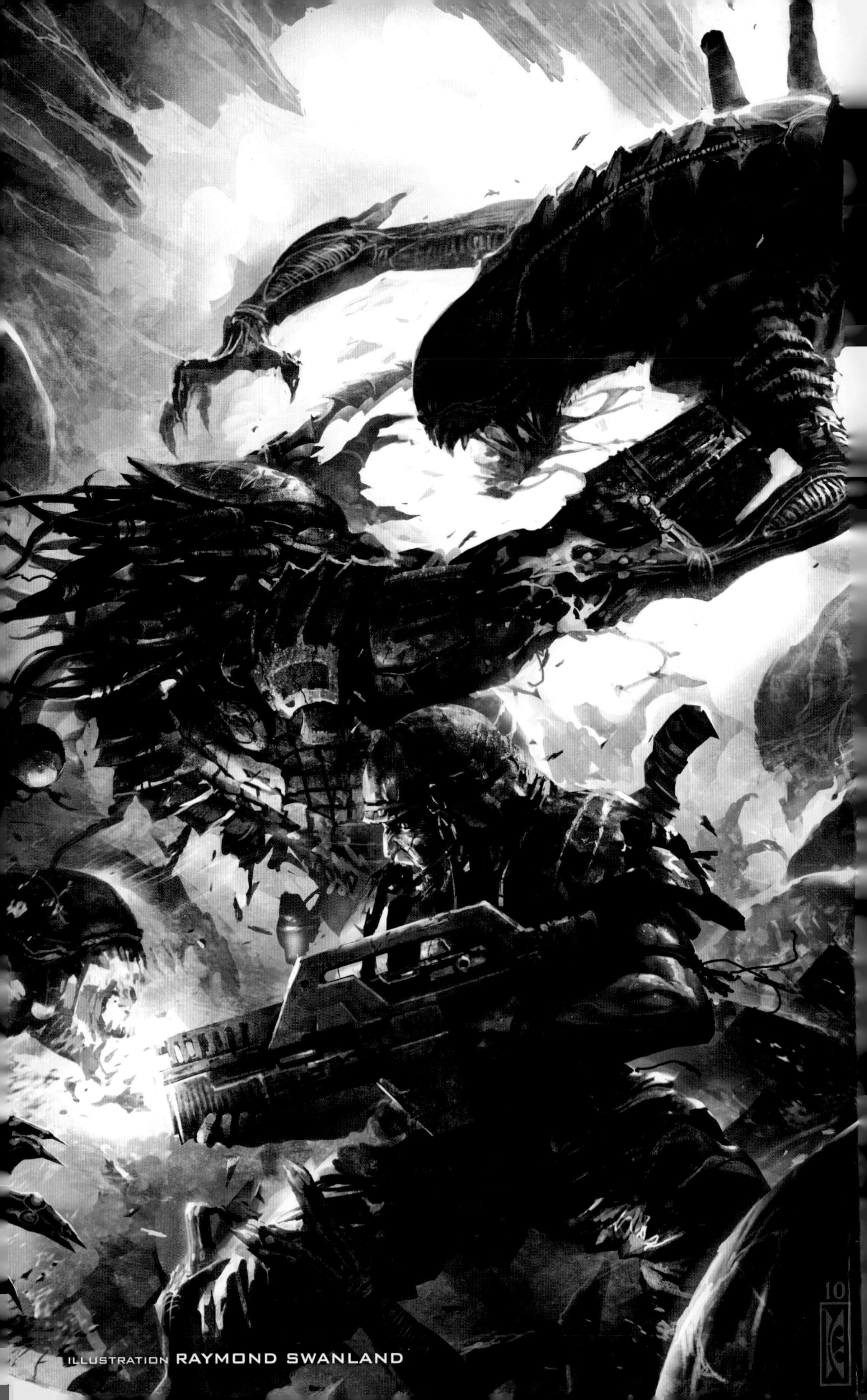

ILLUSTRATION RAYMOND SWANLAND

ALIENS VS. PREDATOR
THREE WORLD WAR

SCRIPT
RANDY STRADLEY

PENCILS
RICK LEONARDI

INKS
MARK PENNINGTON

COLORS
WES DZIOBA

LETTERING
BLAMBOT®

COVER ILLUSTRATION
RAYMOND SWANLAND

PUBLISHER	EDITOR	ASSOCIATE EDITOR	DESIGNER
MIKE RICHARDSON	CHRIS WARNER	SAMANTHA ROBERTSON	KAT LARSON

SPECIAL THANKS TO DEBBIE OLSHAN AT TWENTIETH CENTURY FOX LICENSING

This volume collects issues one through six of the Dark Horse
comic-book series *Aliens vs. Predator: Three World War.*

ALIENS VS. PREDATOR: THREE WORLD WAR

NEIL HANKERSON Executive Vice President • TOM WEDDLE Chief Financial Officer •
RANDY STRADLEY Vice President of Publishing • MICHAEL MARTENS Vice President of
Book Trade Sales • SCOTT ALLIE Editor in Chief • MATT PARKINSON Vice President of
Marketing • DAVID SCROGGY Vice President of Product Development • DALE LAFOUNTAIN
Vice President of Information Technology • DARLENE VOGEL Senior Director of Print,
Design, and Production • KEN LIZZI General Counsel • DAVEY ESTRADA Editorial Director
• CHRIS WARNER Senior Books Editor• DIANA SCHUTZ Executive Editor • CARY GRAZZINI
Director of Print and Development • LIA RIBACCHI Art Director • CARA NIECE Director
of Scheduling • MARK BERNARDI Director of Digital Publishing

Dark Horse Books
A division of Dark Horse Comics, Inc.
10956 SE Main Street
Milwaukie, OR 97222

DarkHorse.com

FoxMovies.com

To find a comics shop in your area, call the Comic Shop Locator Service
toll-free at 1-888-266-4226

First edition: June 2011
ISBN 978-1-59582-702-9

5 7 9 10 8 6 4

Printed in China

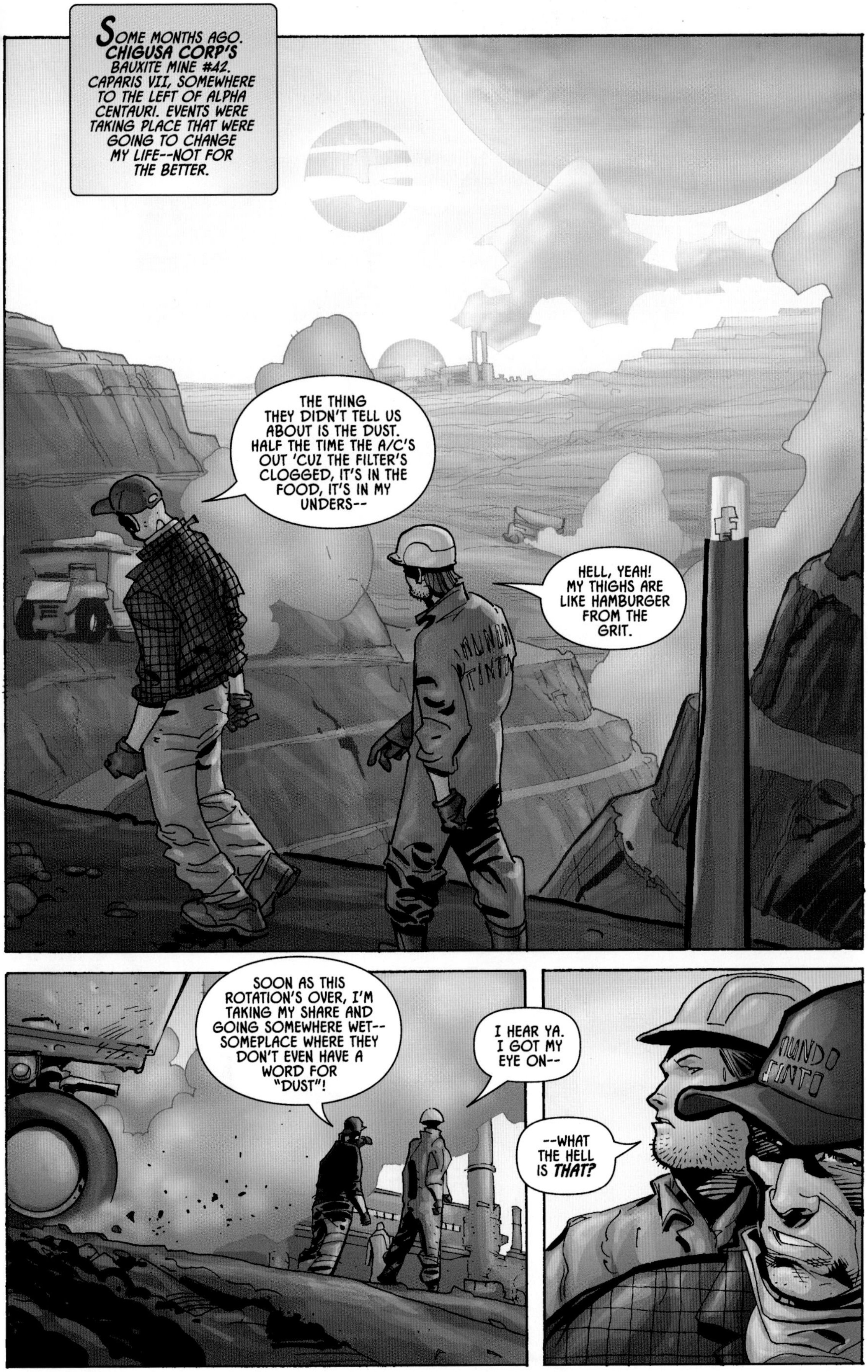
SOME MONTHS AGO. **CHIGUSA CORP'S** BAUXITE MINE #42. CAPARIS VII, SOMEWHERE TO THE LEFT OF ALPHA CENTAURI. EVENTS WERE TAKING PLACE THAT WERE GOING TO CHANGE MY LIFE--NOT FOR THE BETTER.
THE THING THEY DIDN'T TELL US ABOUT IS THE DUST. HALF THE TIME THE A/C'S OUT 'CUZ THE FILTER'S CLOGGED, IT'S IN THE FOOD, IT'S IN MY UNDERS--
HELL, YEAH! MY THIGHS ARE LIKE HAMBURGER FROM THE GRIT.
SOON AS THIS ROTATION'S OVER, I'M TAKING MY SHARE AND GOING SOMEWHERE WET-- SOMEPLACE WHERE THEY DON'T EVEN HAVE A WORD FOR "DUST"!
I HEAR YA. I GOT MY EYE ON--
MUNDO TINTO
--WHAT THE HELL IS ***THAT?***

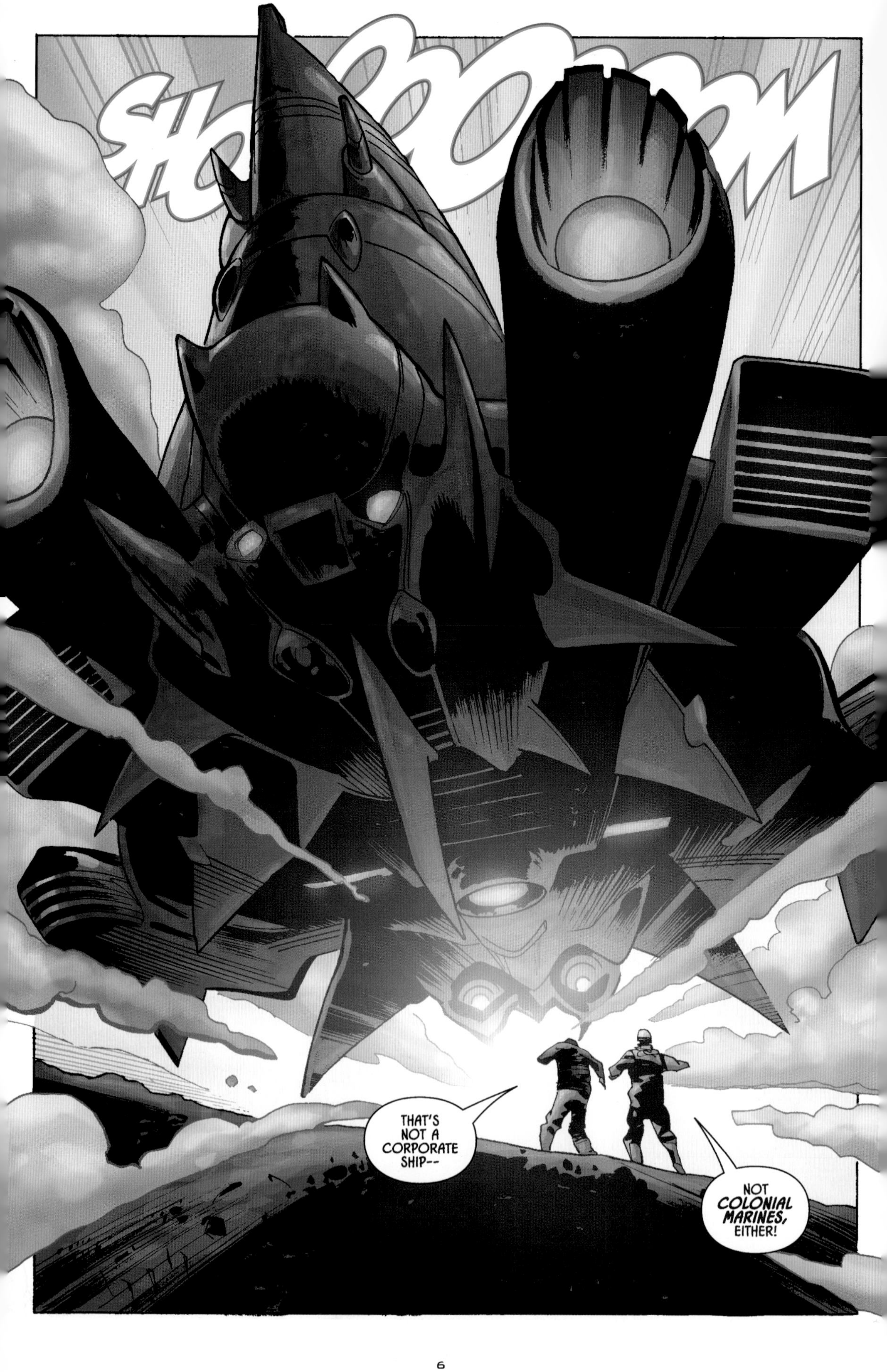
THAT'S NOT A CORPORATE SHIP--
NOT COLONIAL MARINES, EITHER!

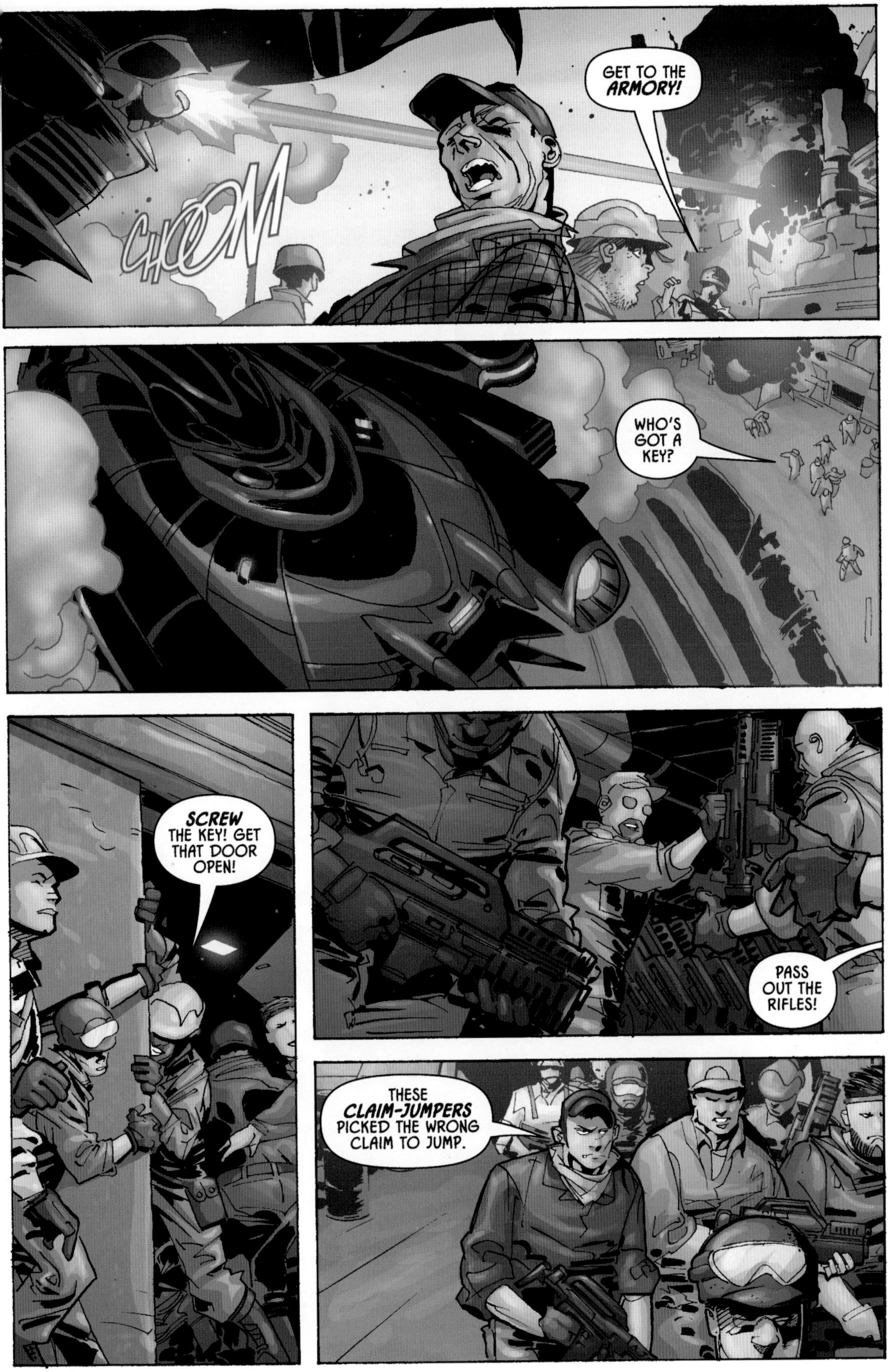
GET TO THE ARMORY!
CHOOM
WHO'S GOT A KEY?
SCREW THE KEY! GET THAT DOOR OPEN!
PASS OUT THE RIFLES!
THESE CLAIM-JUMPERS PICKED THE WRONG CLAIM TO JUMP.

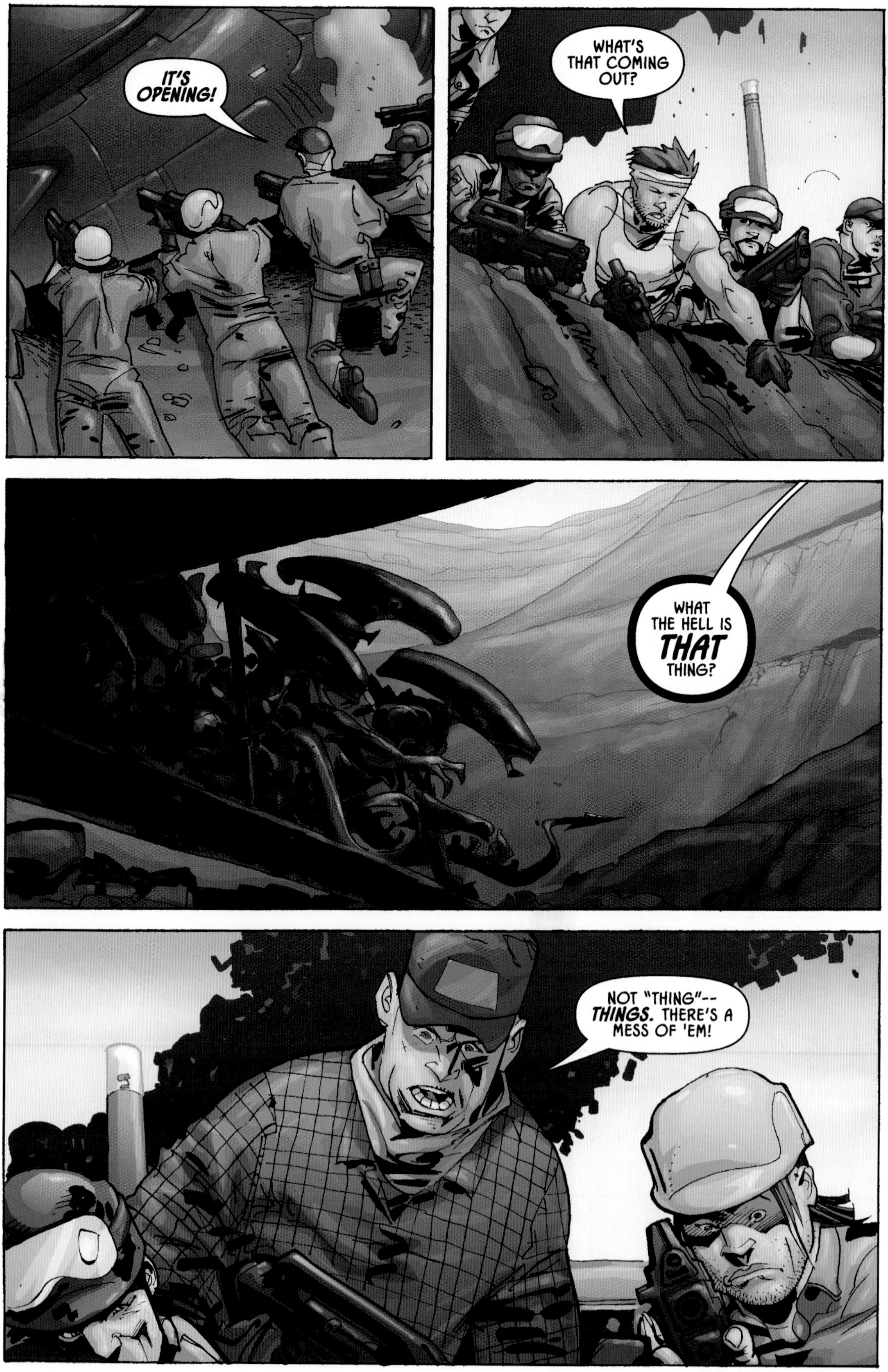
IT'S OPENING!
WHAT'S THAT COMING OUT?
WHAT THE HELL IS THAT THING?
NOT "THING"-- THINGS. THERE'S A MESS OF 'EM!

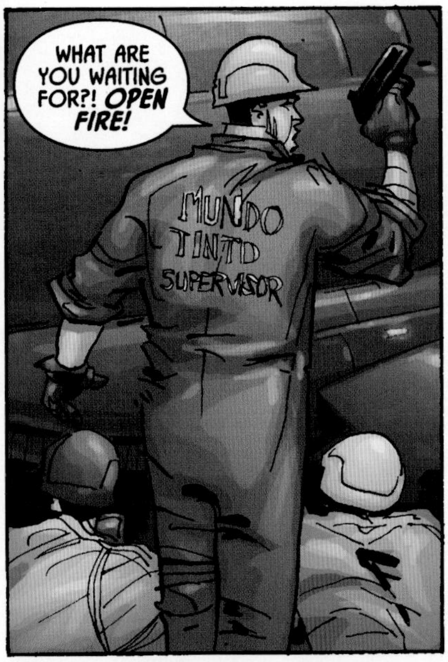
WHAT ARE YOU WAITING FOR?! OPEN FIRE!
MUNDO TINTO SUPERVISOR

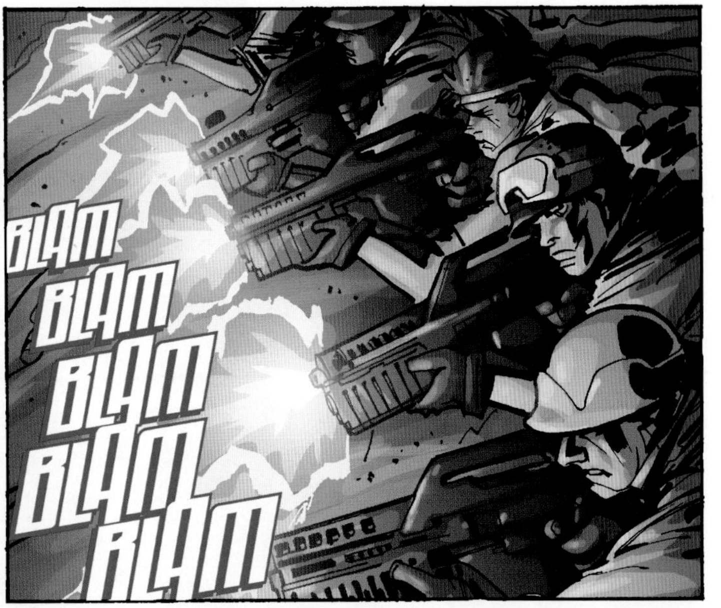
BLAM
BLAM
BLAM
BLAM
BLAM

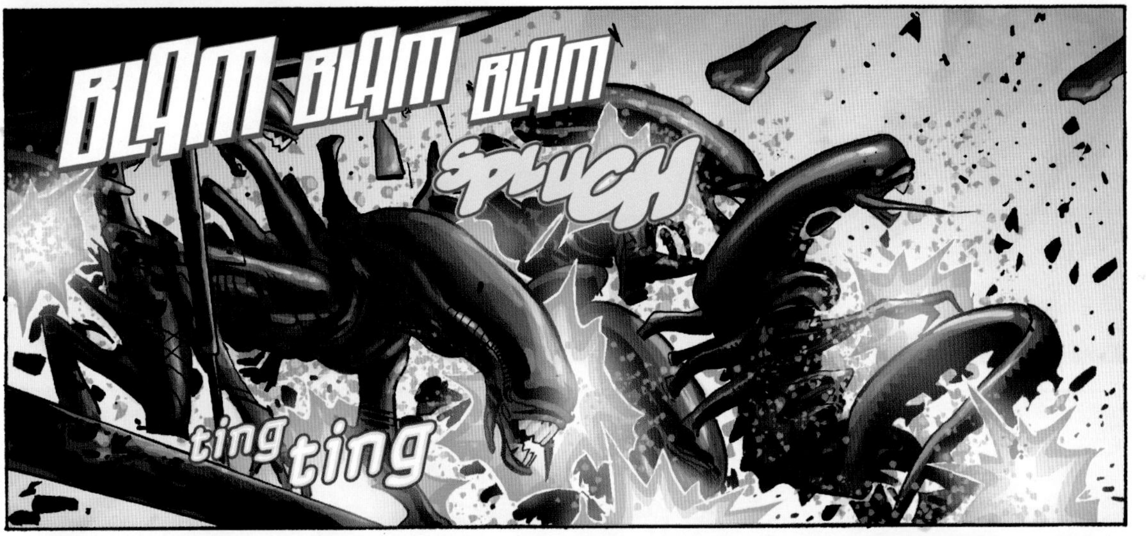
BLAM BLAM BLAM
SPLUCH
ting ting

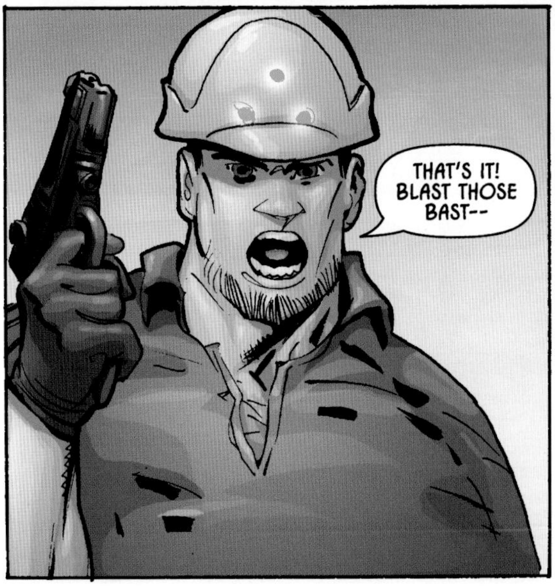
THAT'S IT! BLAST THOSE BAST--

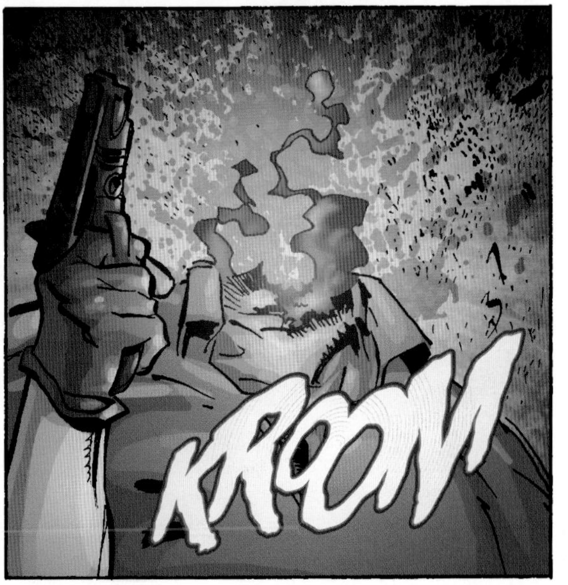
KROOM

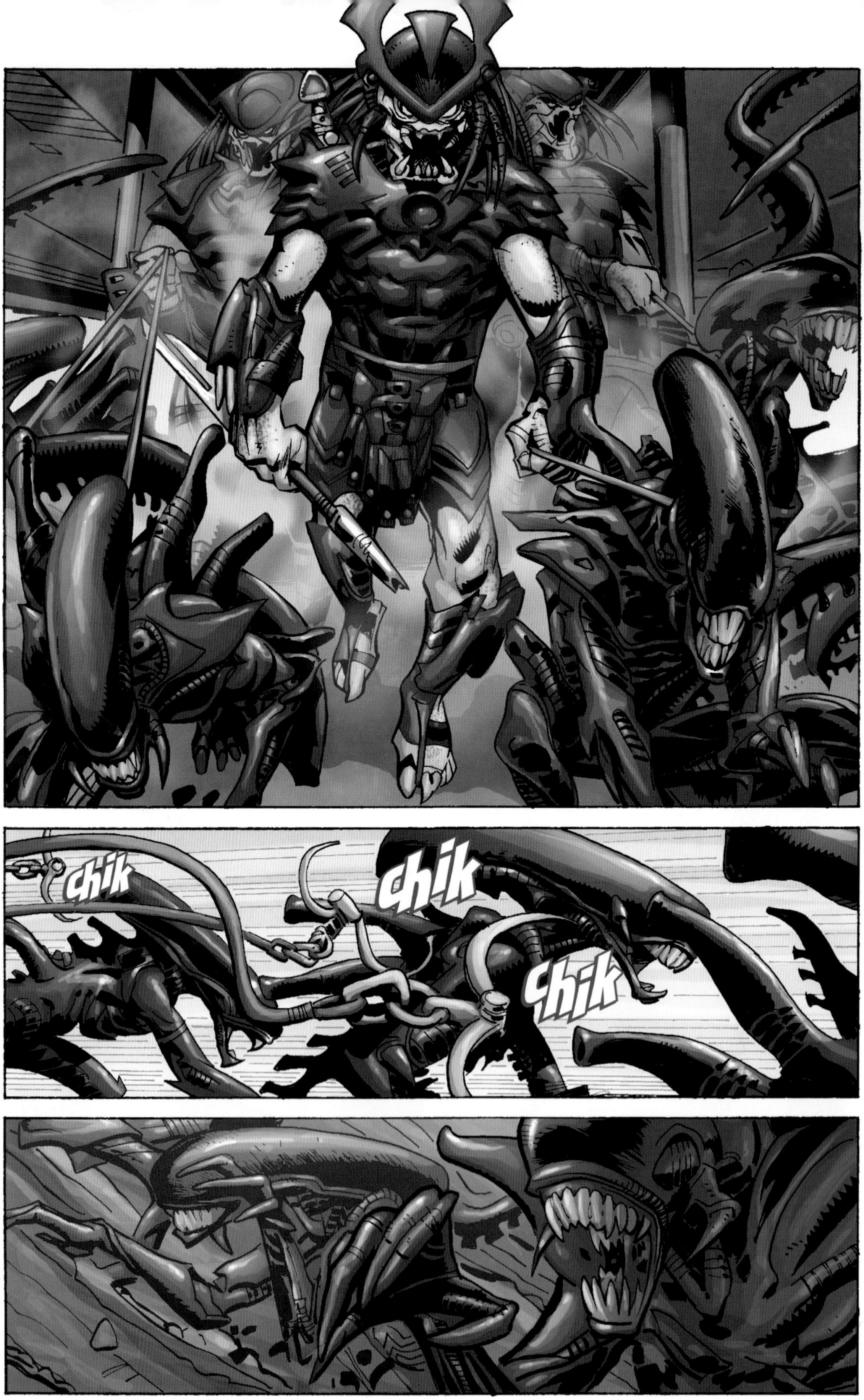
chik
chik
chik

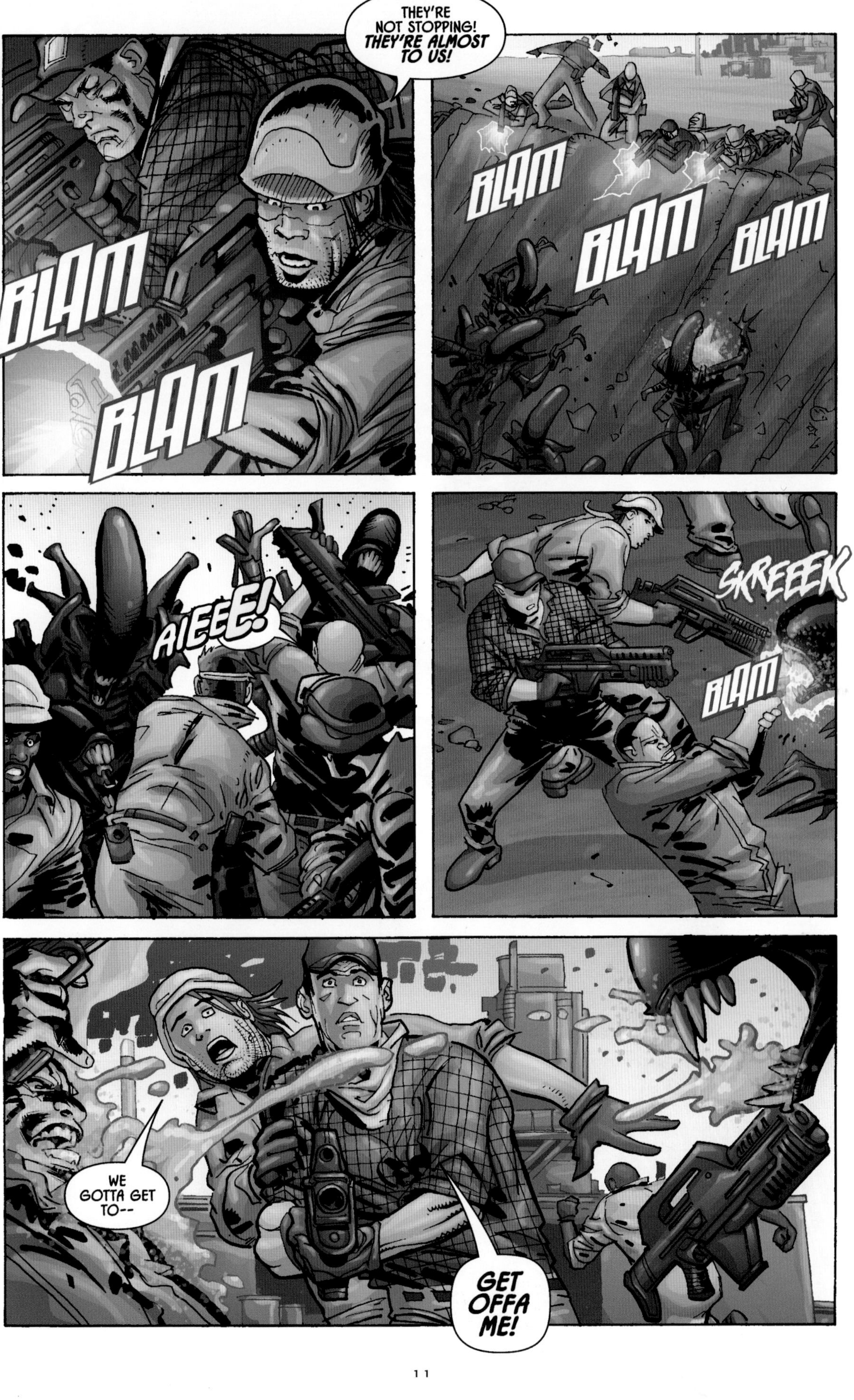
THEY'RE NOT STOPPING! THEY'RE ALMOST TO US!
BLAM
BLAM
BLAM
BLAM
BLAM
AIEEE!
SKREEEK
BLAM
WE GOTTA GET TO--
GET OFFA ME!

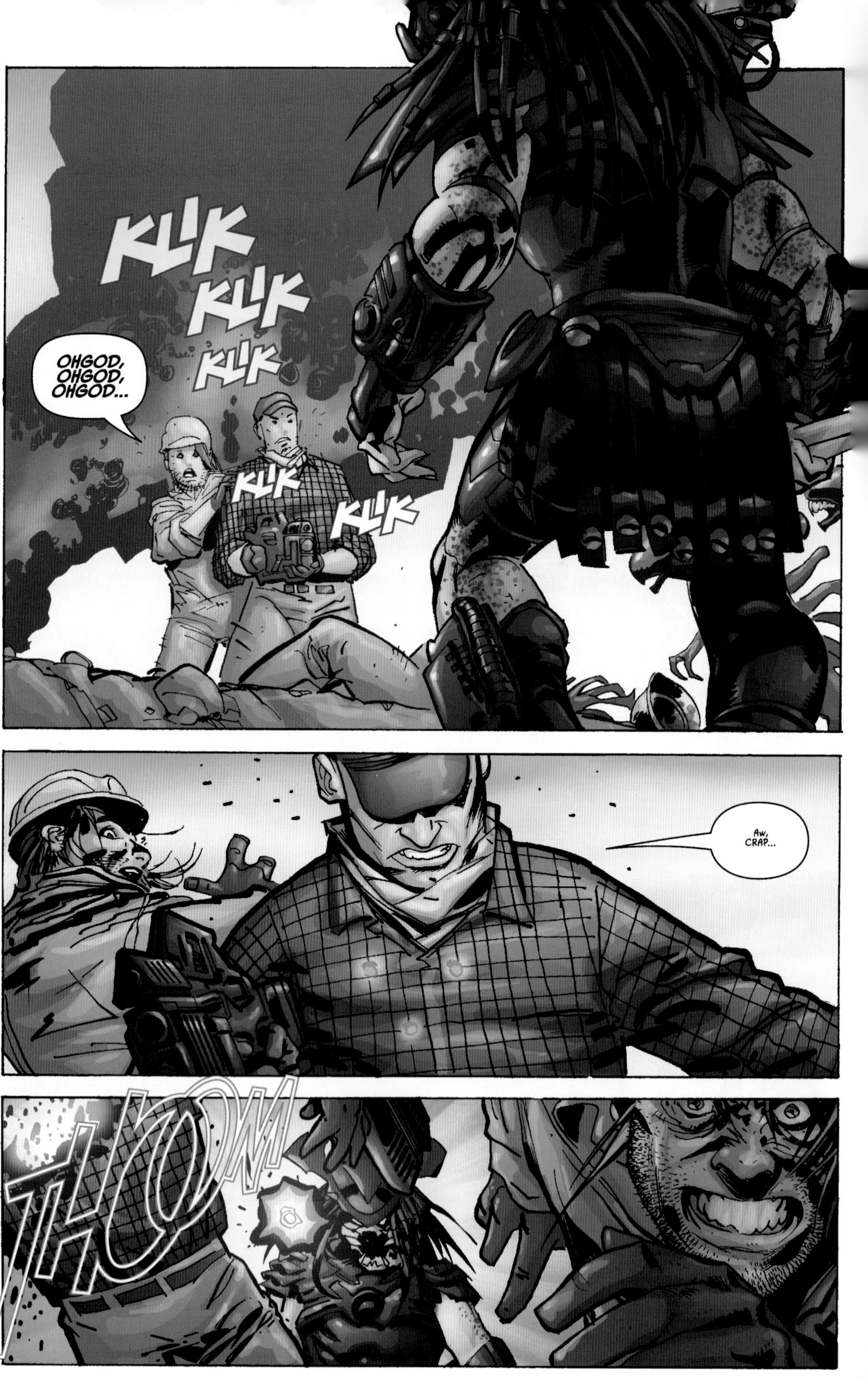
KLIK
KLIK
KLIK
OHGOD, OHGOD, OHGOD...
KLIK
KLIK
AW, CRAP...
THOOM

NO!
KRAK
KRTCH
SPLUT

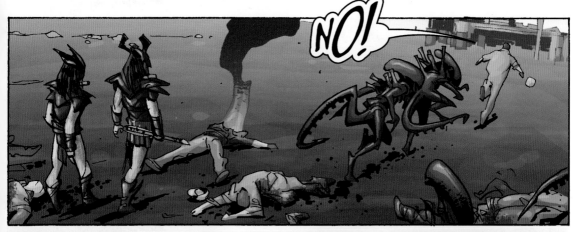

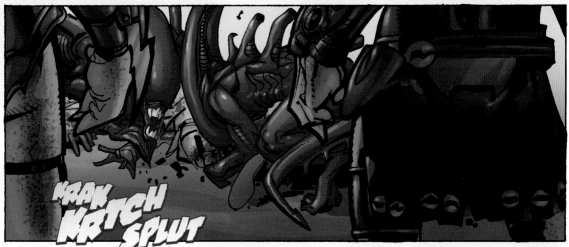

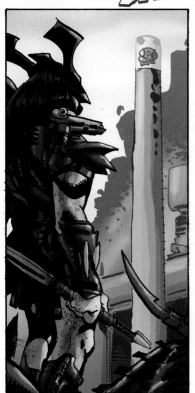

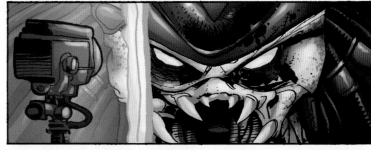

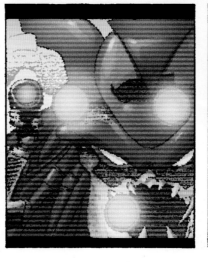

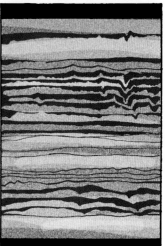

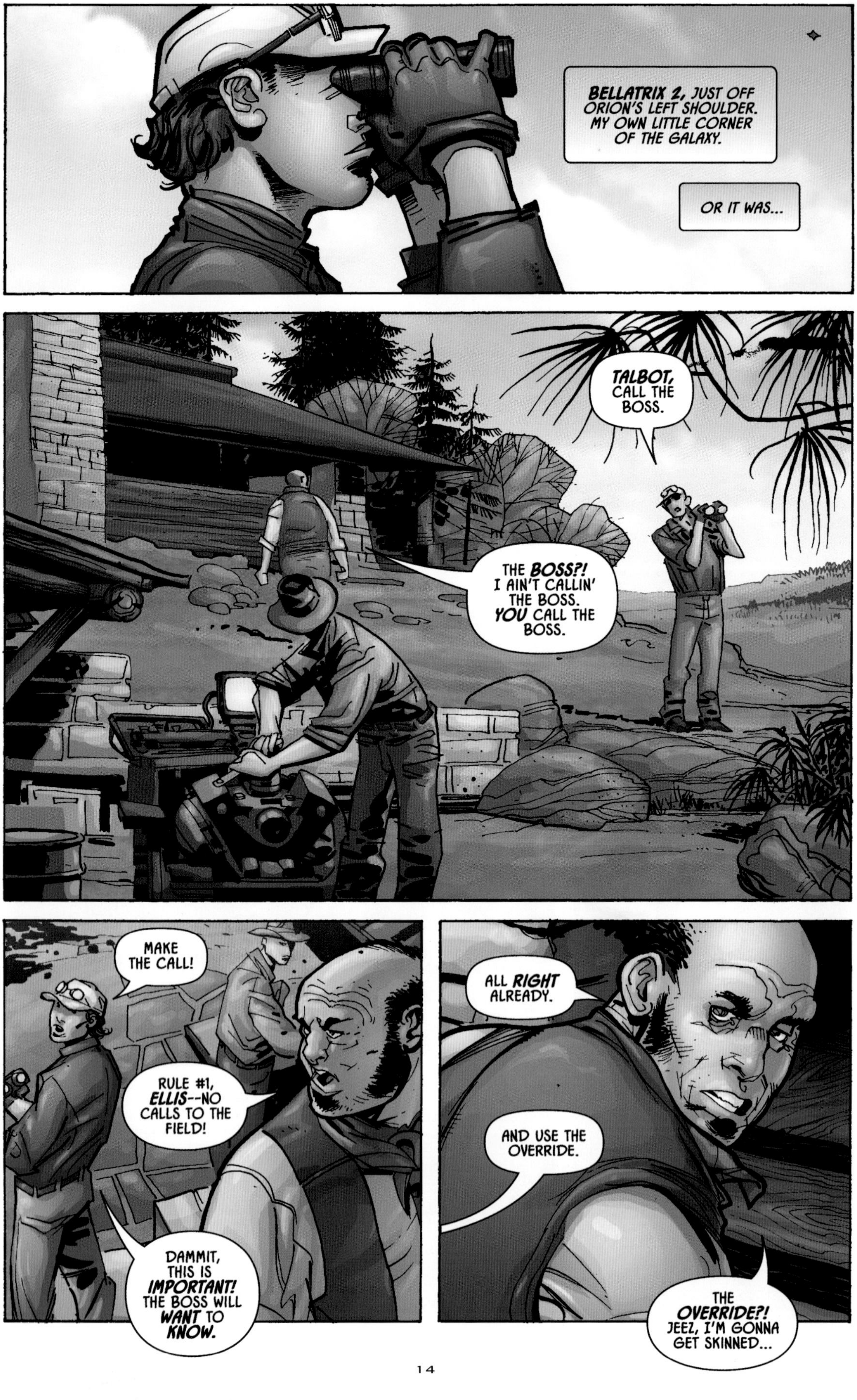
BELLATRIX 2, JUST OFF ORION'S LEFT SHOULDER. MY OWN LITTLE CORNER OF THE GALAXY.
OR IT WAS...
TALBOT, CALL THE BOSS.
THE BOSS?! I AIN'T CALLIN' THE BOSS. YOU CALL THE BOSS.
MAKE THE CALL!
RULE #1, ELLIS--NO CALLS TO THE FIELD!
DAMMIT, THIS IS IMPORTANT! THE BOSS WILL WANT TO KNOW.
ALL RIGHT ALREADY.
AND USE THE OVERRIDE.
THE OVERRIDE?! JEEZ, I'M GONNA GET SKINNED...

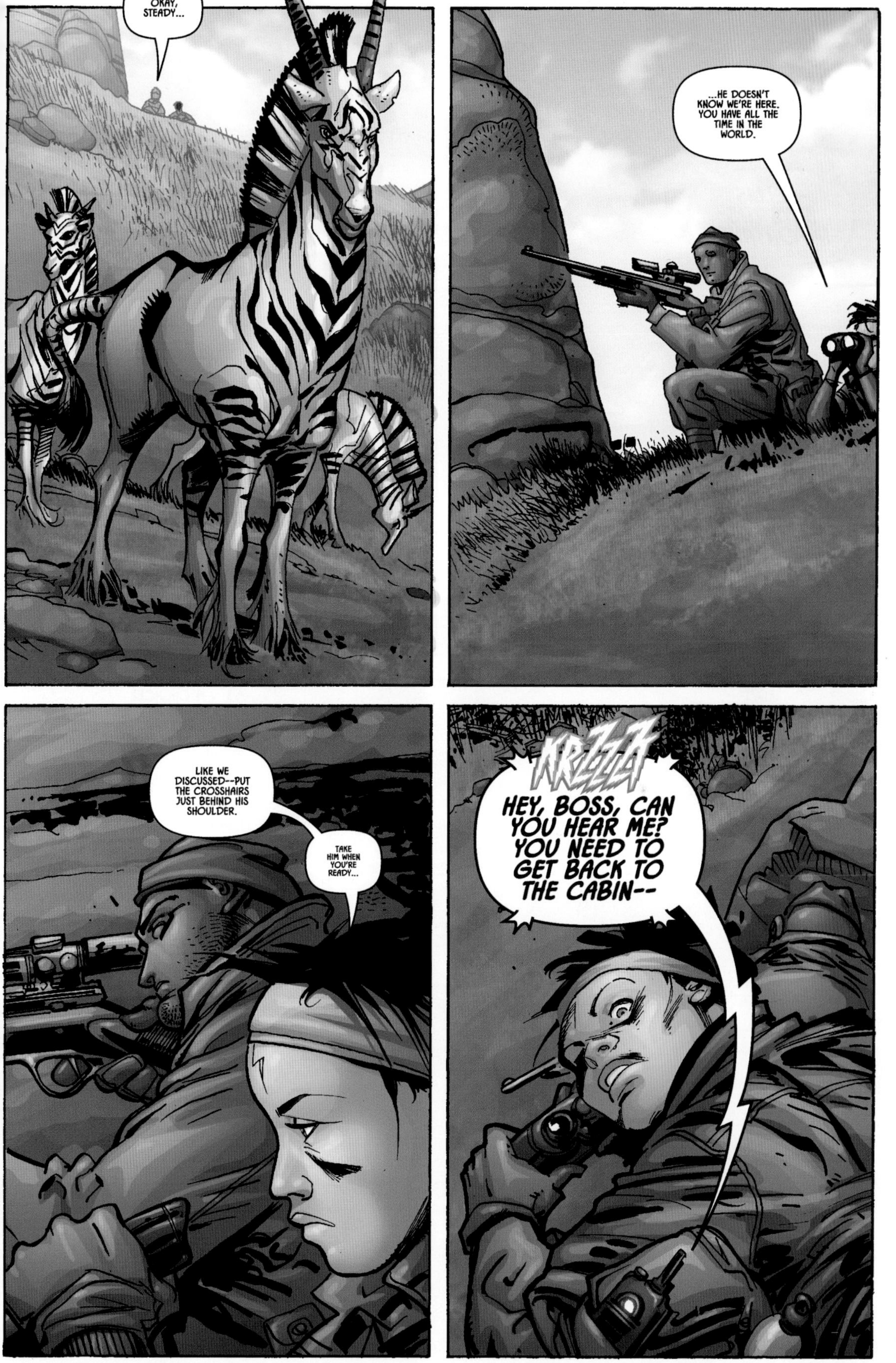
OKAY, STEADY...
...HE DOESN'T KNOW WE'RE HERE. YOU HAVE ALL THE TIME IN THE WORLD.
LIKE WE DISCUSSED--PUT THE CROSSHAIRS JUST BEHIND HIS SHOULDER.
TAKE HIM WHEN YOU'RE READY...
KRZZZT
HEY, BOSS, CAN YOU HEAR ME? YOU NEED TO GET BACK TO THE CABIN--

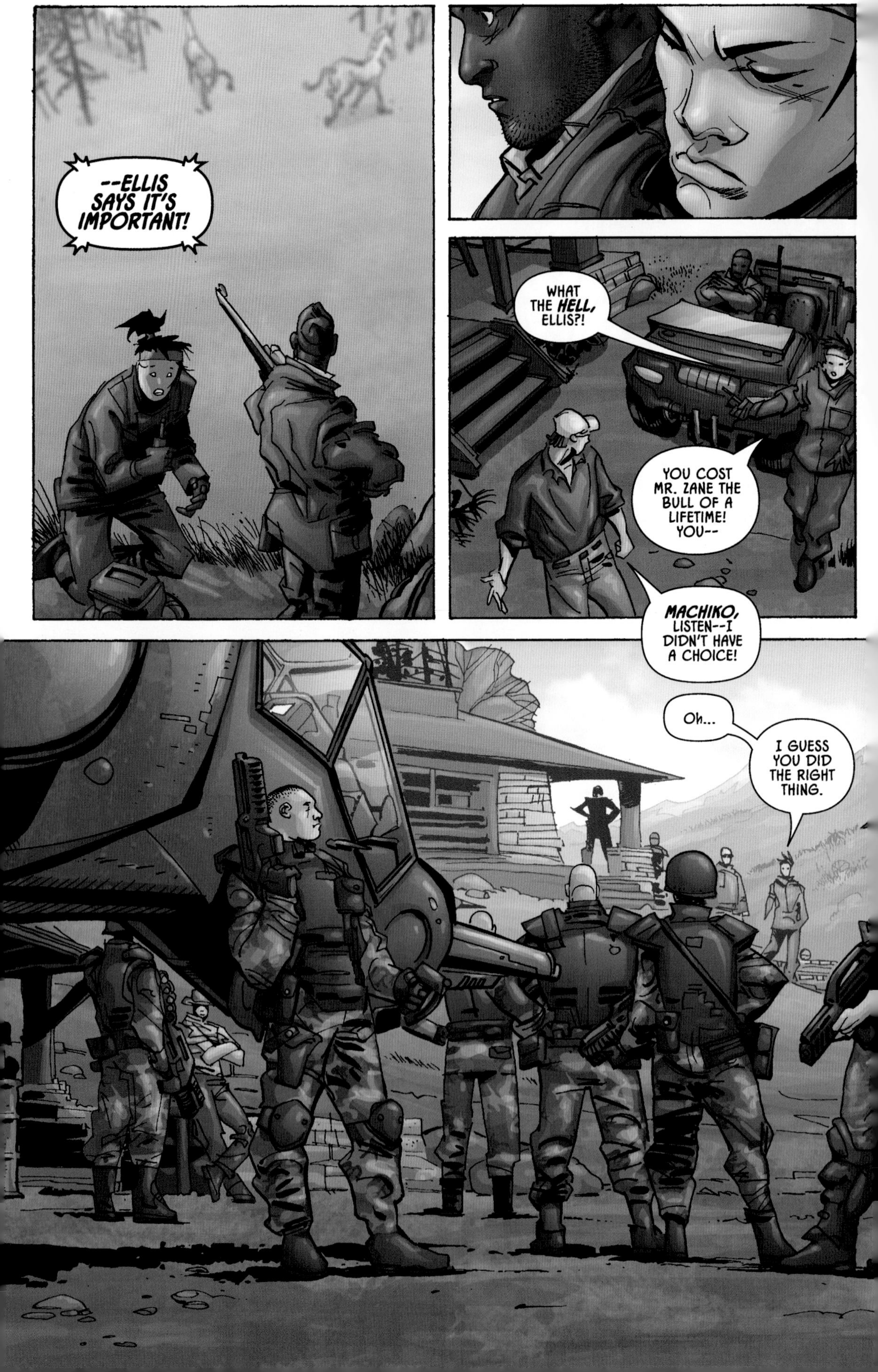
--ELLIS SAYS IT'S IMPORTANT!
WHAT THE HELL, ELLIS?!
YOU COST MR. ZANE THE BULL OF A LIFETIME! YOU--
MACHIKO, LISTEN--I DIDN'T HAVE A CHOICE!
Oh...
I GUESS YOU DID THE RIGHT THING.

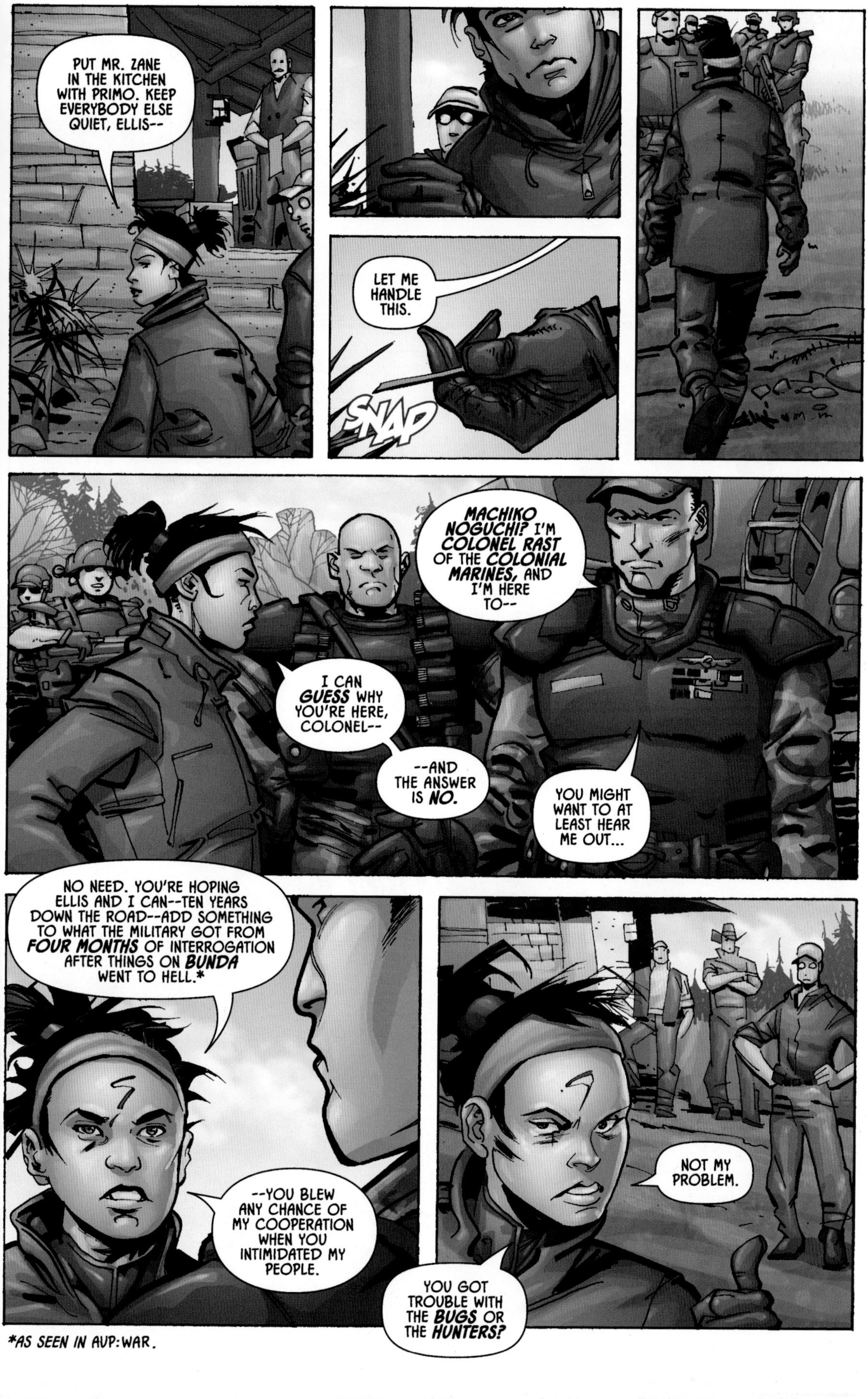
PUT MR. ZANE IN THE KITCHEN WITH PRIMO. KEEP EVERYBODY ELSE QUIET, ELLIS--
LET ME HANDLE THIS.
SNAP
MACHIKO NOGUCHI? I'M COLONEL RAST OF THE COLONIAL MARINES, AND I'M HERE TO--
I CAN GUESS WHY YOU'RE HERE, COLONEL--
--AND THE ANSWER IS NO.
YOU MIGHT WANT TO AT LEAST HEAR ME OUT...
NO NEED. YOU'RE HOPING ELLIS AND I CAN--TEN YEARS DOWN THE ROAD--ADD SOMETHING TO WHAT THE MILITARY GOT FROM FOUR MONTHS OF INTERROGATION AFTER THINGS ON BUNDA WENT TO HELL.*
--YOU BLEW ANY CHANCE OF MY COOPERATION WHEN YOU INTIMIDATED MY PEOPLE.
NOT MY PROBLEM.
YOU GOT TROUBLE WITH THE BUGS OR THE HUNTERS?

*AS SEEN IN AVP: WAR.

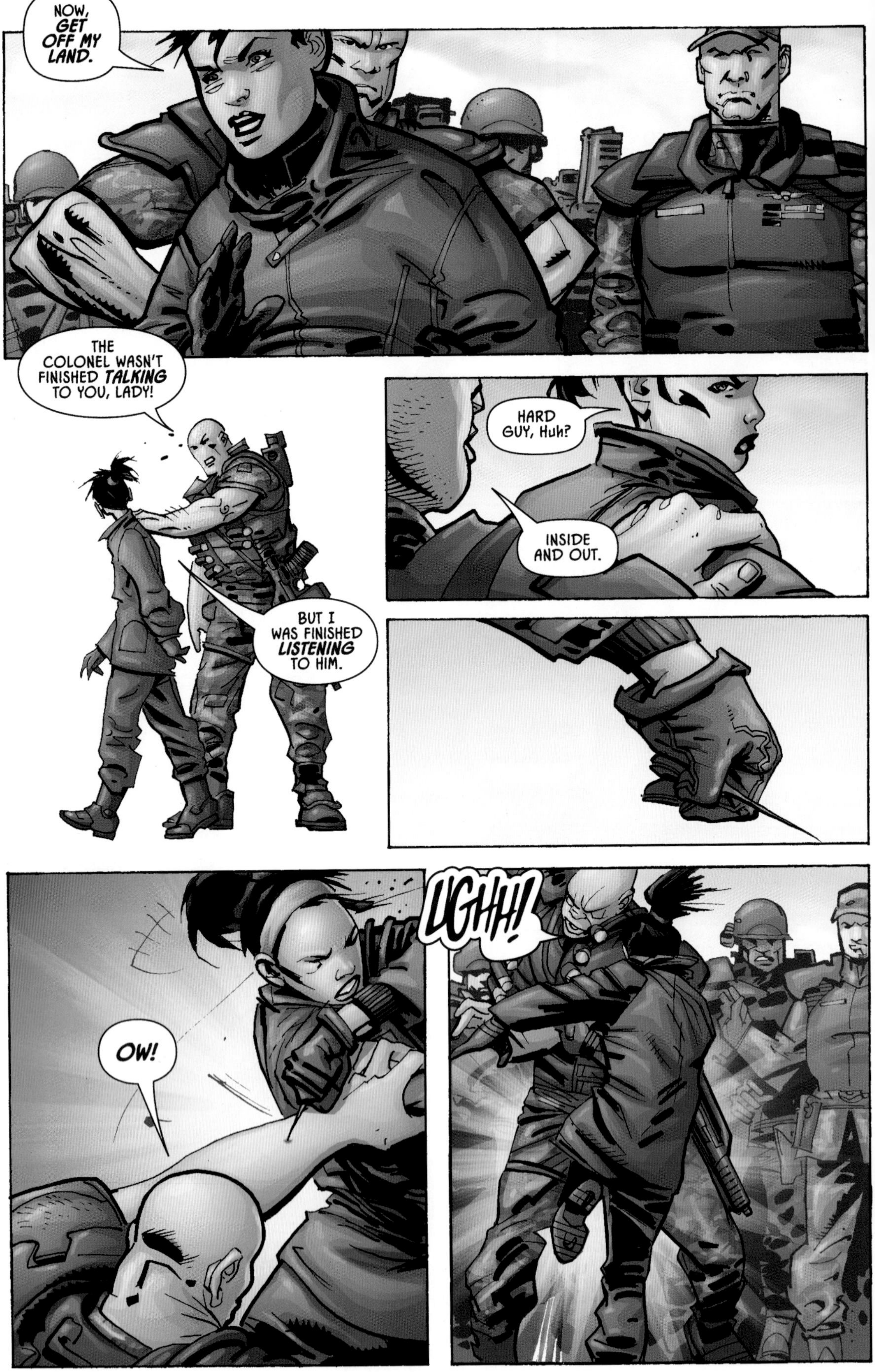
NOW, GET OFF MY LAND.
THE COLONEL WASN'T FINISHED TALKING TO YOU, LADY!
BUT I WAS FINISHED LISTENING TO HIM.
HARD GUY, Huh?
INSIDE AND OUT.
OW!
UGHH!

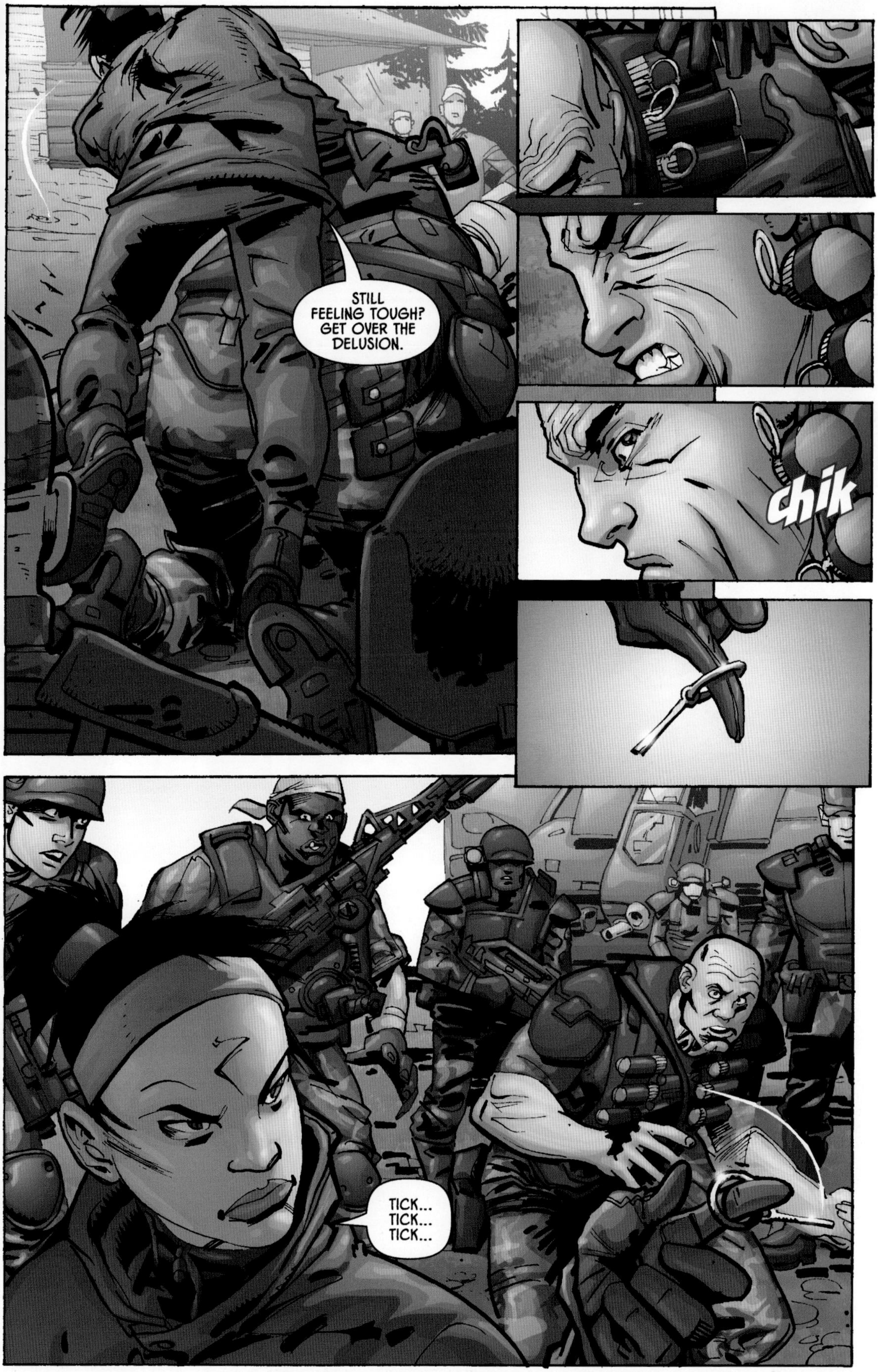
STILL FEELING TOUGH? GET OVER THE DELUSION.
chik
TICK... TICK... TICK...

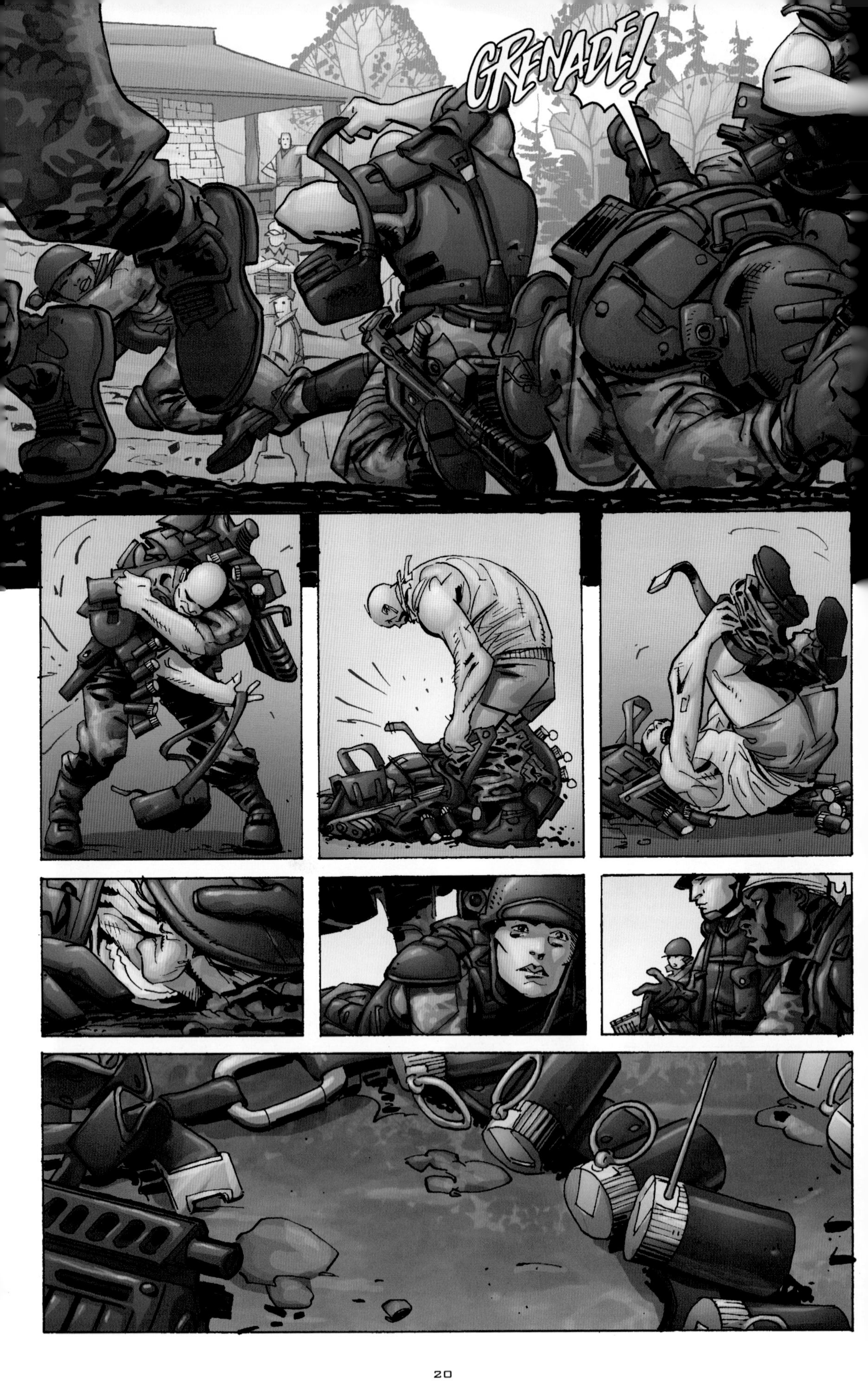
GRENADE!

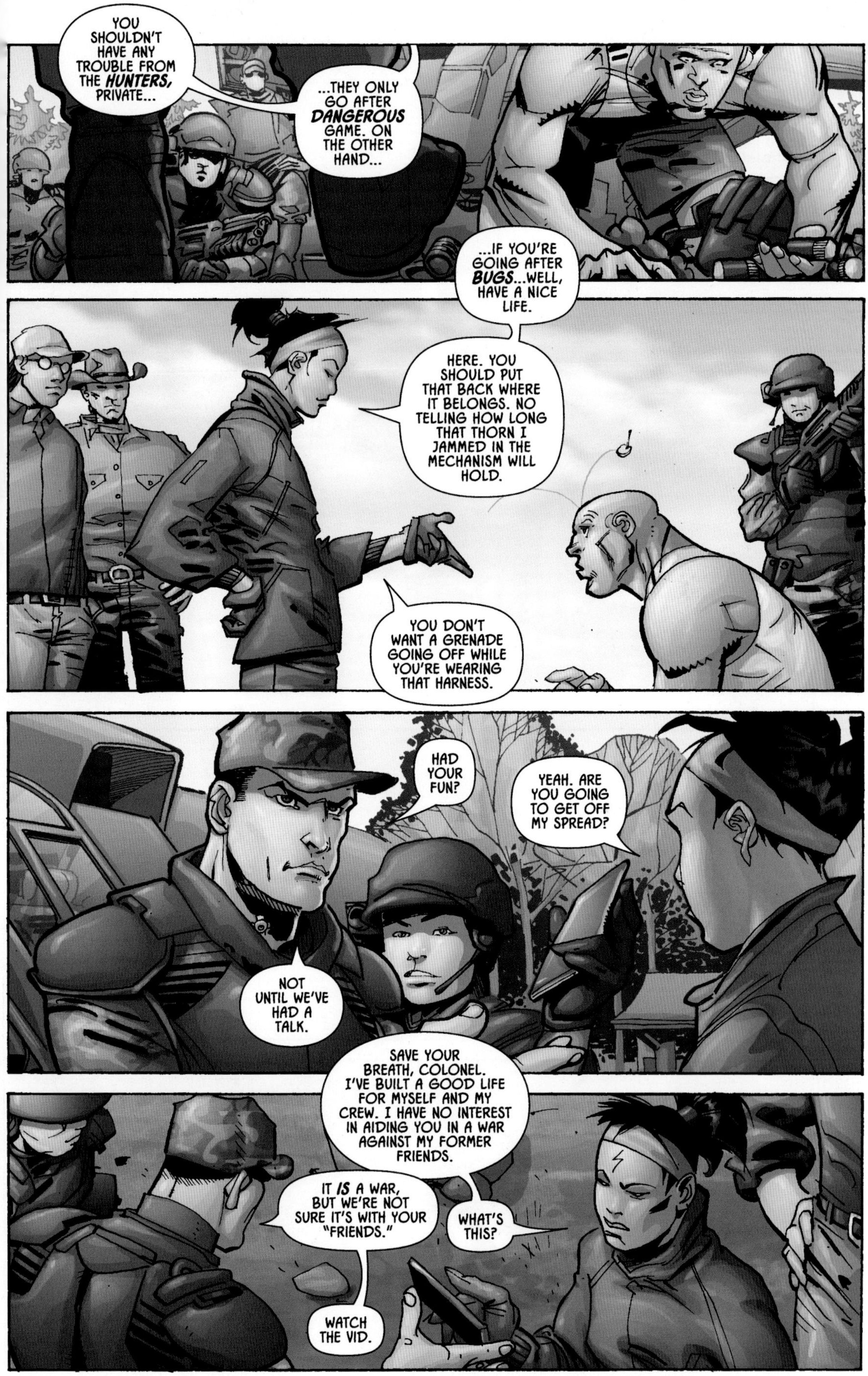
YOU SHOULDN'T HAVE ANY TROUBLE FROM THE HUNTERS, PRIVATE...
...THEY ONLY GO AFTER DANGEROUS GAME. ON THE OTHER HAND...
...IF YOU'RE GOING AFTER BUGS...WELL, HAVE A NICE LIFE.
HERE. YOU SHOULD PUT THAT BACK WHERE IT BELONGS. NO TELLING HOW LONG THAT THORN I JAMMED IN THE MECHANISM WILL HOLD.
YOU DON'T WANT A GRENADE GOING OFF WHILE YOU'RE WEARING THAT HARNESS.
HAD YOUR FUN?
YEAH. ARE YOU GOING TO GET OFF MY SPREAD?
NOT UNTIL WE'VE HAD A TALK.
SAVE YOUR BREATH, COLONEL. I'VE BUILT A GOOD LIFE FOR MYSELF AND MY CREW. I HAVE NO INTEREST IN AIDING YOU IN A WAR AGAINST MY FORMER FRIENDS.
IT IS A WAR, BUT WE'RE NOT SURE IT'S WITH YOUR "FRIENDS."
WHAT'S THIS?
WATCH THE VID.

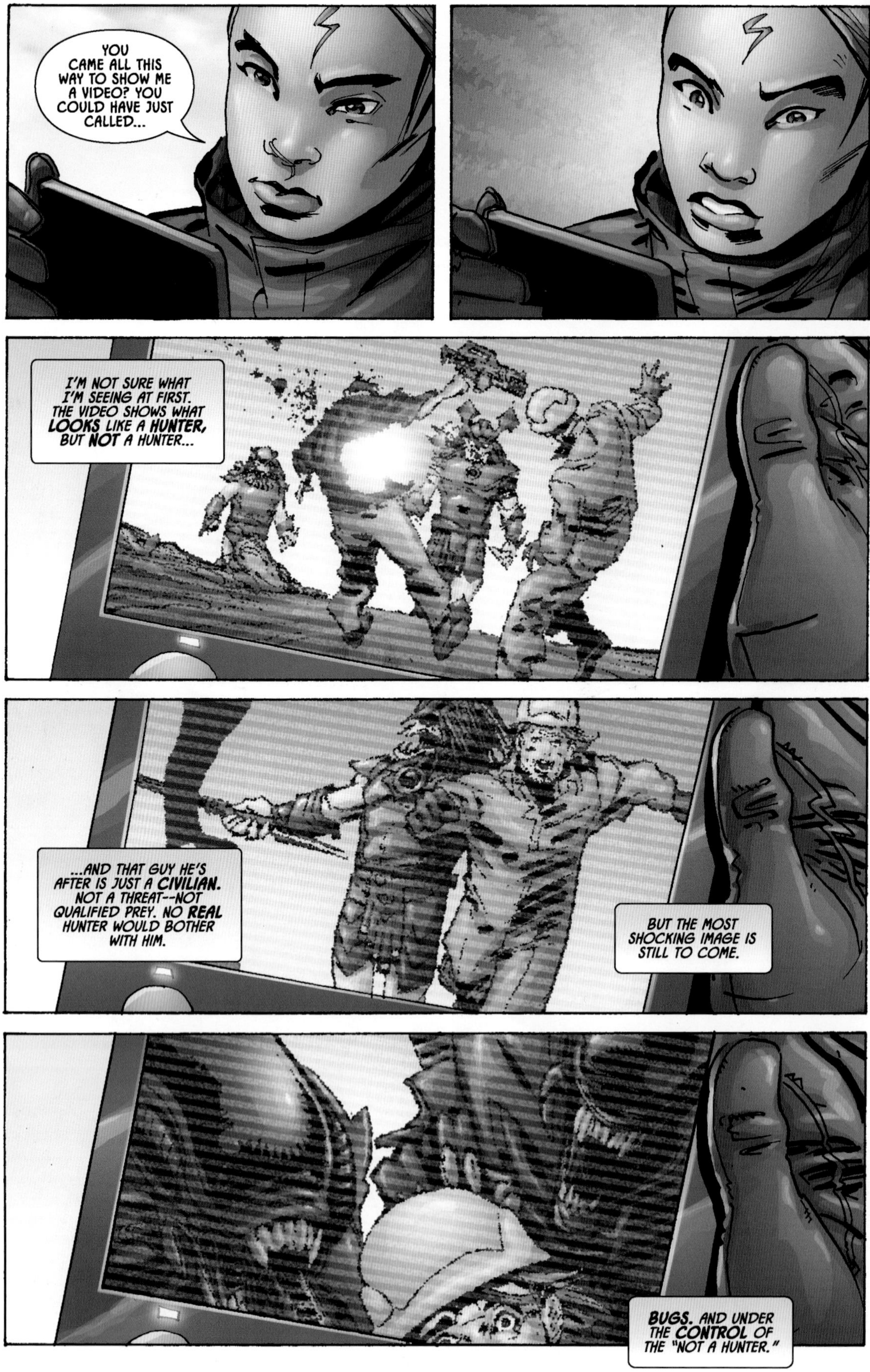
YOU CAME ALL THIS WAY TO SHOW ME A VIDEO? YOU COULD HAVE JUST CALLED...
I'M NOT SURE WHAT I'M SEEING AT FIRST. THE VIDEO SHOWS WHAT LOOKS LIKE A HUNTER, BUT NOT A HUNTER...
...AND THAT GUY HE'S AFTER IS JUST A CIVILIAN. NOT A THREAT--NOT QUALIFIED PREY. NO REAL HUNTER WOULD BOTHER WITH HIM.
BUT THE MOST SHOCKING IMAGE IS STILL TO COME.
BUGS. AND UNDER THE CONTROL OF THE "NOT A HUNTER."

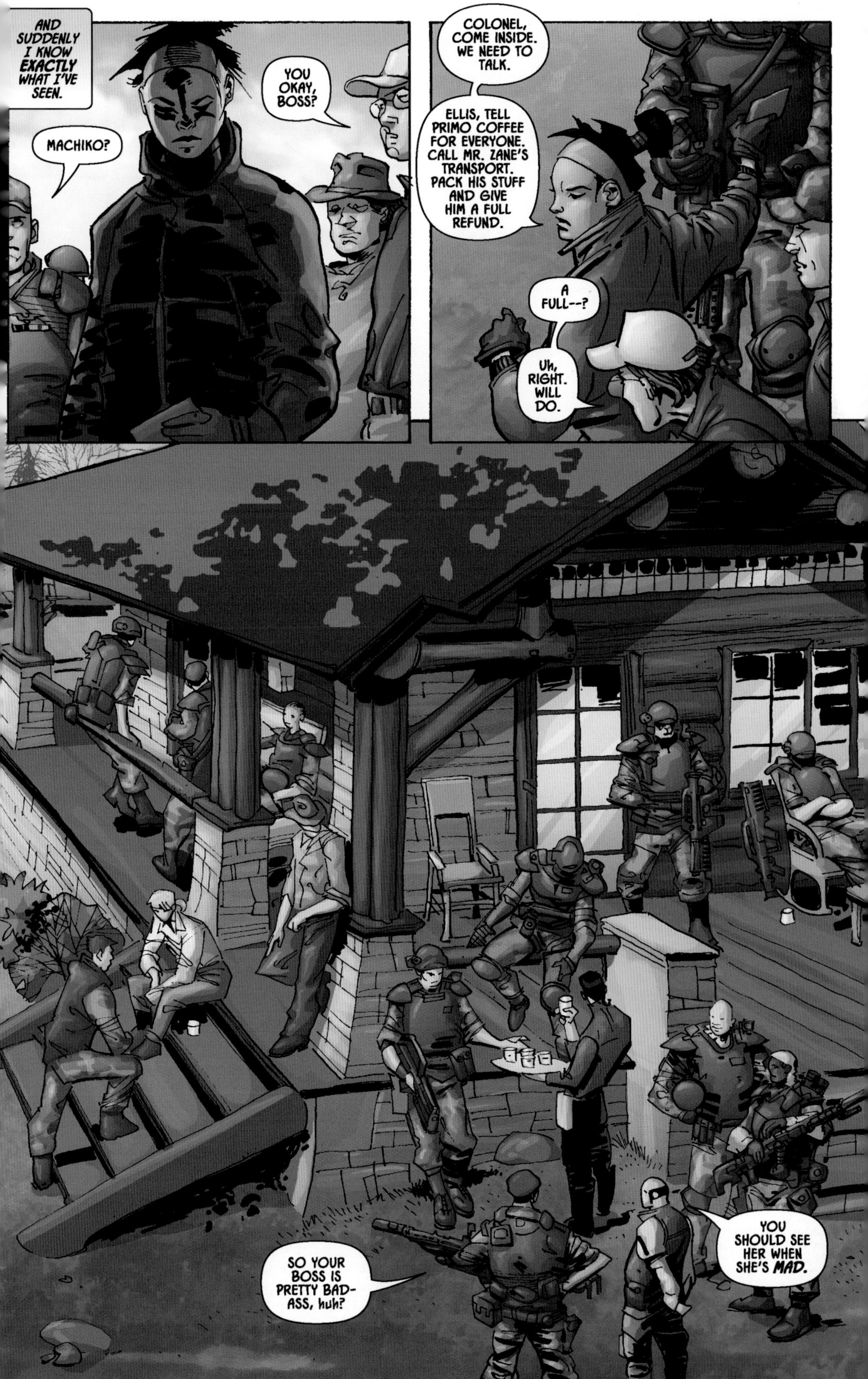

AND SUDDENLY I KNOW *EXACTLY* WHAT I'VE SEEN.
MACHIKO?
YOU OKAY, BOSS?
COLONEL, COME INSIDE. WE NEED TO TALK.
ELLIS, TELL PRIMO COFFEE FOR EVERYONE. CALL MR. ZANE'S TRANSPORT. PACK HIS STUFF AND GIVE HIM A FULL REFUND.
A FULL--?
Uh, RIGHT. WILL DO.
SO YOUR BOSS IS PRETTY BAD-ASS, huh?
YOU SHOULD SEE HER WHEN SHE'S *MAD*.

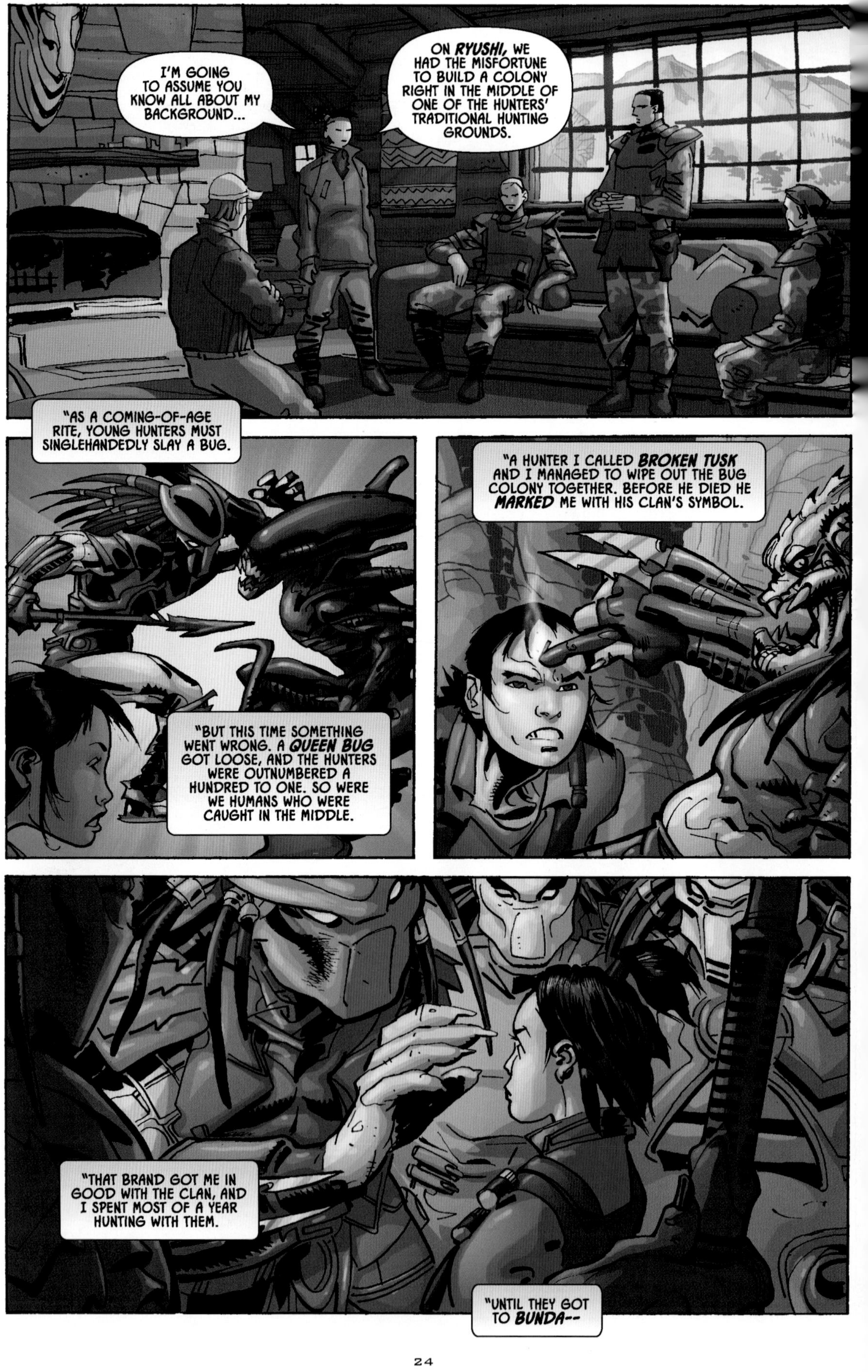
I'M GOING TO ASSUME YOU KNOW ALL ABOUT MY BACKGROUND...
ON RYUSHI, WE HAD THE MISFORTUNE TO BUILD A COLONY RIGHT IN THE MIDDLE OF ONE OF THE HUNTERS' TRADITIONAL HUNTING GROUNDS.
"AS A COMING-OF-AGE RITE, YOUNG HUNTERS MUST SINGLEHANDEDLY SLAY A BUG.
"BUT THIS TIME SOMETHING WENT WRONG. A QUEEN BUG GOT LOOSE, AND THE HUNTERS WERE OUTNUMBERED A HUNDRED TO ONE. SO WERE WE HUMANS WHO WERE CAUGHT IN THE MIDDLE.
"A HUNTER I CALLED BROKEN TUSK AND I MANAGED TO WIPE OUT THE BUG COLONY TOGETHER. BEFORE HE DIED HE MARKED ME WITH HIS CLAN'S SYMBOL.
"THAT BRAND GOT ME IN GOOD WITH THE CLAN, AND I SPENT MOST OF A YEAR HUNTING WITH THEM.
"UNTIL THEY GOT TO BUNDA--

"--AND STARTED KILLING HUMANS.

"I WENT TO WAR WITH THEM, THEN."

"THAT'S WHERE I RAN INTO *ELLIS* AND HIS FRIENDS. THEY'D JUST BEEN THROUGH THEIR OWN HELLISH ENCOUNTER WITH THE BUGS..."

THE BUNDA INCIDENT REALLY BLEW THE LID OFF OUR COVERT OPS. AFTER THAT, EVERY REPORTER AND HIS BROTHER WANTED A STORY ABOUT "ALIEN LIFE FORMS" AND THE THREAT THEY POSE.

WELL, HANG ON, COLONEL. IT'S GOING TO GET WORSE.

THAT FOOTAGE YOU SHOWED ME--WHERE IT LOOKED LIKE THE HUNTERS AND BUGS WERE WORKING *TOGETHER?*

IT'S PROOF THAT ONE OF THE OLD STORIES THE HUNTERS TELL IS *MORE* THAN JUST A LEGEND.

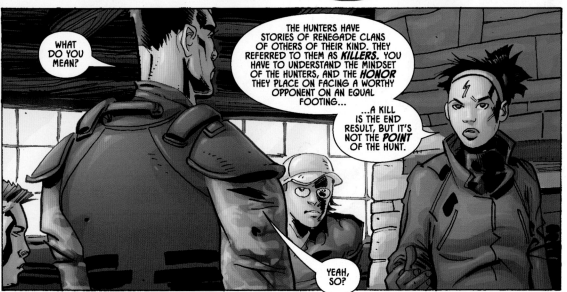

WHAT DO YOU MEAN?

THE HUNTERS HAVE STORIES OF RENEGADE CLANS OF OTHERS OF THEIR KIND. THEY REFERRED TO THEM AS *KILLERS.* YOU HAVE TO UNDERSTAND THE MINDSET OF THE HUNTERS, AND THE *HONOR* THEY PLACE ON FACING A WORTHY OPPONENT ON AN EQUAL FOOTING...

...A KILL IS THE END RESULT, BUT IT'S NOT THE *POINT* OF THE HUNT.

YEAH, SO?

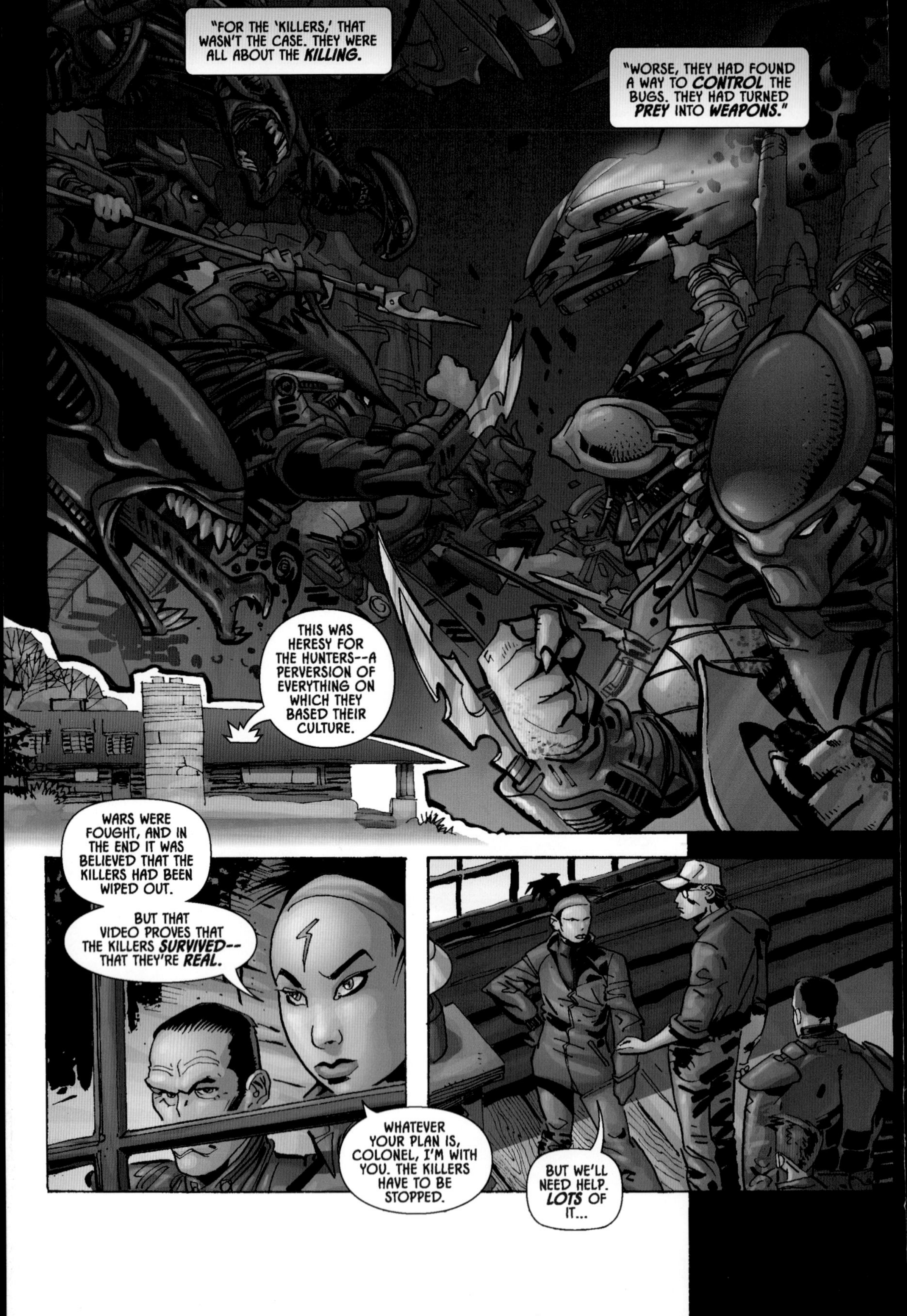
"FOR THE 'KILLERS,' THAT WASN'T THE CASE. THEY WERE ALL ABOUT THE KILLING.
"WORSE, THEY HAD FOUND A WAY TO CONTROL THE BUGS. THEY HAD TURNED PREY INTO WEAPONS."
THIS WAS HERESY FOR THE HUNTERS--A PERVERSION OF EVERYTHING ON WHICH THEY BASED THEIR CULTURE.
WARS WERE FOUGHT, AND IN THE END IT WAS BELIEVED THAT THE KILLERS HAD BEEN WIPED OUT.
BUT THAT VIDEO PROVES THAT THE KILLERS SURVIVED--THAT THEY'RE REAL.
WHATEVER YOUR PLAN IS, COLONEL, I'M WITH YOU. THE KILLERS HAVE TO BE STOPPED.
BUT WE'LL NEED HELP. LOTS OF IT...

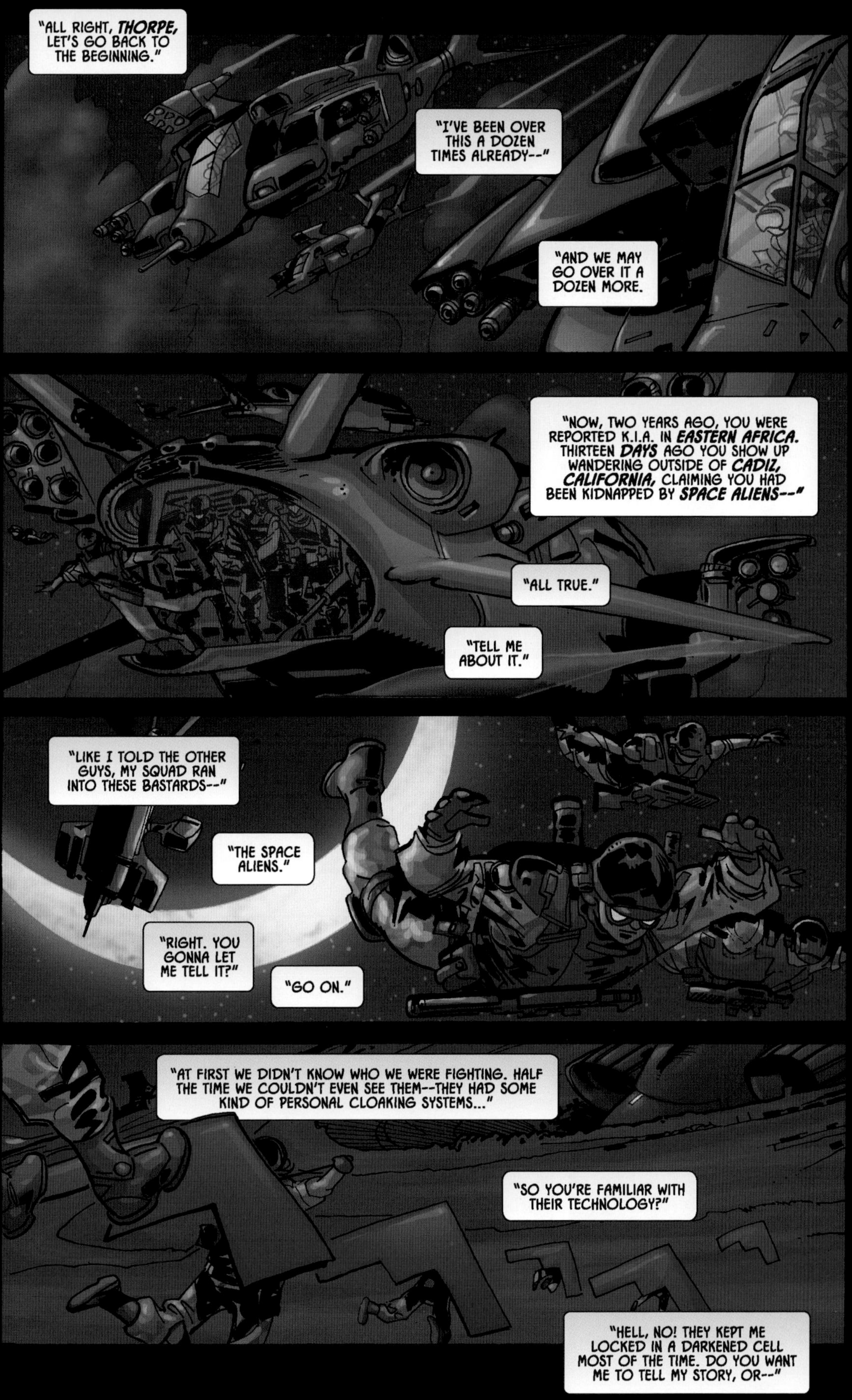
"ALL RIGHT, THORPE, LET'S GO BACK TO THE BEGINNING."
"I'VE BEEN OVER THIS A DOZEN TIMES ALREADY--"
"AND WE MAY GO OVER IT A DOZEN MORE.
"NOW, TWO YEARS AGO, YOU WERE REPORTED K.I.A. IN EASTERN AFRICA. THIRTEEN DAYS AGO YOU SHOW UP WANDERING OUTSIDE OF CADIZ, CALIFORNIA, CLAIMING YOU HAD BEEN KIDNAPPED BY SPACE ALIENS--"
"ALL TRUE."
"TELL ME ABOUT IT."
"LIKE I TOLD THE OTHER GUYS, MY SQUAD RAN INTO THESE BASTARDS--"
"THE SPACE ALIENS."
"RIGHT. YOU GONNA LET ME TELL IT?"
"GO ON."
"AT FIRST WE DIDN'T KNOW WHO WE WERE FIGHTING. HALF THE TIME WE COULDN'T EVEN SEE THEM--THEY HAD SOME KIND OF PERSONAL CLOAKING SYSTEMS..."
"SO YOU'RE FAMILIAR WITH THEIR TECHNOLOGY?"
"HELL, NO! THEY KEPT ME LOCKED IN A DARKENED CELL MOST OF THE TIME. DO YOU WANT ME TO TELL MY STORY, OR--"

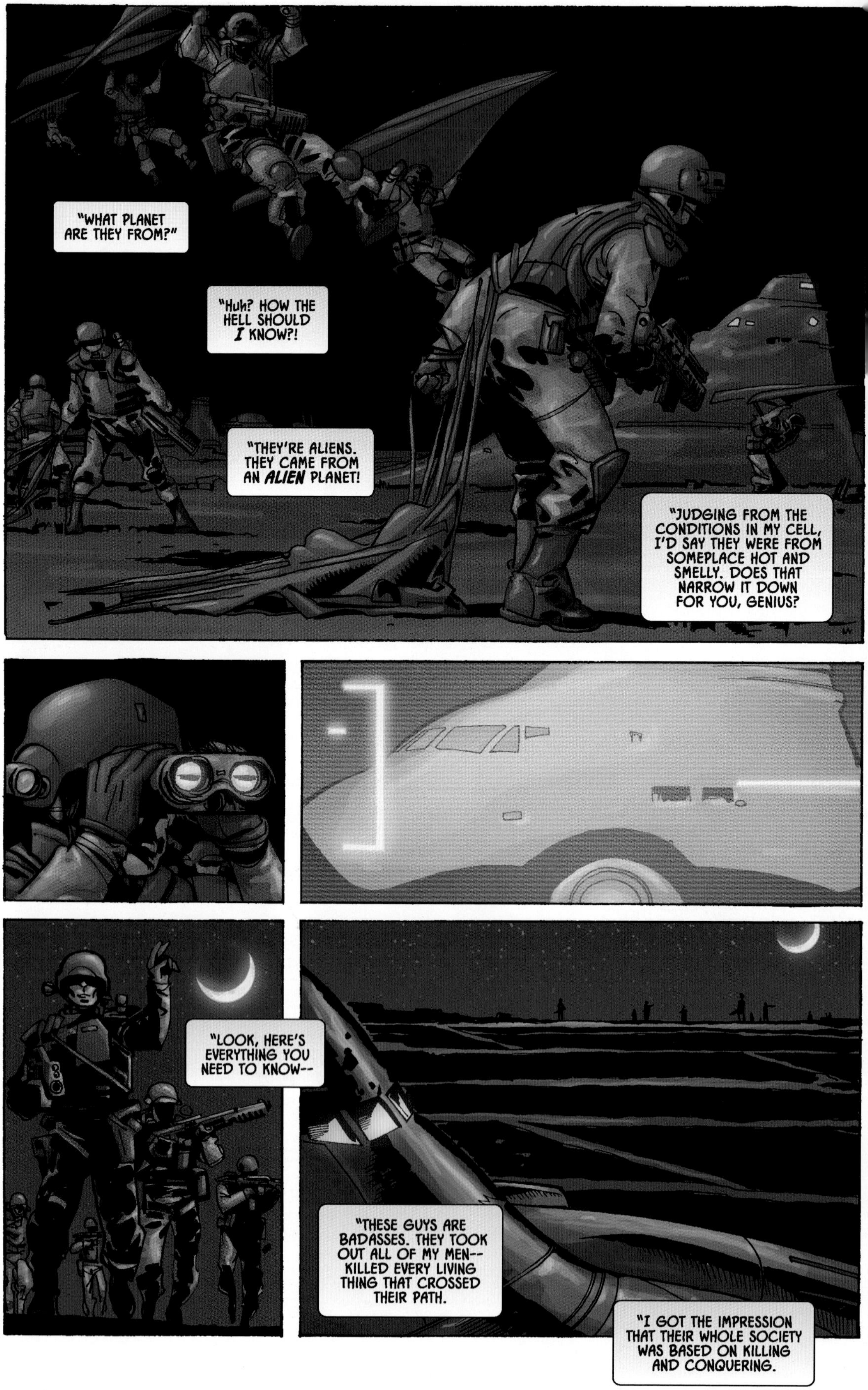
"WHAT PLANET ARE THEY FROM?"
"Huh? HOW THE HELL SHOULD *I* KNOW?!
"THEY'RE ALIENS. THEY CAME FROM AN *ALIEN* PLANET!
"JUDGING FROM THE CONDITIONS IN MY CELL, I'D SAY THEY WERE FROM SOMEPLACE HOT AND SMELLY. DOES THAT NARROW IT DOWN FOR YOU, GENIUS?
"LOOK, HERE'S EVERYTHING YOU NEED TO KNOW--
"THESE GUYS ARE BADASSES. THEY TOOK OUT ALL OF MY MEN--KILLED EVERY LIVING THING THAT CROSSED THEIR PATH.
"I GOT THE IMPRESSION THAT THEIR WHOLE SOCIETY WAS BASED ON KILLING AND CONQUERING.

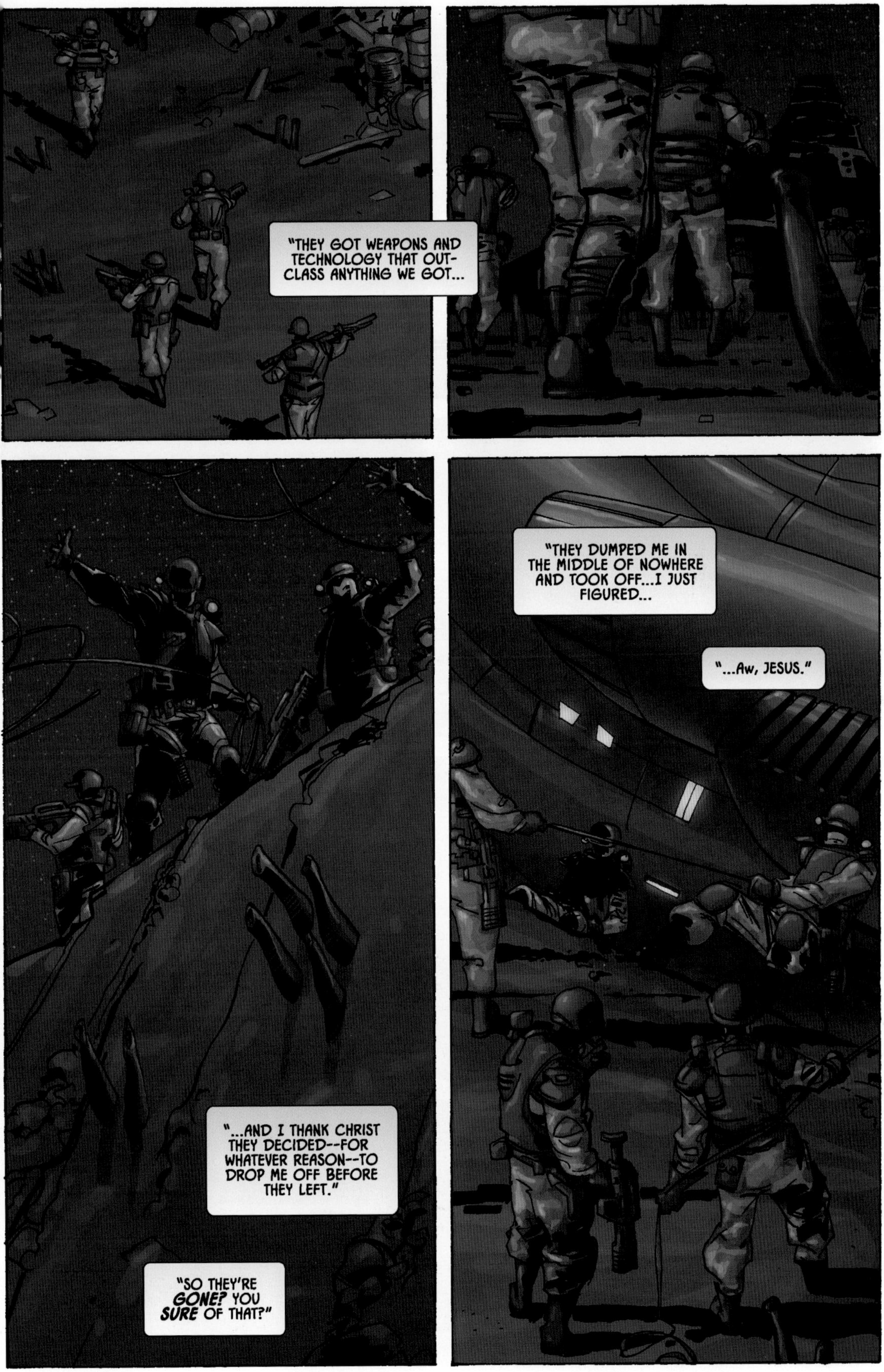
"THEY GOT WEAPONS AND TECHNOLOGY THAT OUT-CLASS ANYTHING WE GOT...
"...AND I THANK CHRIST THEY DECIDED--FOR WHATEVER REASON--TO DROP ME OFF BEFORE THEY LEFT."
"SO THEY'RE GONE? YOU SURE OF THAT?"
"THEY DUMPED ME IN THE MIDDLE OF NOWHERE AND TOOK OFF...I JUST FIGURED...
"...Aw, JESUS."

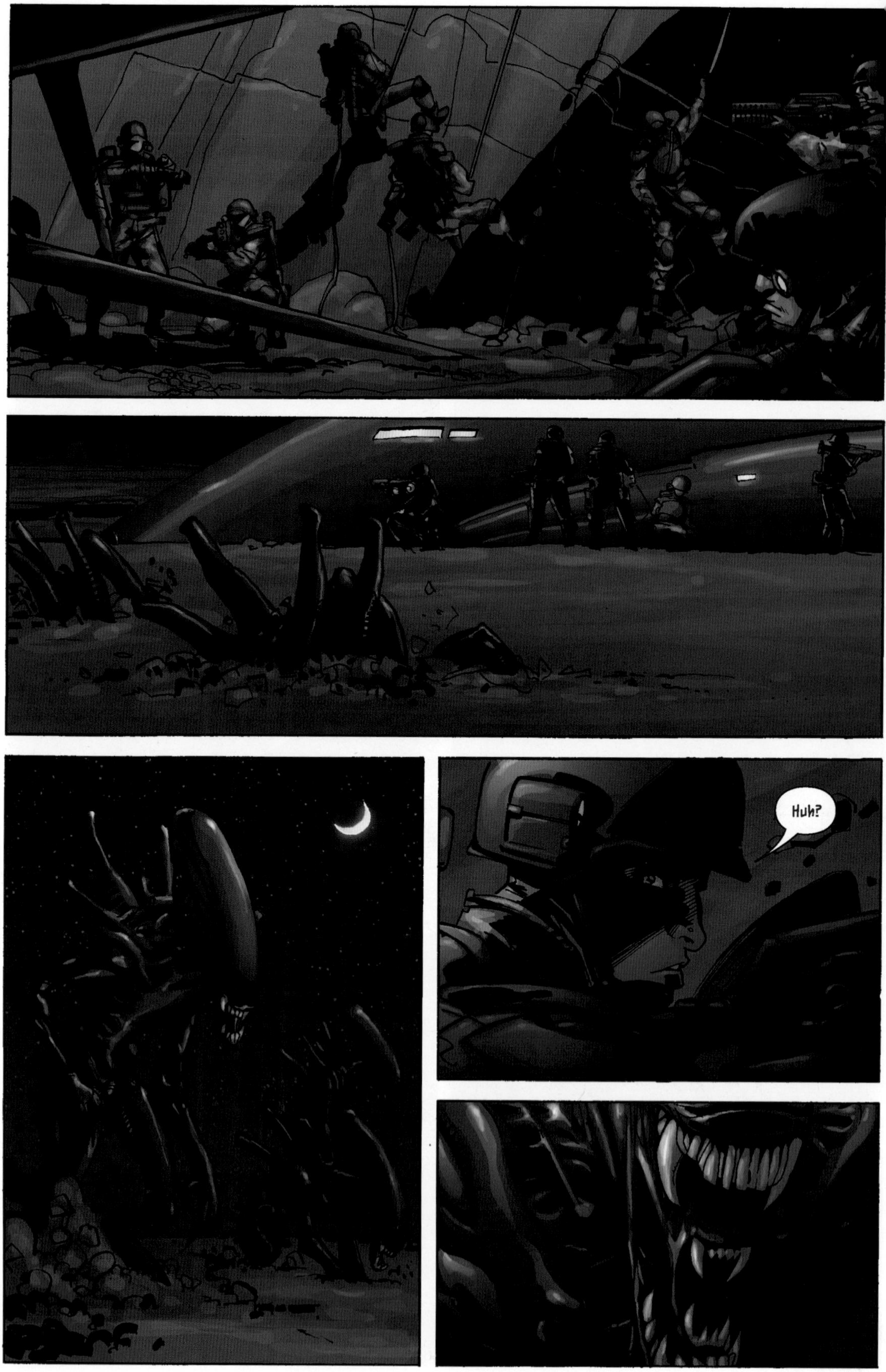
Huh?

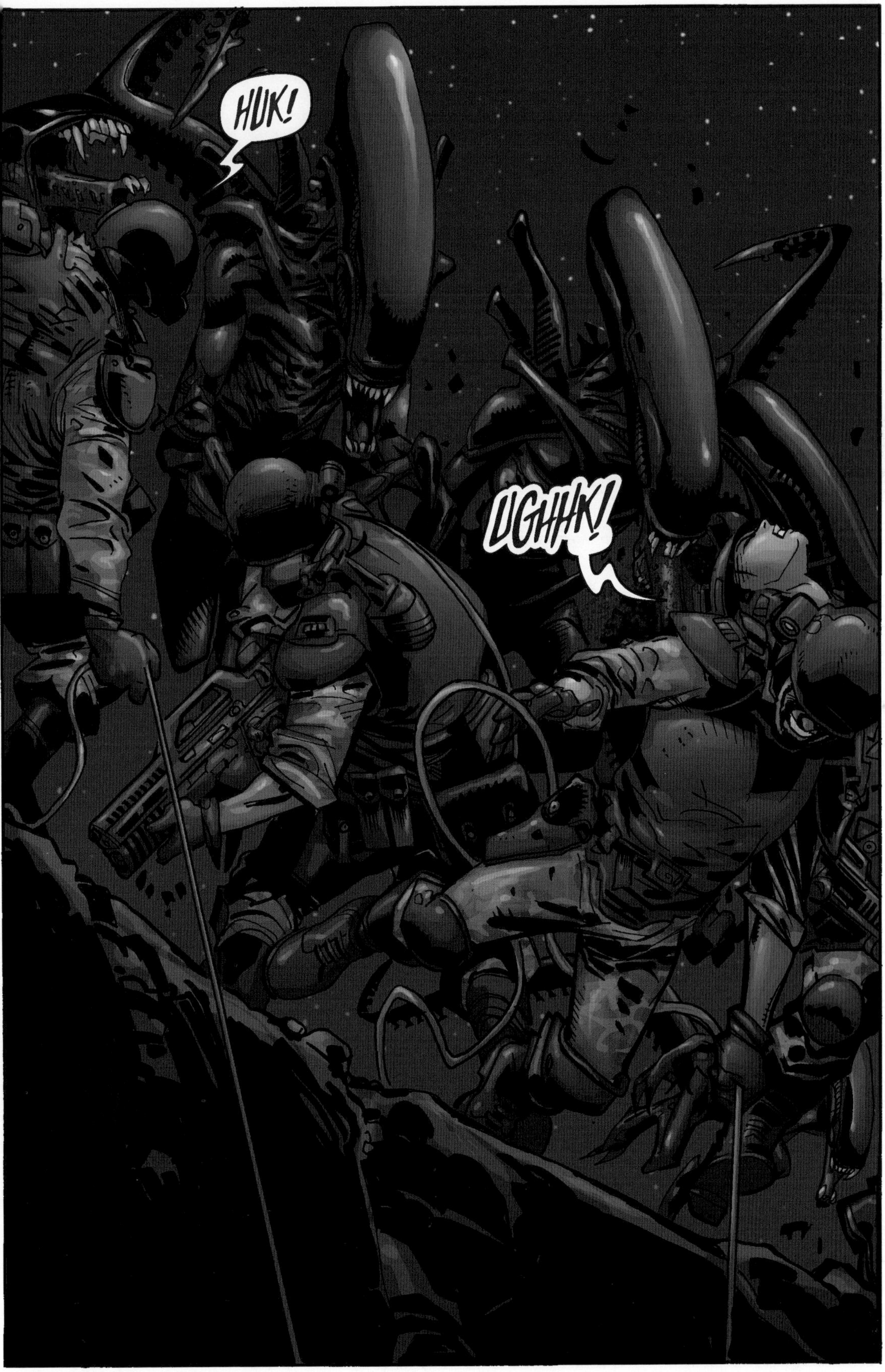
HUK!
UGHHK!

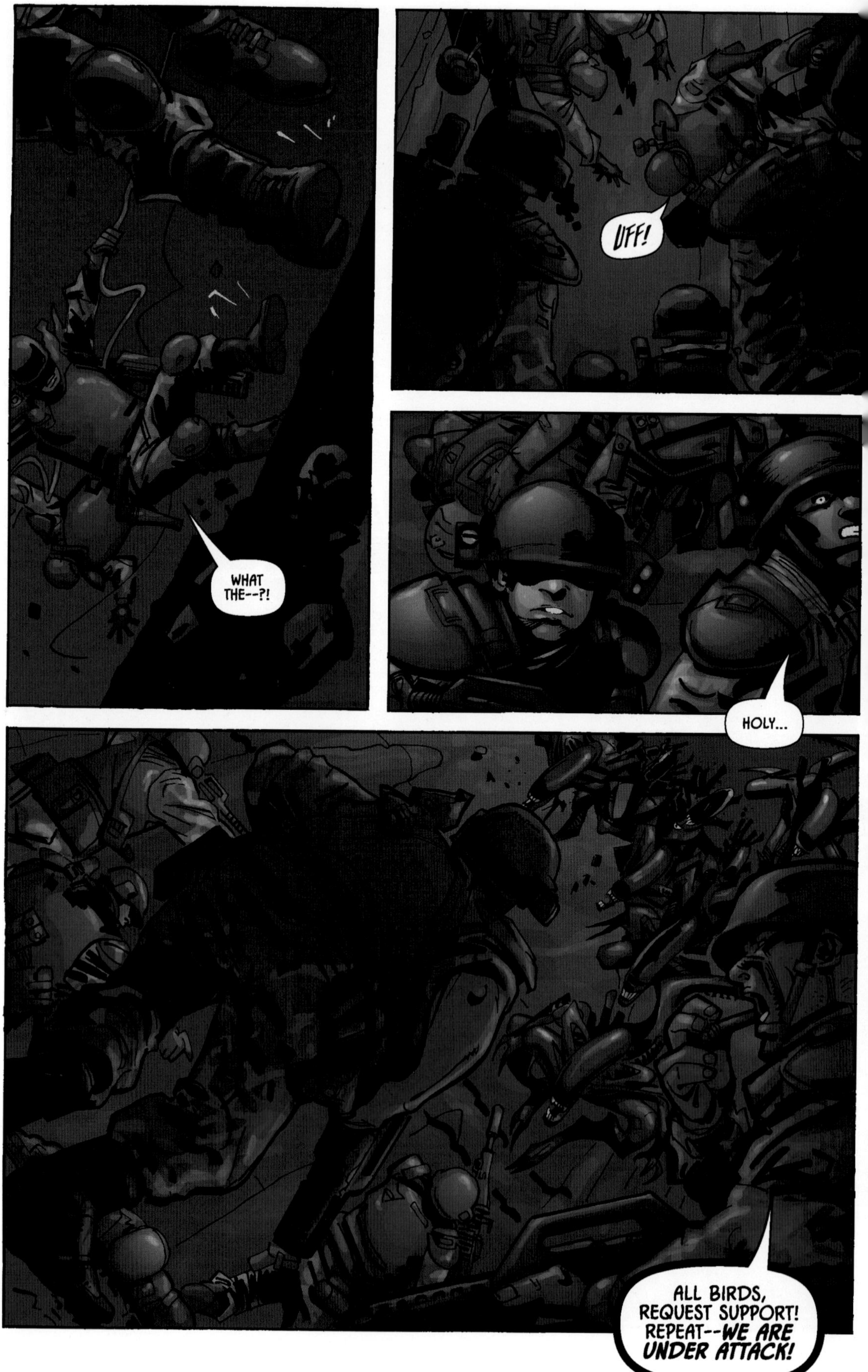
WHAT THE--?!
UFF!
HOLY...
ALL BIRDS, REQUEST SUPPORT! REPEAT--WE ARE UNDER ATTACK!

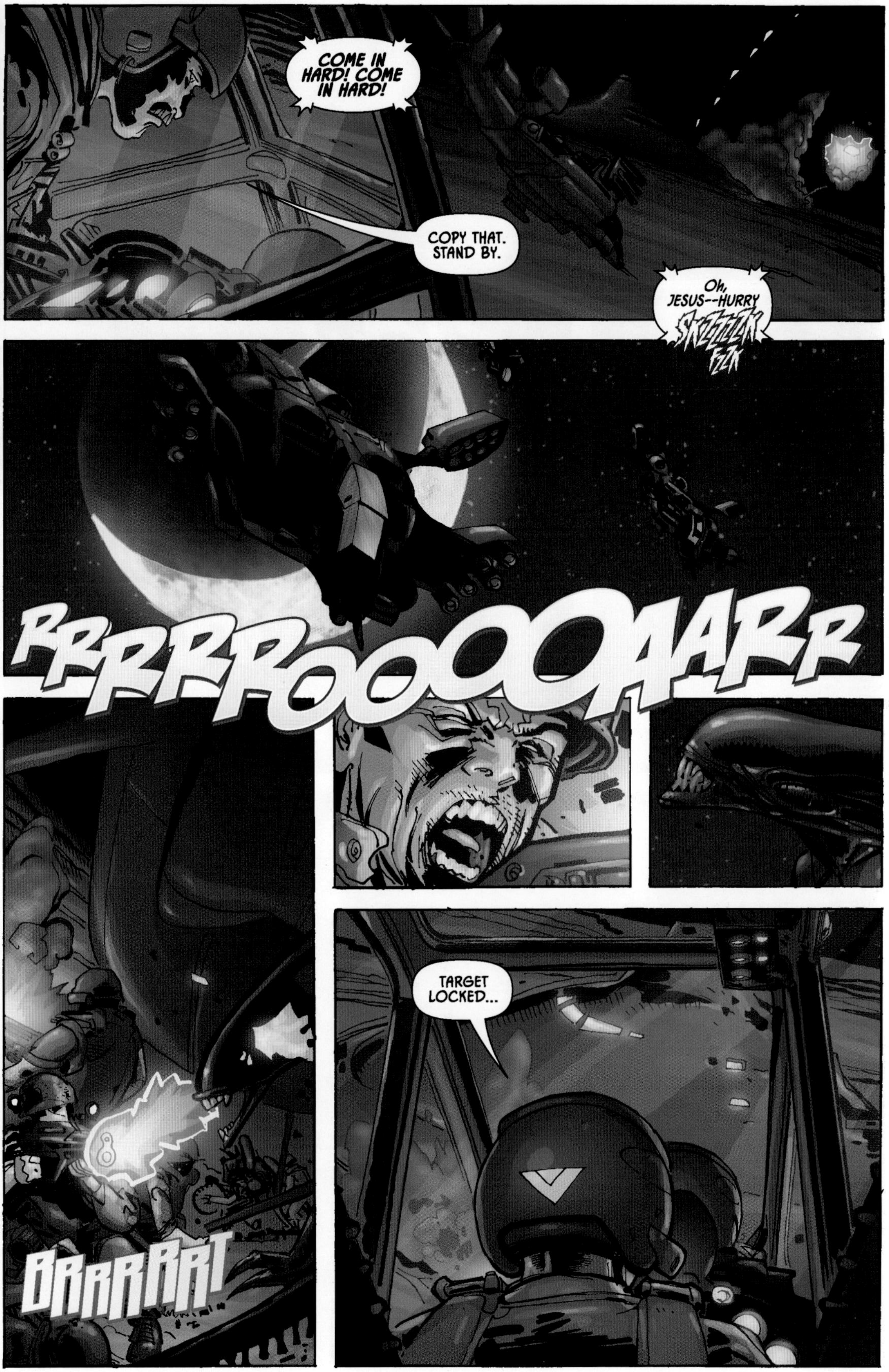
COME IN HARD! COME IN HARD!
COPY THAT. STAND BY.
Oh, JESUS--HURRY
SKZZZZZZK FZZK
RRRRROOOOOAARR
BRRRRRT
TARGET LOCKED...

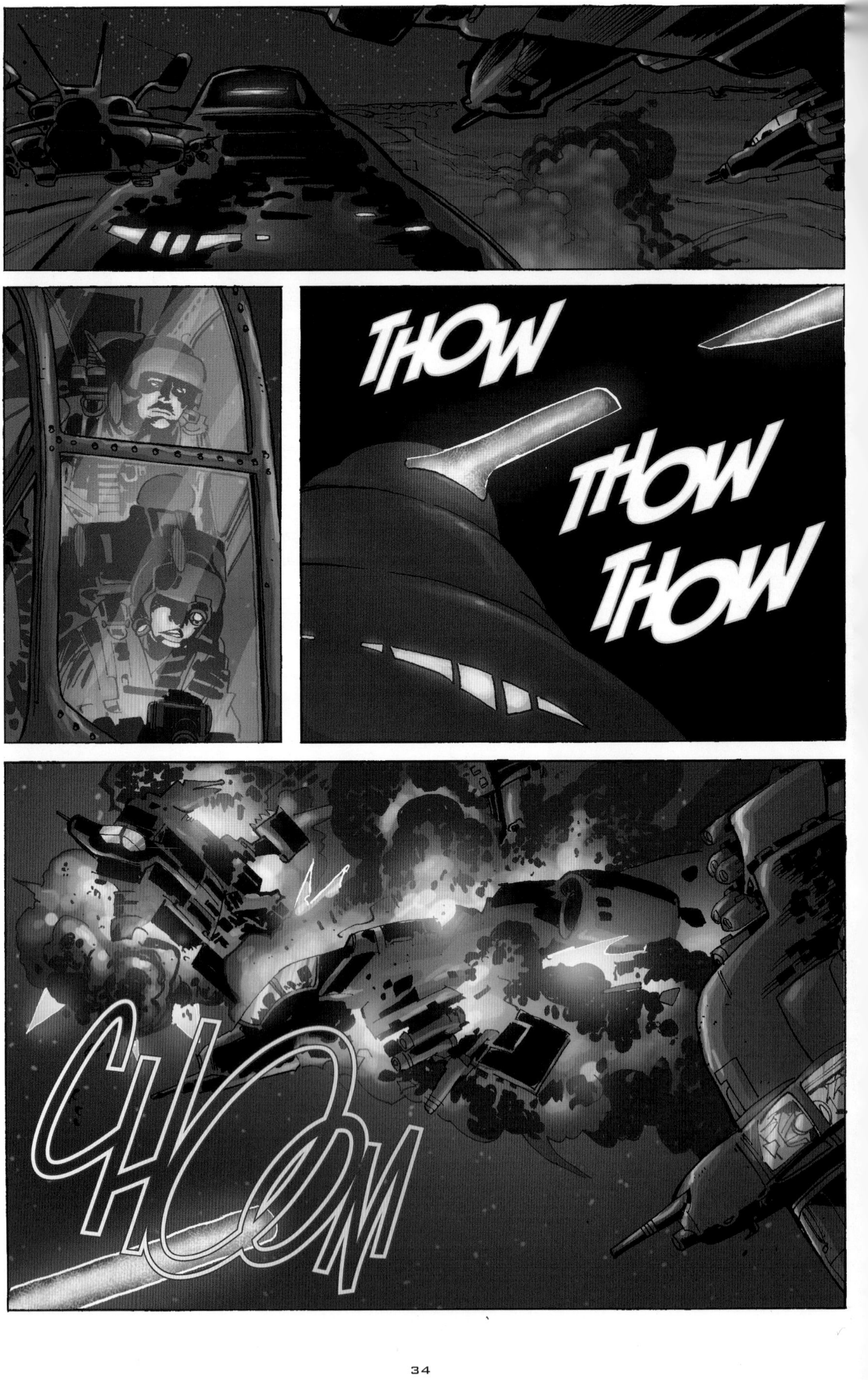
THOW
THOW
THOW
CHOOM

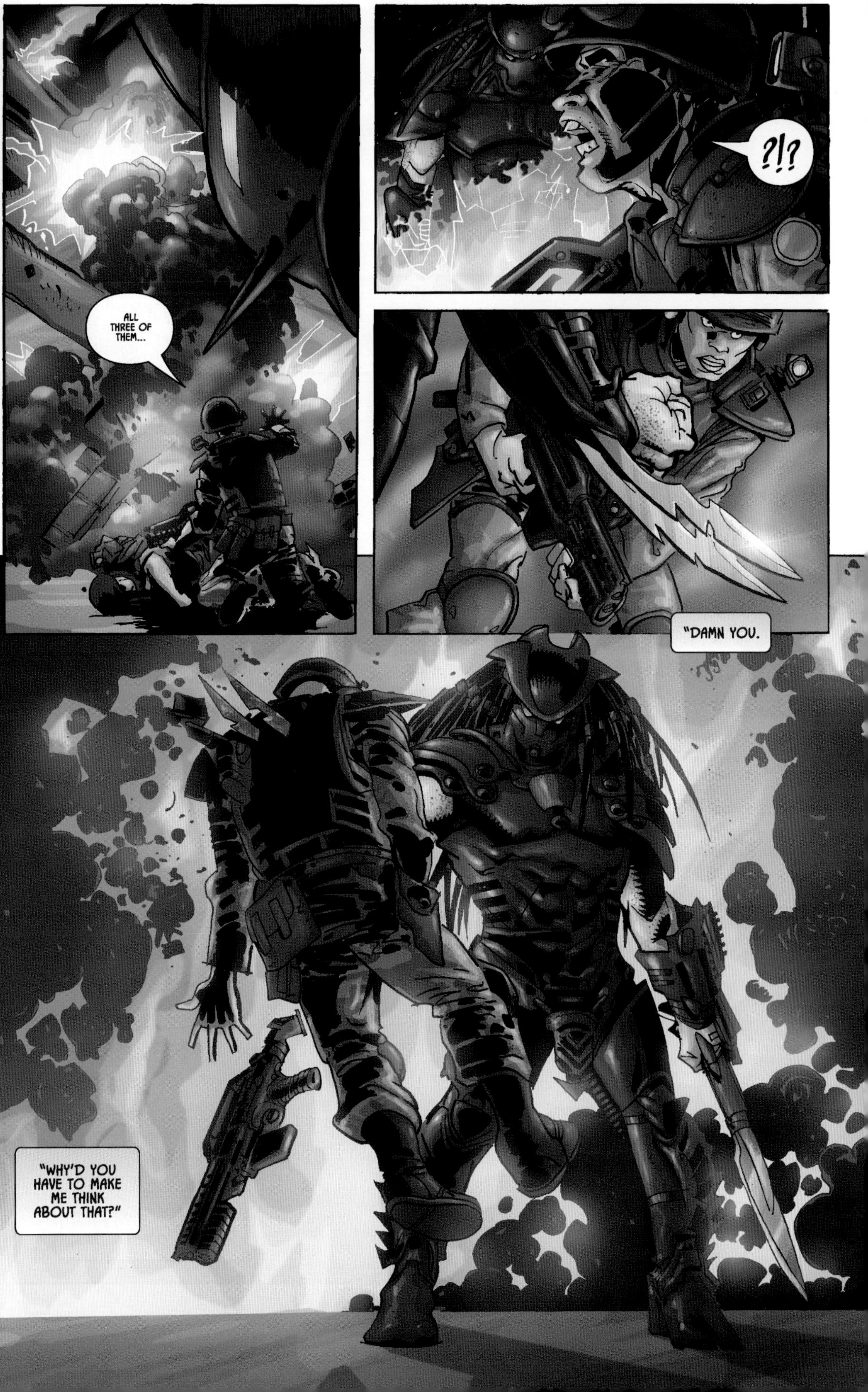

?!?
ALL THREE OF THEM...
"DAMN YOU.
"WHY'D YOU HAVE TO MAKE ME THINK ABOUT THAT?"

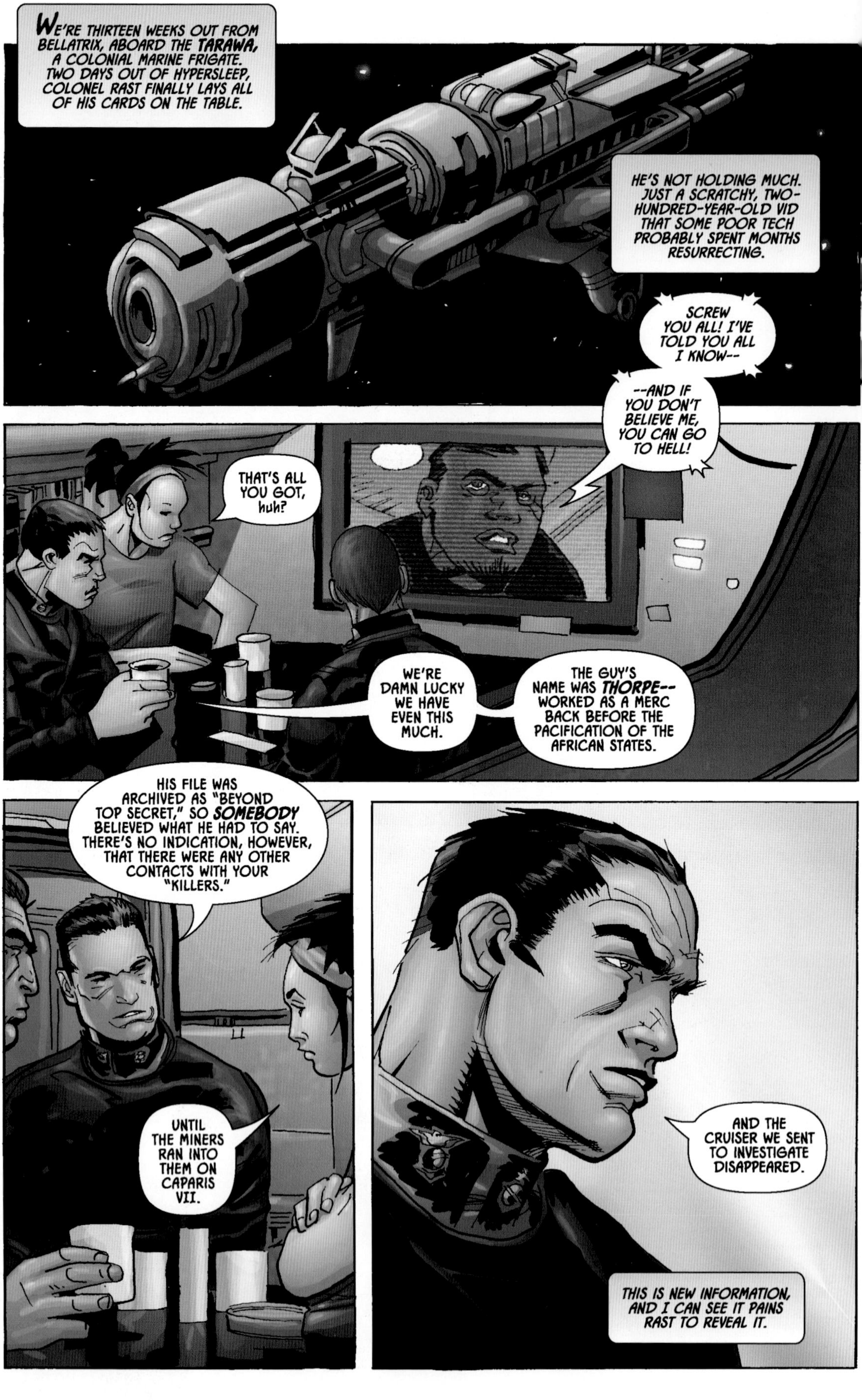
WE'RE THIRTEEN WEEKS OUT FROM BELLATRIX, ABOARD THE TARAWA, A COLONIAL MARINE FRIGATE. TWO DAYS OUT OF HYPERSLEEP, COLONEL RAST FINALLY LAYS ALL OF HIS CARDS ON THE TABLE.
HE'S NOT HOLDING MUCH. JUST A SCRATCHY, TWO-HUNDRED-YEAR-OLD VID THAT SOME POOR TECH PROBABLY SPENT MONTHS RESURRECTING.
SCREW YOU ALL! I'VE TOLD YOU ALL I KNOW--
--AND IF YOU DON'T BELIEVE ME, YOU CAN GO TO HELL!
THAT'S ALL YOU GOT, huh?
WE'RE DAMN LUCKY WE HAVE EVEN THIS MUCH.
THE GUY'S NAME WAS THORPE-- WORKED AS A MERC BACK BEFORE THE PACIFICATION OF THE AFRICAN STATES.
HIS FILE WAS ARCHIVED AS "BEYOND TOP SECRET," SO SOMEBODY BELIEVED WHAT HE HAD TO SAY. THERE'S NO INDICATION, HOWEVER, THAT THERE WERE ANY OTHER CONTACTS WITH YOUR "KILLERS."
UNTIL THE MINERS RAN INTO THEM ON CAPARIS VII.
AND THE CRUISER WE SENT TO INVESTIGATE DISAPPEARED.
THIS IS NEW INFORMATION, AND I CAN SEE IT PAINS RAST TO REVEAL IT.

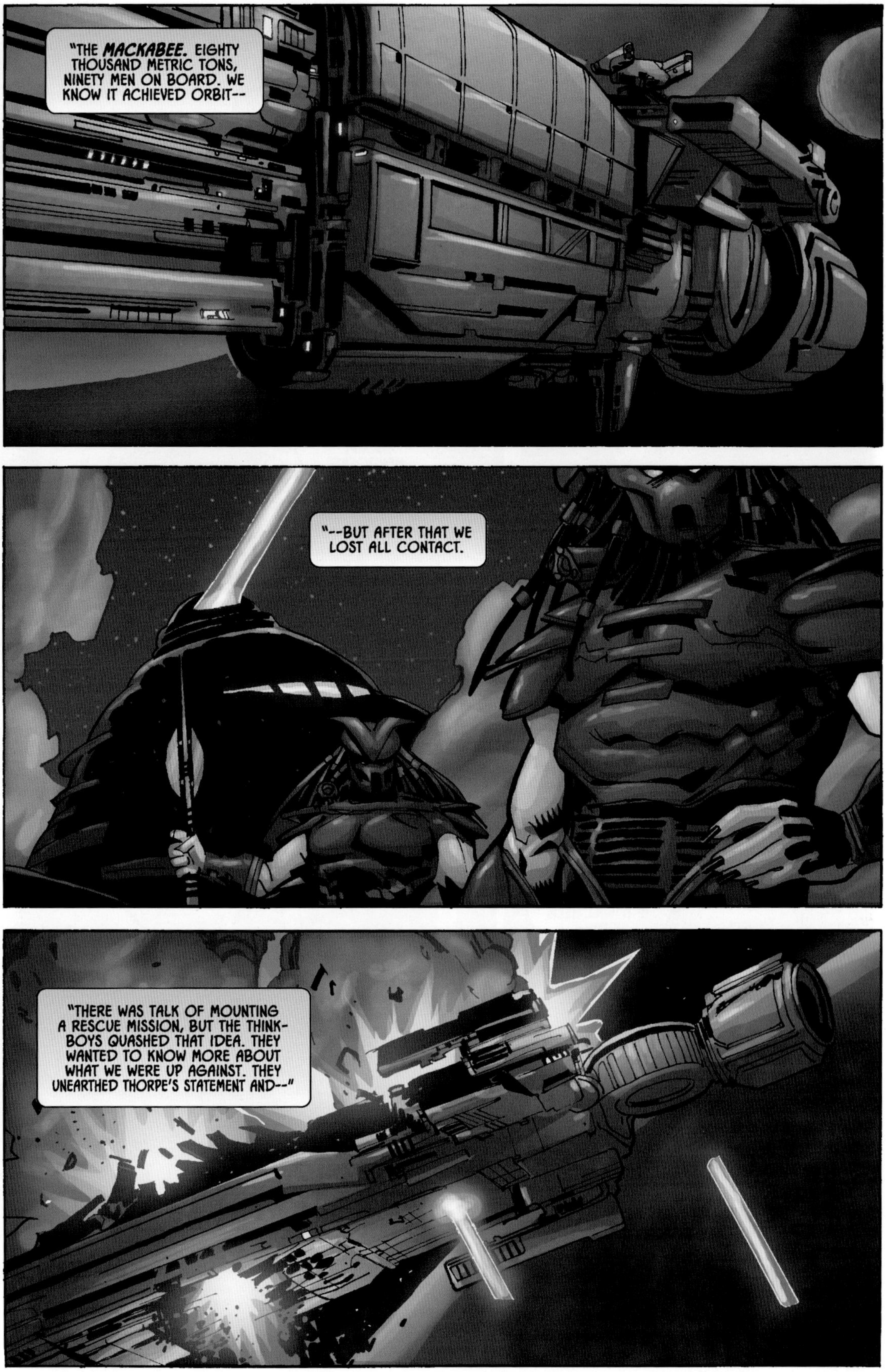
"THE MACKABEE. EIGHTY THOUSAND METRIC TONS, NINETY MEN ON BOARD. WE KNOW IT ACHIEVED ORBIT--
"--BUT AFTER THAT WE LOST ALL CONTACT.
"THERE WAS TALK OF MOUNTING A RESCUE MISSION, BUT THE THINK-BOYS QUASHED THAT IDEA. THEY WANTED TO KNOW MORE ABOUT WHAT WE WERE UP AGAINST. THEY UNEARTHED THORPE'S STATEMENT AND--"

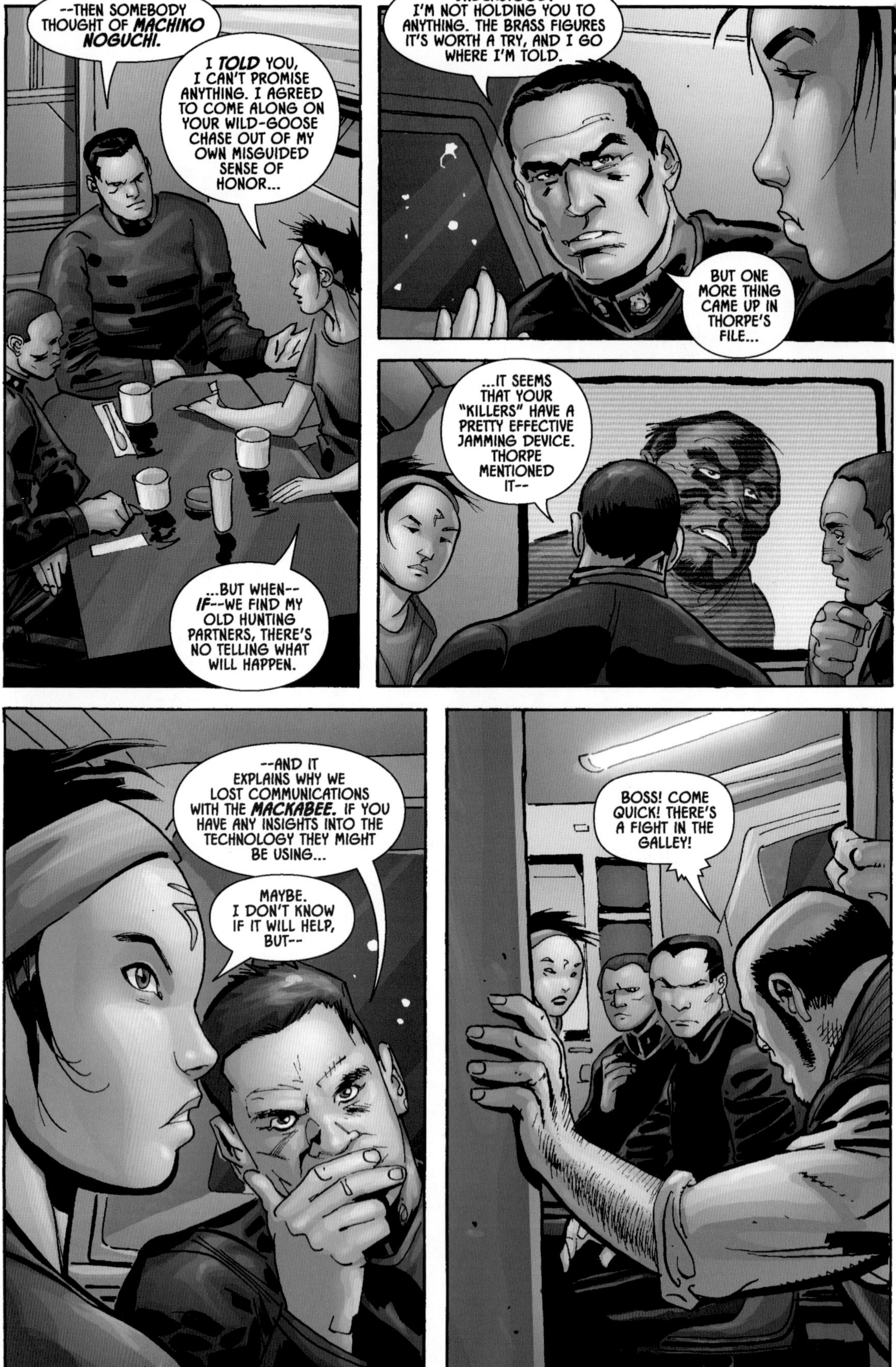
--THEN SOMEBODY THOUGHT OF MACHIKO NOGUCHI.
I TOLD YOU, I CAN'T PROMISE ANYTHING. I AGREED TO COME ALONG ON YOUR WILD-GOOSE CHASE OUT OF MY OWN MISGUIDED SENSE OF HONOR...
...BUT WHEN--IF--WE FIND MY OLD HUNTING PARTNERS, THERE'S NO TELLING WHAT WILL HAPPEN.
UNDERSTOOD. I'M NOT HOLDING YOU TO ANYTHING. THE BRASS FIGURES IT'S WORTH A TRY, AND I GO WHERE I'M TOLD.
BUT ONE MORE THING CAME UP IN THORPE'S FILE...
...IT SEEMS THAT YOUR "KILLERS" HAVE A PRETTY EFFECTIVE JAMMING DEVICE. THORPE MENTIONED IT--
--AND IT EXPLAINS WHY WE LOST COMMUNICATIONS WITH THE MACKABEE. IF YOU HAVE ANY INSIGHTS INTO THE TECHNOLOGY THEY MIGHT BE USING...
MAYBE. I DON'T KNOW IF IT WILL HELP, BUT--
BOSS! COME QUICK! THERE'S A FIGHT IN THE GALLEY!

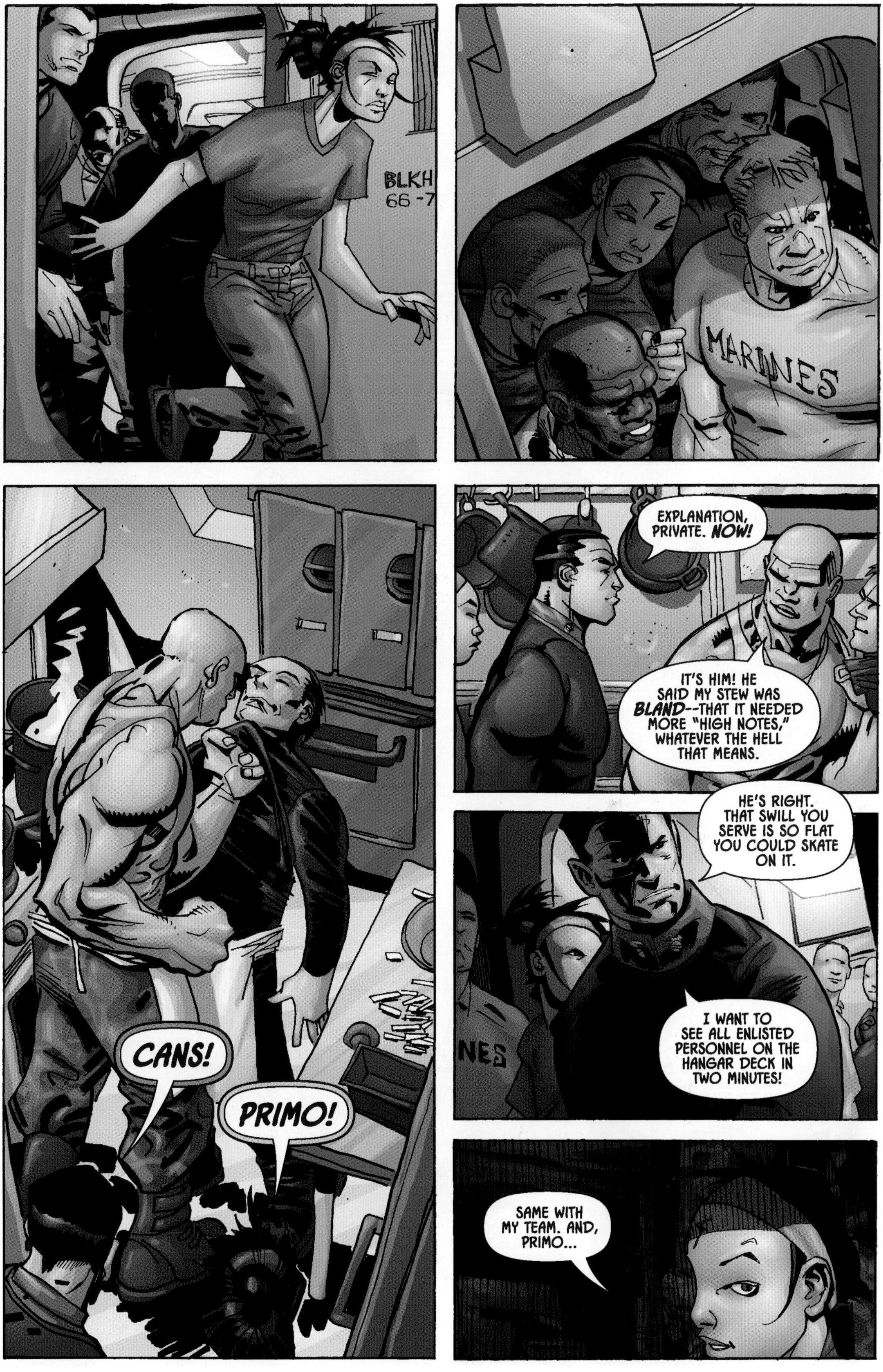

BLKH
66-7
MARINES
CANS!
PRIMO!
EXPLANATION, PRIVATE. NOW!
IT'S HIM! HE SAID MY STEW WAS BLAND--THAT IT NEEDED MORE "HIGH NOTES," WHATEVER THE HELL THAT MEANS.
HE'S RIGHT. THAT SWILL YOU SERVE IS SO FLAT YOU COULD SKATE ON IT.
I WANT TO SEE ALL ENLISTED PERSONNEL ON THE HANGAR DECK IN TWO MINUTES!
SAME WITH MY TEAM. AND, PRIMO...

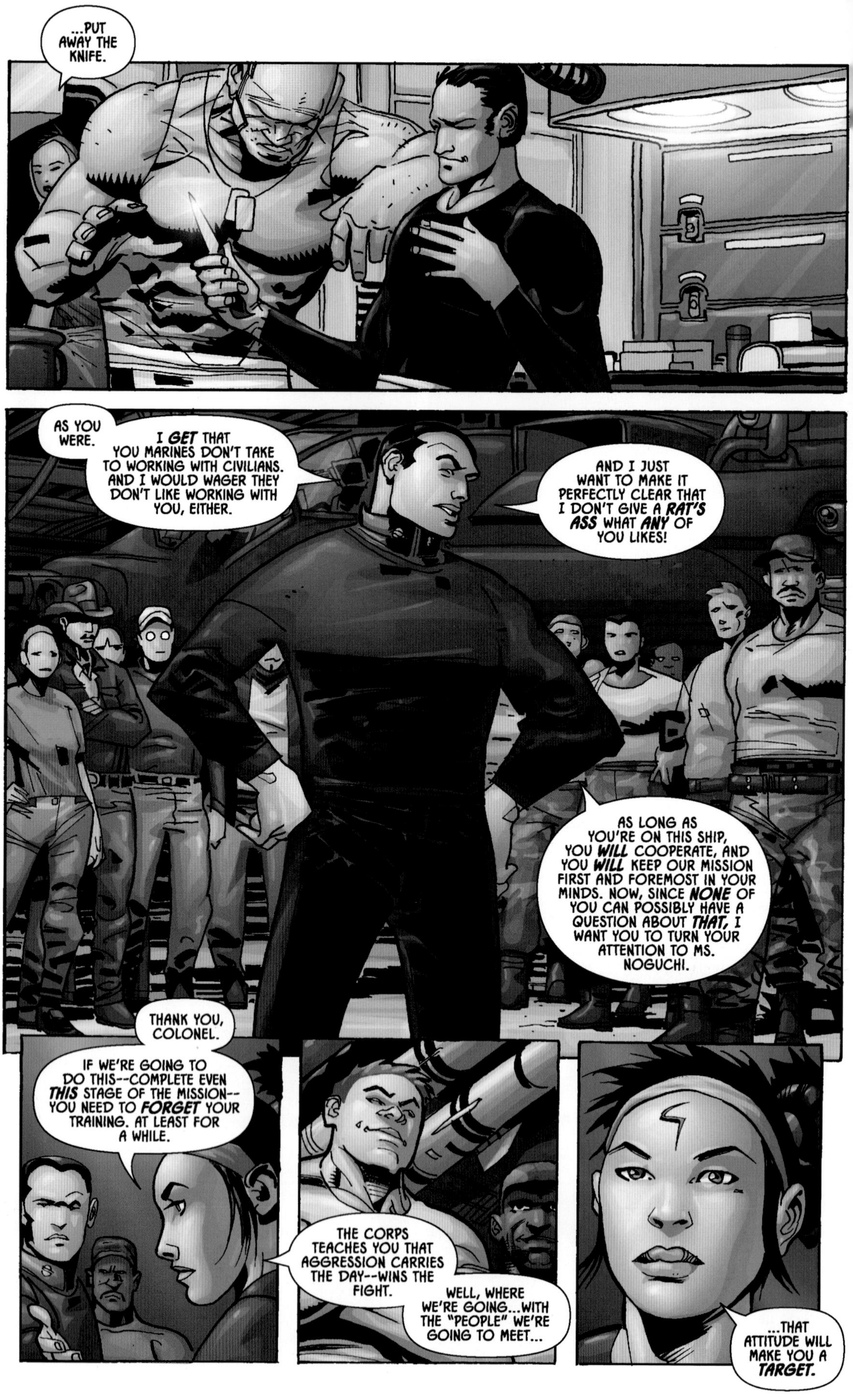
...PUT AWAY THE KNIFE.
AS YOU WERE.
I GET THAT YOU MARINES DON'T TAKE TO WORKING WITH CIVILIANS. AND I WOULD WAGER THEY DON'T LIKE WORKING WITH YOU, EITHER.
AND I JUST WANT TO MAKE IT PERFECTLY CLEAR THAT I DON'T GIVE A RAT'S ASS WHAT ANY OF YOU LIKES!
AS LONG AS YOU'RE ON THIS SHIP, YOU WILL COOPERATE, AND YOU WILL KEEP OUR MISSION FIRST AND FOREMOST IN YOUR MINDS. NOW, SINCE NONE OF YOU CAN POSSIBLY HAVE A QUESTION ABOUT THAT, I WANT YOU TO TURN YOUR ATTENTION TO MS. NOGUCHI.
THANK YOU, COLONEL.
IF WE'RE GOING TO DO THIS--COMPLETE EVEN THIS STAGE OF THE MISSION--YOU NEED TO FORGET YOUR TRAINING. AT LEAST FOR A WHILE.
THE CORPS TEACHES YOU THAT AGGRESSION CARRIES THE DAY--WINS THE FIGHT.
WELL, WHERE WE'RE GOING...WITH THE "PEOPLE" WE'RE GOING TO MEET...
...THAT ATTITUDE WILL MAKE YOU A TARGET.

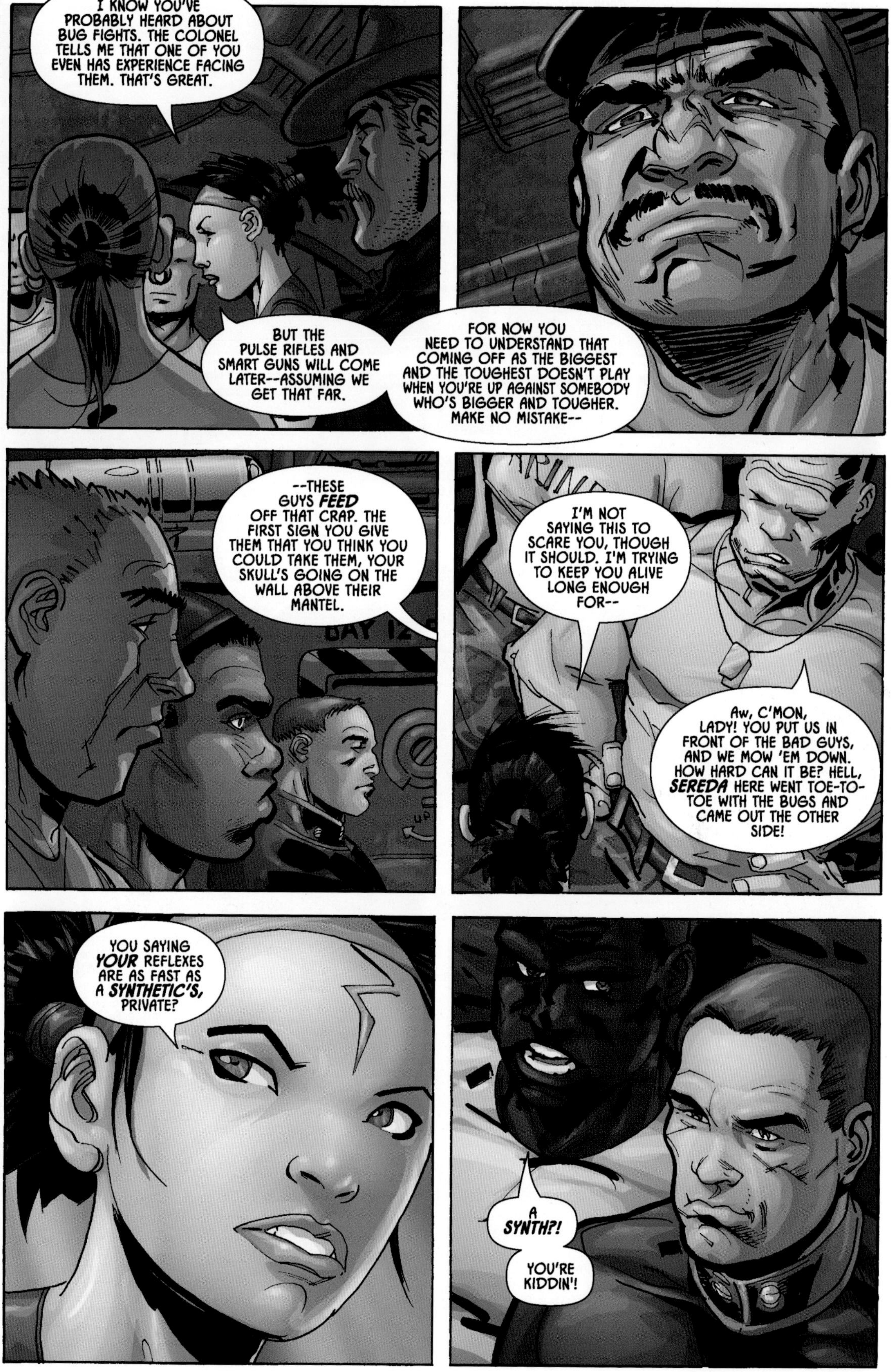
I KNOW YOU'VE PROBABLY HEARD ABOUT BUG FIGHTS. THE COLONEL TELLS ME THAT ONE OF YOU EVEN HAS EXPERIENCE FACING THEM. THAT'S GREAT.
BUT THE PULSE RIFLES AND SMART GUNS WILL COME LATER--ASSUMING WE GET THAT FAR.
FOR NOW YOU NEED TO UNDERSTAND THAT COMING OFF AS THE BIGGEST AND THE TOUGHEST DOESN'T PLAY WHEN YOU'RE UP AGAINST SOMEBODY WHO'S BIGGER AND TOUGHER. MAKE NO MISTAKE--
--THESE GUYS *FEED* OFF THAT CRAP. THE FIRST SIGN YOU GIVE THEM THAT YOU THINK YOU COULD TAKE THEM, YOUR SKULL'S GOING ON THE WALL ABOVE THEIR MANTEL.
I'M NOT SAYING THIS TO SCARE YOU, THOUGH IT SHOULD. I'M TRYING TO KEEP YOU ALIVE LONG ENOUGH FOR--
AW, C'MON, LADY! YOU PUT US IN FRONT OF THE BAD GUYS, AND WE MOW 'EM DOWN. HOW HARD CAN IT BE? HELL, *SEREDA* HERE WENT TOE-TO-TOE WITH THE BUGS AND CAME OUT THE OTHER SIDE!
YOU SAYING *YOUR* REFLEXES ARE AS FAST AS A *SYNTHETIC'S,* PRIVATE?
A *SYNTH?!*
YOU'RE KIDDIN'!

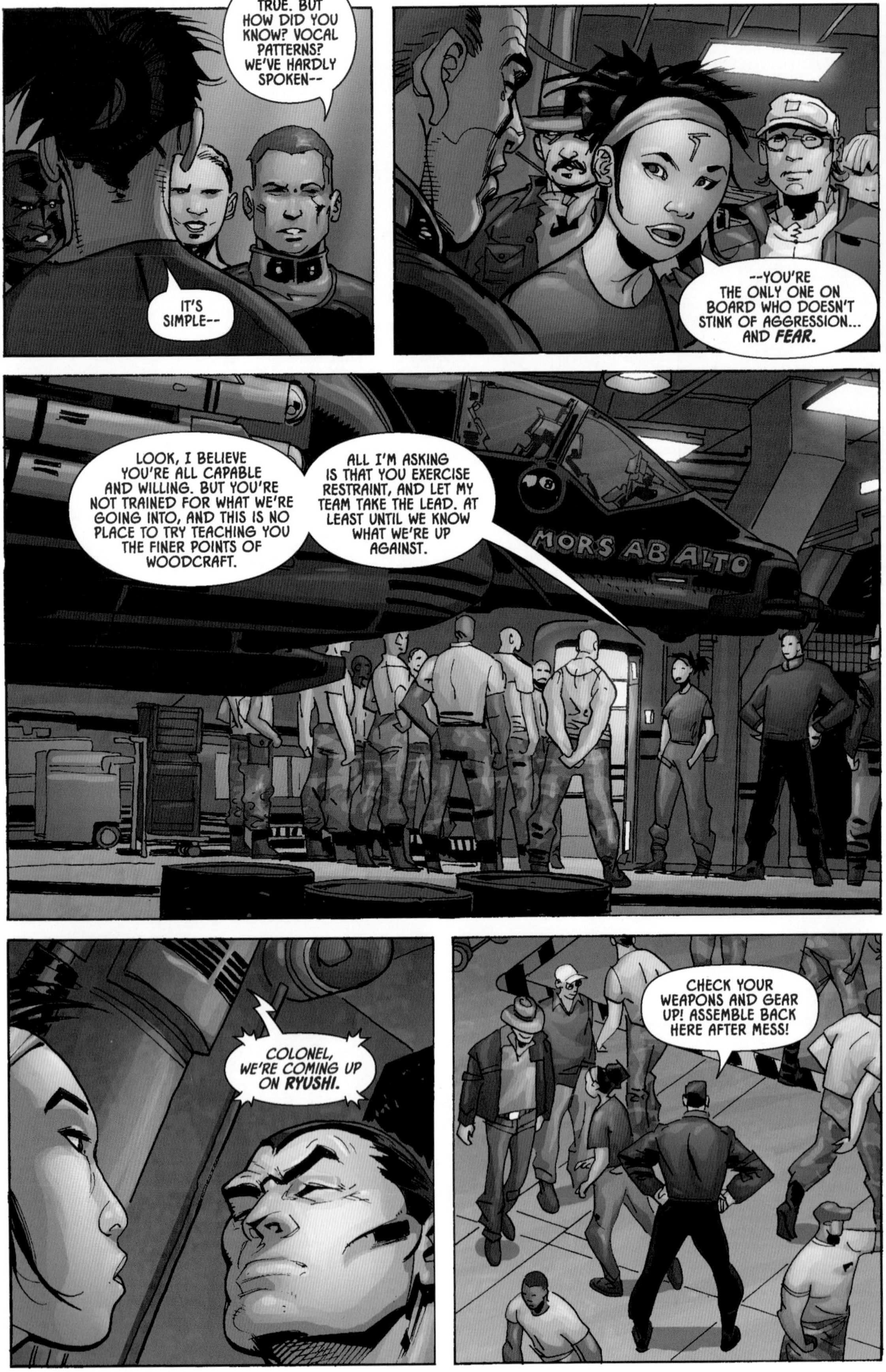
IT'S TRUE. BUT HOW DID YOU KNOW? VOCAL PATTERNS? WE'VE HARDLY SPOKEN--
IT'S SIMPLE--
--YOU'RE THE ONLY ONE ON BOARD WHO DOESN'T STINK OF AGGRESSION... AND FEAR.
LOOK, I BELIEVE YOU'RE ALL CAPABLE AND WILLING. BUT YOU'RE NOT TRAINED FOR WHAT WE'RE GOING INTO, AND THIS IS NO PLACE TO TRY TEACHING YOU THE FINER POINTS OF WOODCRAFT.
ALL I'M ASKING IS THAT YOU EXERCISE RESTRAINT, AND LET MY TEAM TAKE THE LEAD. AT LEAST UNTIL WE KNOW WHAT WE'RE UP AGAINST.
MORS AB ALTO
COLONEL, WE'RE COMING UP ON RYUSHI.
CHECK YOUR WEAPONS AND GEAR UP! ASSEMBLE BACK HERE AFTER MESS!

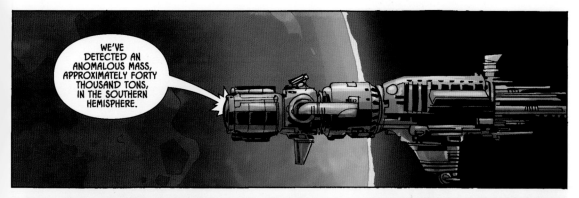

WE'VE DETECTED AN ANOMALOUS MASS, APPROXIMATELY FORTY THOUSAND TONS, IN THE SOUTHERN HEMISPHERE.

THAT'S THEM.

WON'T IT PROVOKE AN ATTACK IF WE SHOW UP UNANNOUNCED?

CORPORAL GARMAN AND ELLIS HAD AN IDEA ABOUT THAT. THERE'S NO WAY TO ESTABLISH VOCAL CONTACT WITH THE HUNTERS, BUT--

WE THOUGHT BY USING A FEW OF THE SHIP'S NIGHTBREAKER FLARES, WE COULD SEND A *VISUAL* MESSAGE. IT'S ALMOST DAWN WHERE THEY ARE...

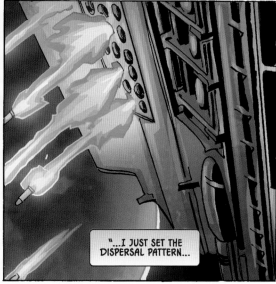

"...I JUST SET THE DISPERSAL PATTERN...

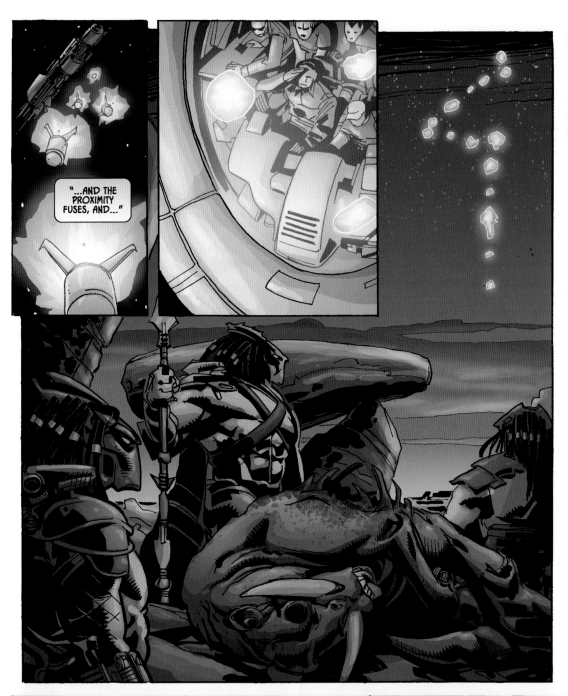

"...AND THE PROXIMITY FUSES, AND..."

WHAT THE HELL IS SHE WEARIN'?

IT'S THE GEAR THE *HUNTERS* WEAR. IT WAS GIVEN TO HER WHEN SHE LIVED WITH THEM.

SHE WENT "NATIVE," eh?

WHEN IN ROME, HARVALD.

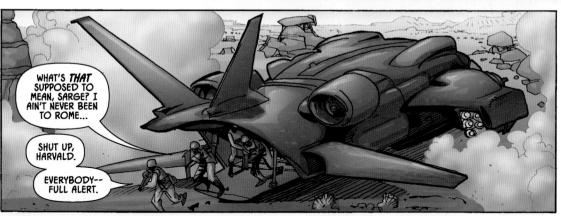

WHAT'S *THAT* SUPPOSED TO MEAN, SARGE? I AIN'T NEVER BEEN TO ROME...

SHUT UP, HARVALD.

EVERYBODY-- FULL ALERT.

AS WE DISCUSSED--MY TEAM TAKES THE LEAD. NOBODY FIRES A WEAPON UNLESS MY GUYS SHOOT FIRST.

HEAR THAT GUYS? NOBODY SHOOTS.

BE CAREFUL, MACHIKO. THERE'S NO GUARANTEE THEY'LL HONOR YOUR PAST RELATIONSHIP WITH THEM, EVEN IF WE DO FIND THEM.

WE'LL FIND OUT SOON ENOUGH...

45

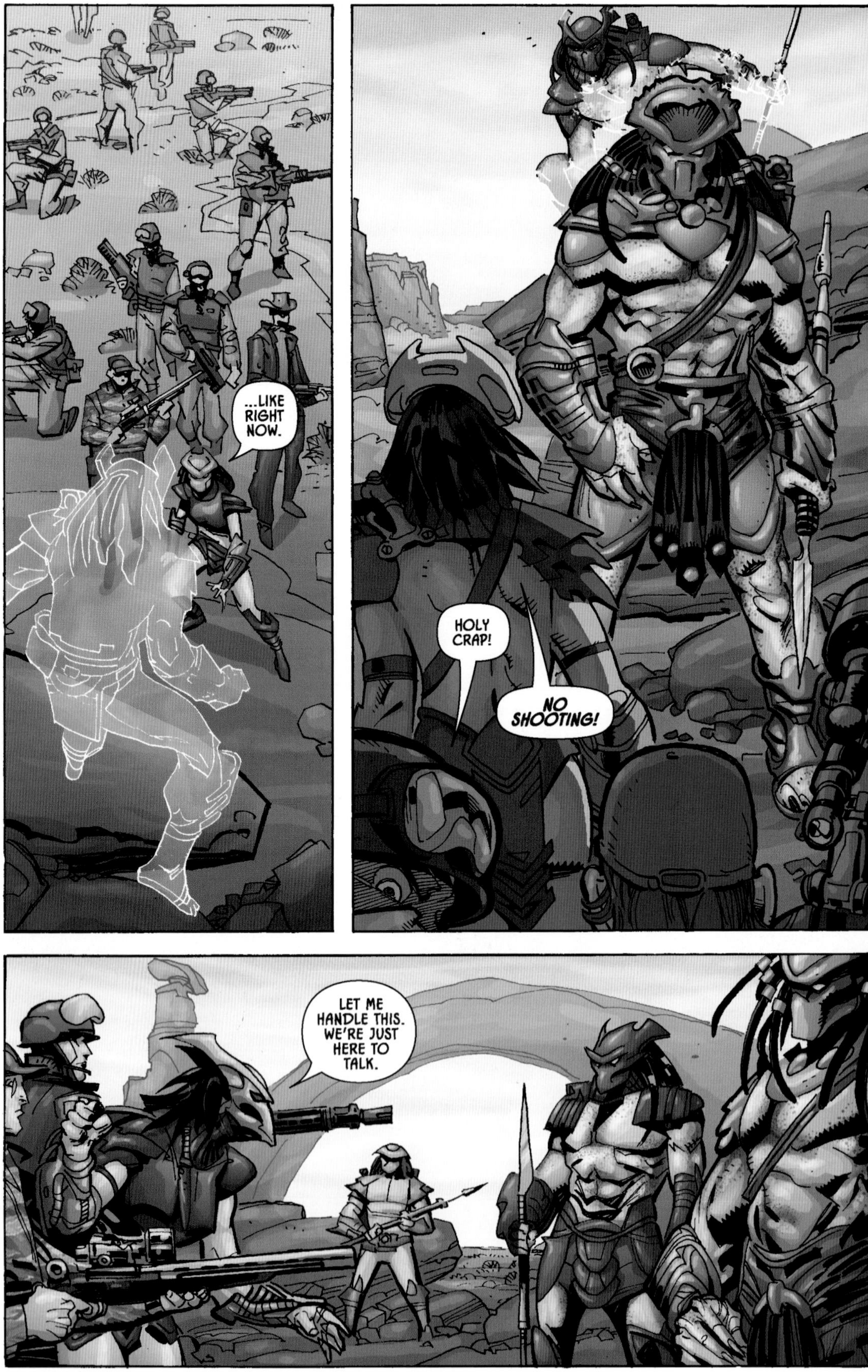
...LIKE RIGHT NOW.
HOLY CRAP!
NO SHOOTING!
LET ME HANDLE THIS. WE'RE JUST HERE TO TALK.

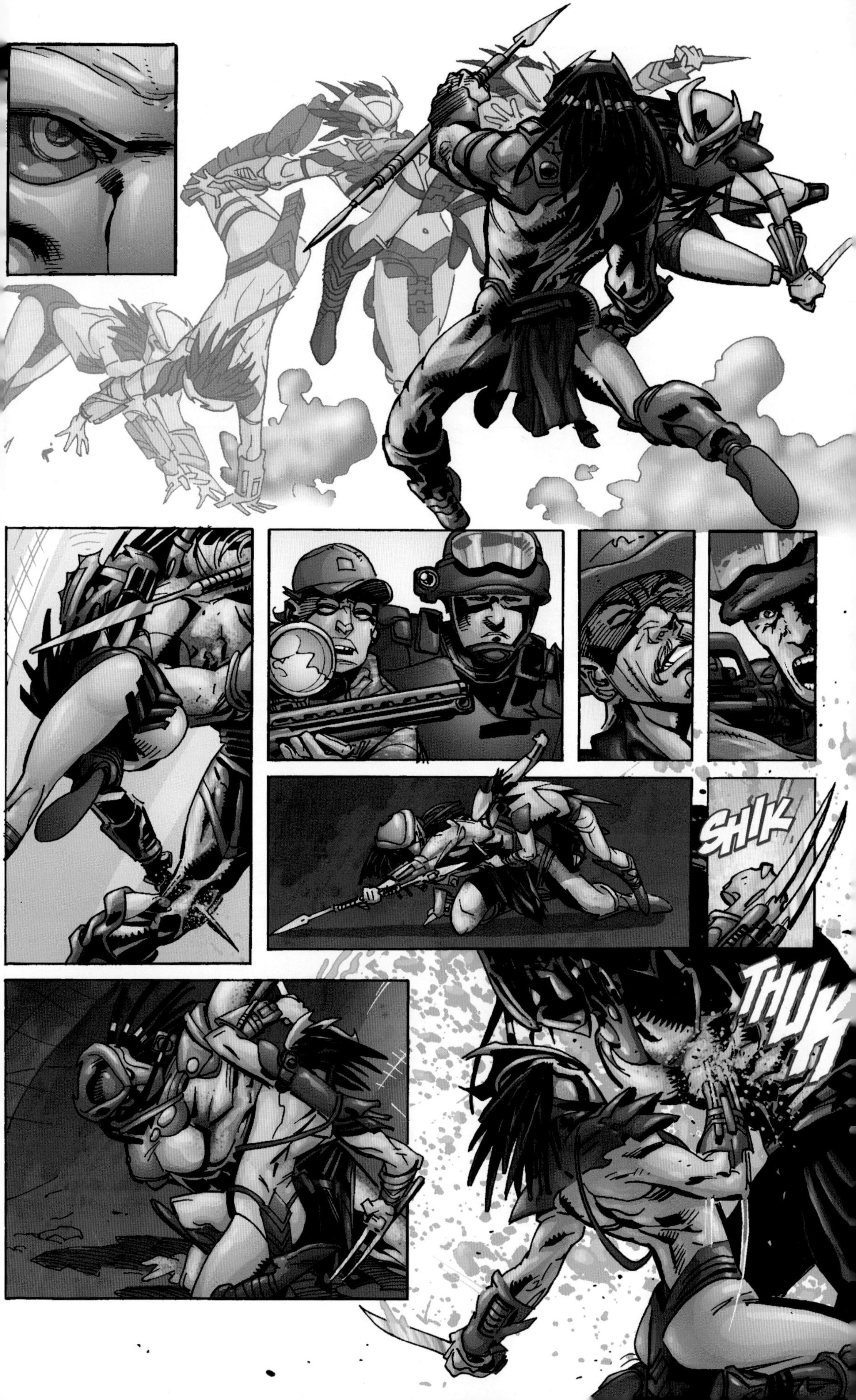
SHIK
THUK

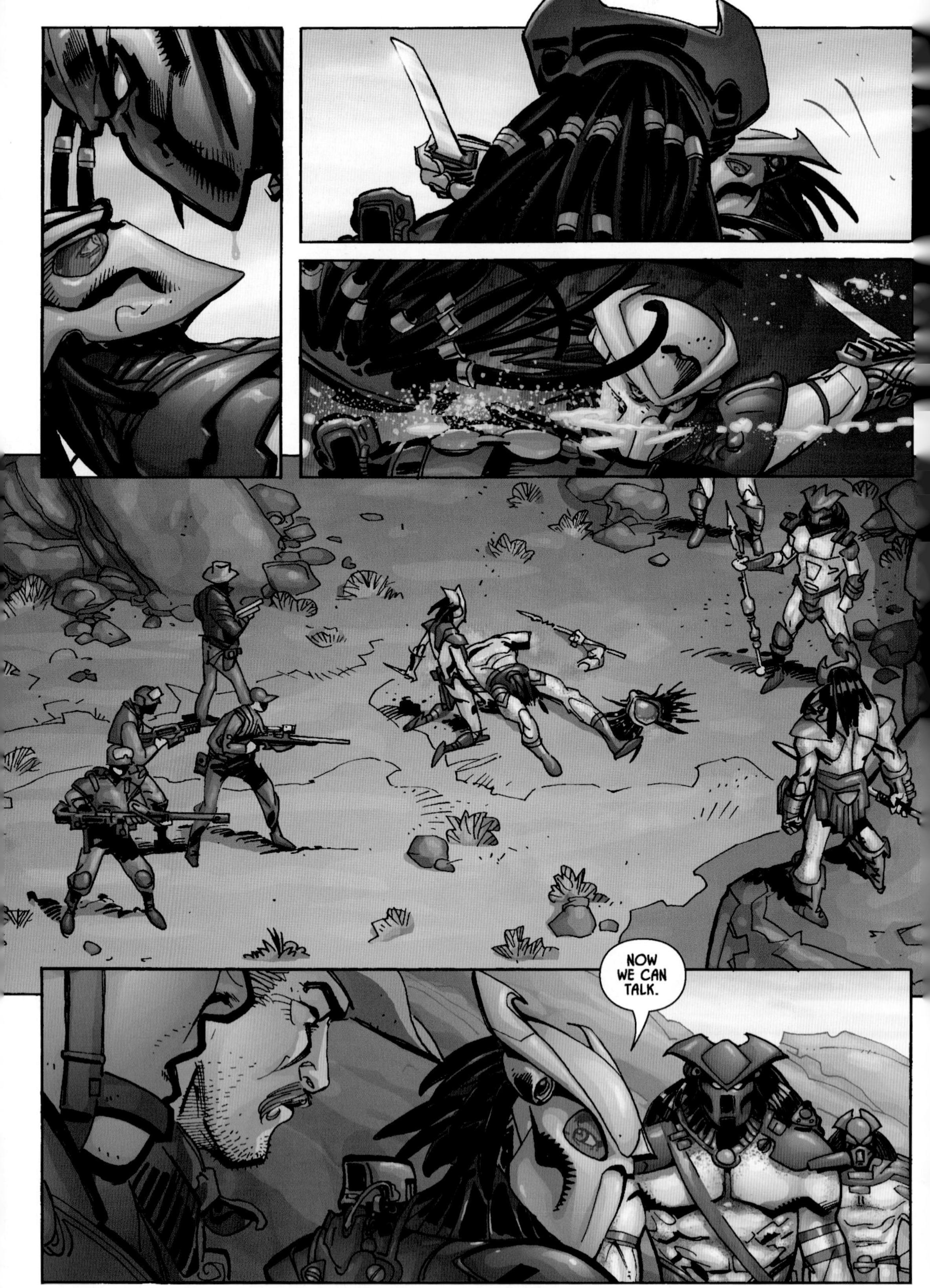
NOW WE CAN TALK.

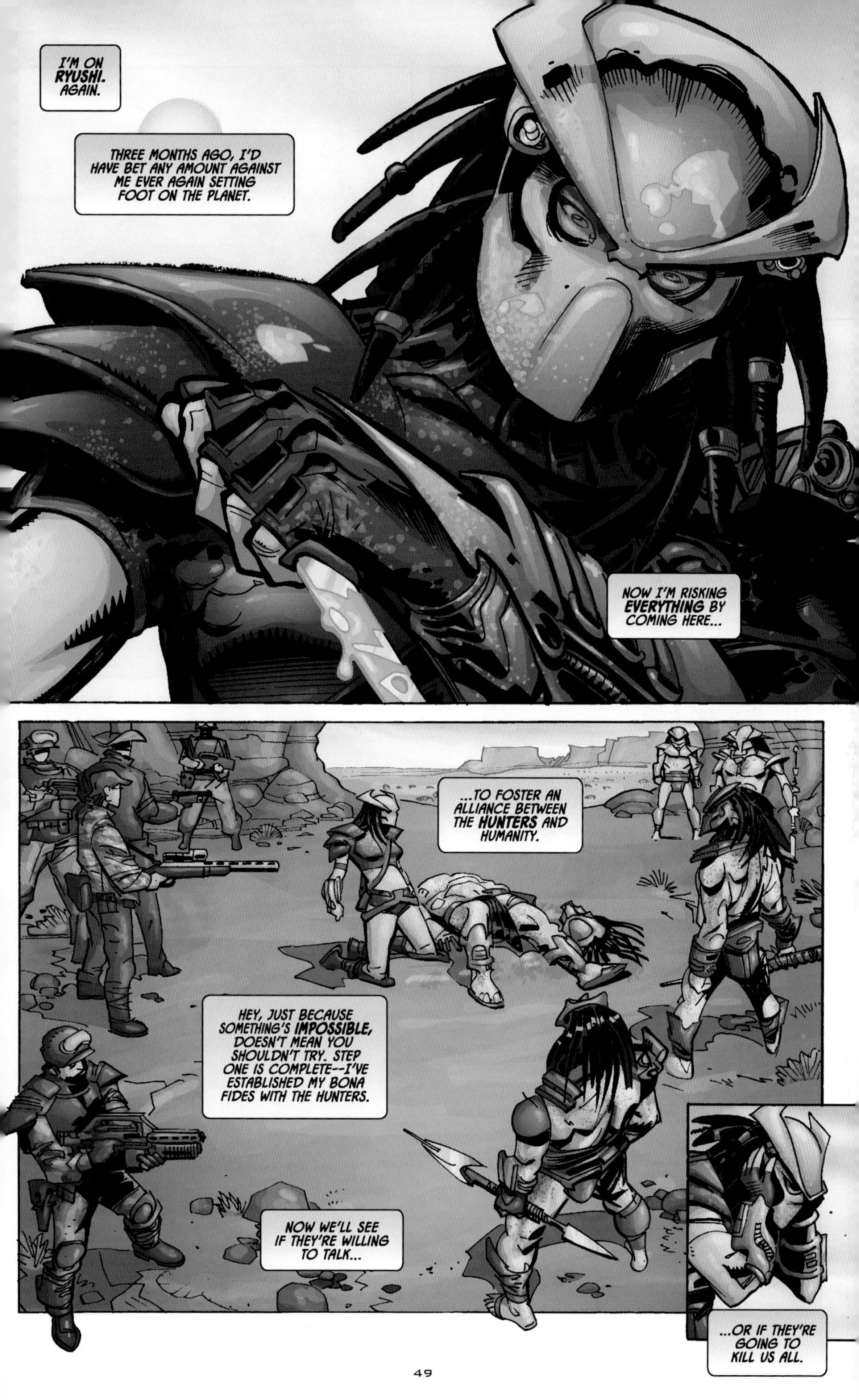
I'M ON RYUSHI. AGAIN.
THREE MONTHS AGO, I'D HAVE BET ANY AMOUNT AGAINST ME EVER AGAIN SETTING FOOT ON THE PLANET.
NOW I'M RISKING EVERYTHING BY COMING HERE...
...TO FOSTER AN ALLIANCE BETWEEN THE HUNTERS AND HUMANITY.
HEY, JUST BECAUSE SOMETHING'S IMPOSSIBLE, DOESN'T MEAN YOU SHOULDN'T TRY. STEP ONE IS COMPLETE--I'VE ESTABLISHED MY BONA FIDES WITH THE HUNTERS.
NOW WE'LL SEE IF THEY'RE WILLING TO TALK...
...OR IF THEY'RE GOING TO KILL US ALL.

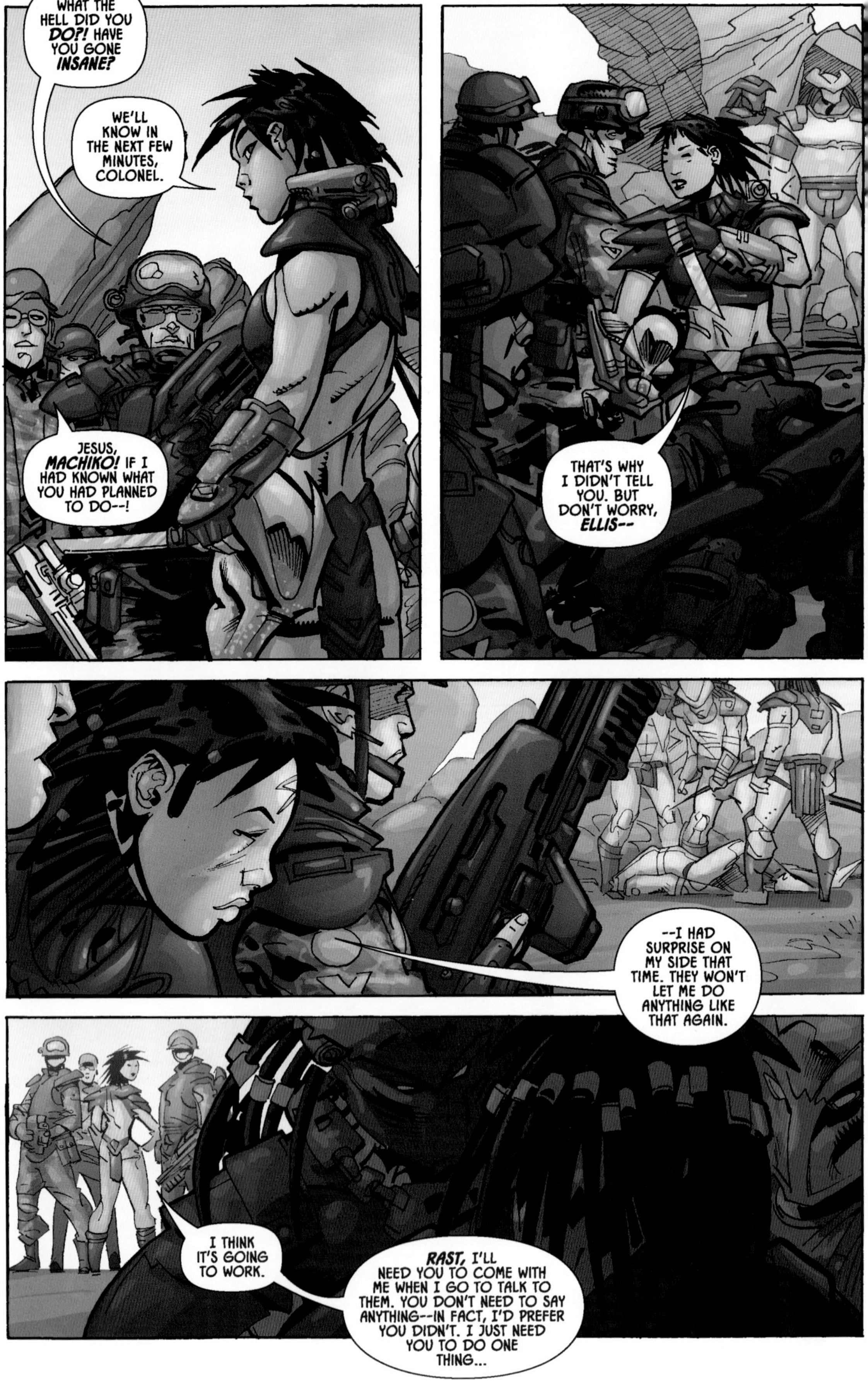
WHAT THE HELL DID YOU DO?! HAVE YOU GONE INSANE?
WE'LL KNOW IN THE NEXT FEW MINUTES, COLONEL.
JESUS, MACHIKO! IF I HAD KNOWN WHAT YOU HAD PLANNED TO DO--!
THAT'S WHY I DIDN'T TELL YOU. BUT DON'T WORRY, ELLIS--
--I HAD SURPRISE ON MY SIDE THAT TIME. THEY WON'T LET ME DO ANYTHING LIKE THAT AGAIN.
I THINK IT'S GOING TO WORK.
RAST, I'LL NEED YOU TO COME WITH ME WHEN I GO TO TALK TO THEM. YOU DON'T NEED TO SAY ANYTHING--IN FACT, I'D PREFER YOU DIDN'T. I JUST NEED YOU TO DO ONE THING...

...ACT LIKE YOU'RE IN *CHARGE* OF THIS MISSION.

WHA--?!

I *AM* IN CHARGE!

IT'S CUTE THAT YOU THINK SO. BUT WE NEED THE *HUNTERS* TO THINK SO, TOO.

ELLIS, I NEED YOU TO HANG BACK...

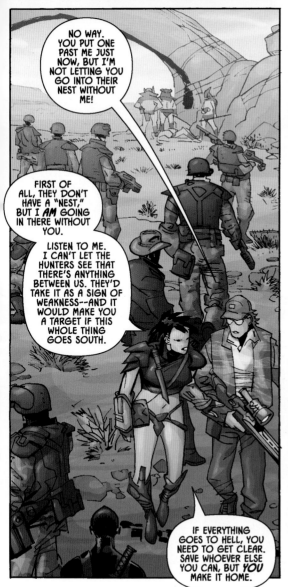

NO WAY. YOU PUT ONE PAST ME JUST NOW, BUT I'M NOT LETTING YOU GO INTO THEIR NEST WITHOUT ME!

FIRST OF ALL, THEY DON'T HAVE A "NEST," BUT I *AM* GOING IN THERE WITHOUT YOU.

LISTEN TO ME. I CAN'T LET THE HUNTERS SEE THAT THERE'S ANYTHING BETWEEN US. THEY'D TAKE IT AS A SIGN OF WEAKNESS--AND IT WOULD MAKE YOU A TARGET IF THIS WHOLE THING GOES SOUTH.

IF EVERYTHING GOES TO HELL, YOU NEED TO GET CLEAR. SAVE WHOEVER ELSE YOU CAN, BUT *YOU* MAKE IT HOME.

PROMISE ME. I CAN'T DO THIS NEXT PART--I WON'T HAVE THE STRENGTH FOR IT--UNLESS YOU PROMISE.

OKAY.

OKAY, RAST! LET'S GET THIS STARTED.

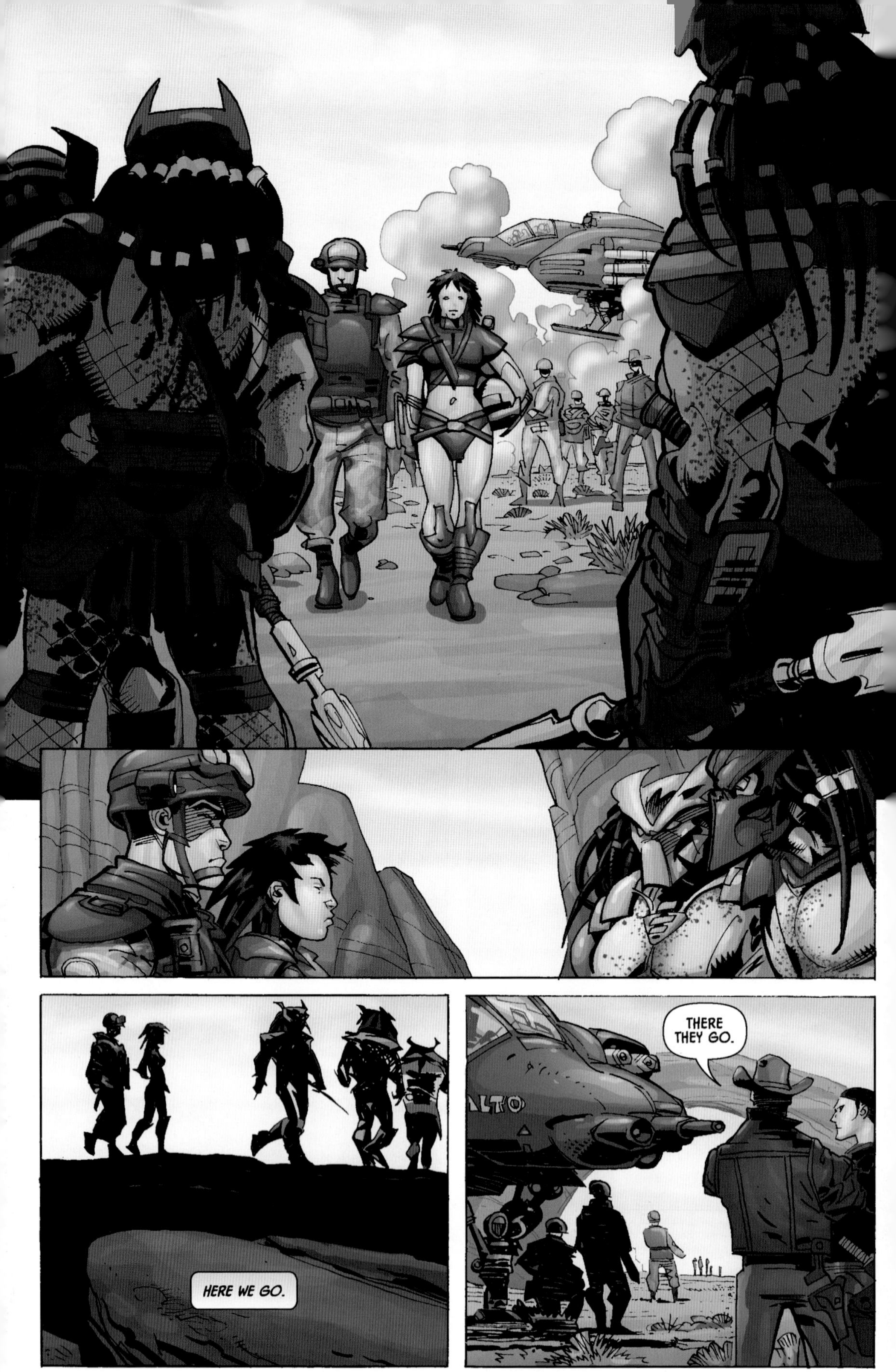
HERE WE GO.
THERE THEY GO.

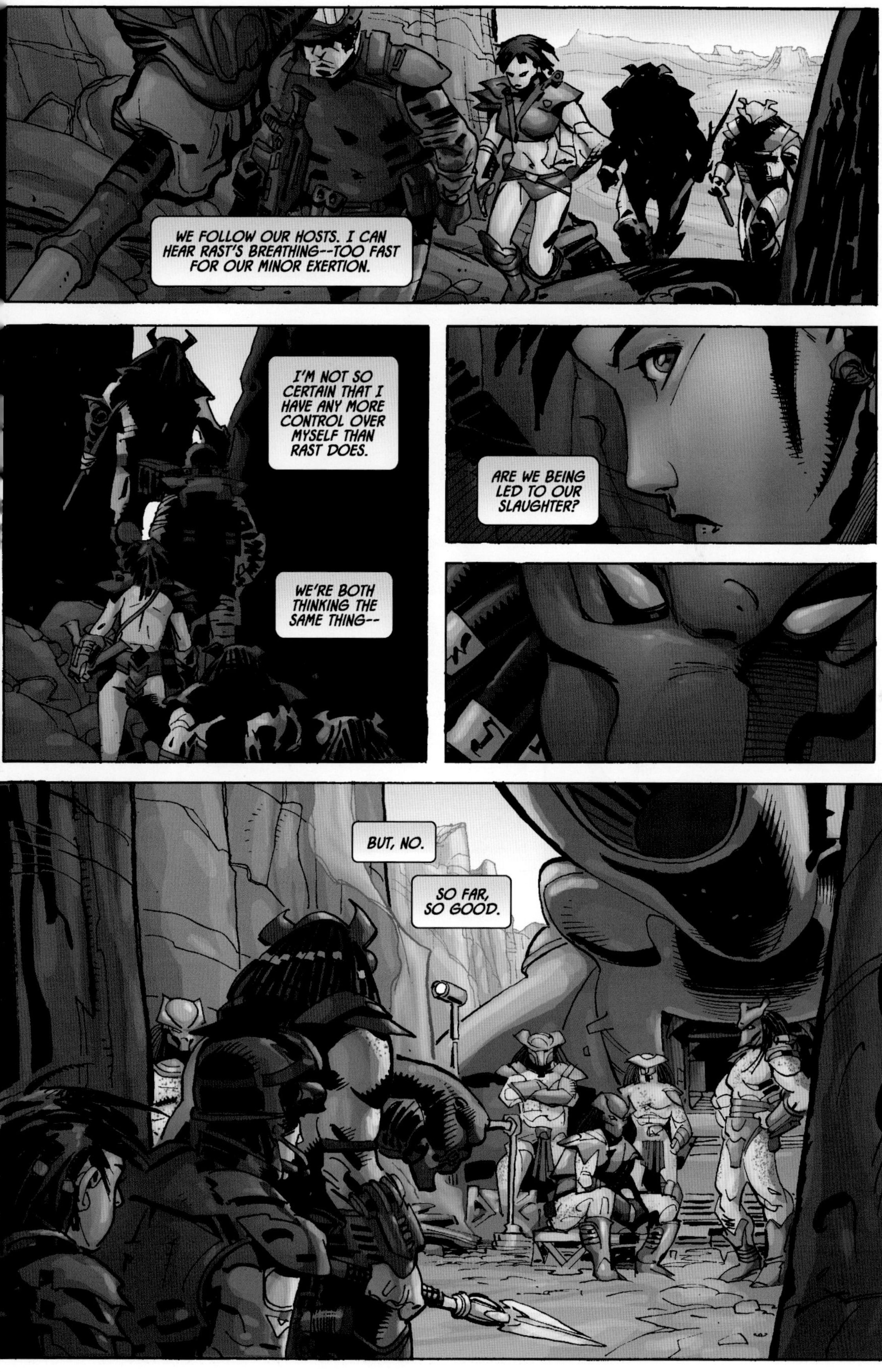
WE FOLLOW OUR HOSTS. I CAN HEAR RAST'S BREATHING--TOO FAST FOR OUR MINOR EXERTION.
I'M NOT SO CERTAIN THAT I HAVE ANY MORE CONTROL OVER MYSELF THAN RAST DOES.
WE'RE BOTH THINKING THE SAME THING--
ARE WE BEING LED TO OUR SLAUGHTER?
BUT, NO.
SO FAR, SO GOOD.

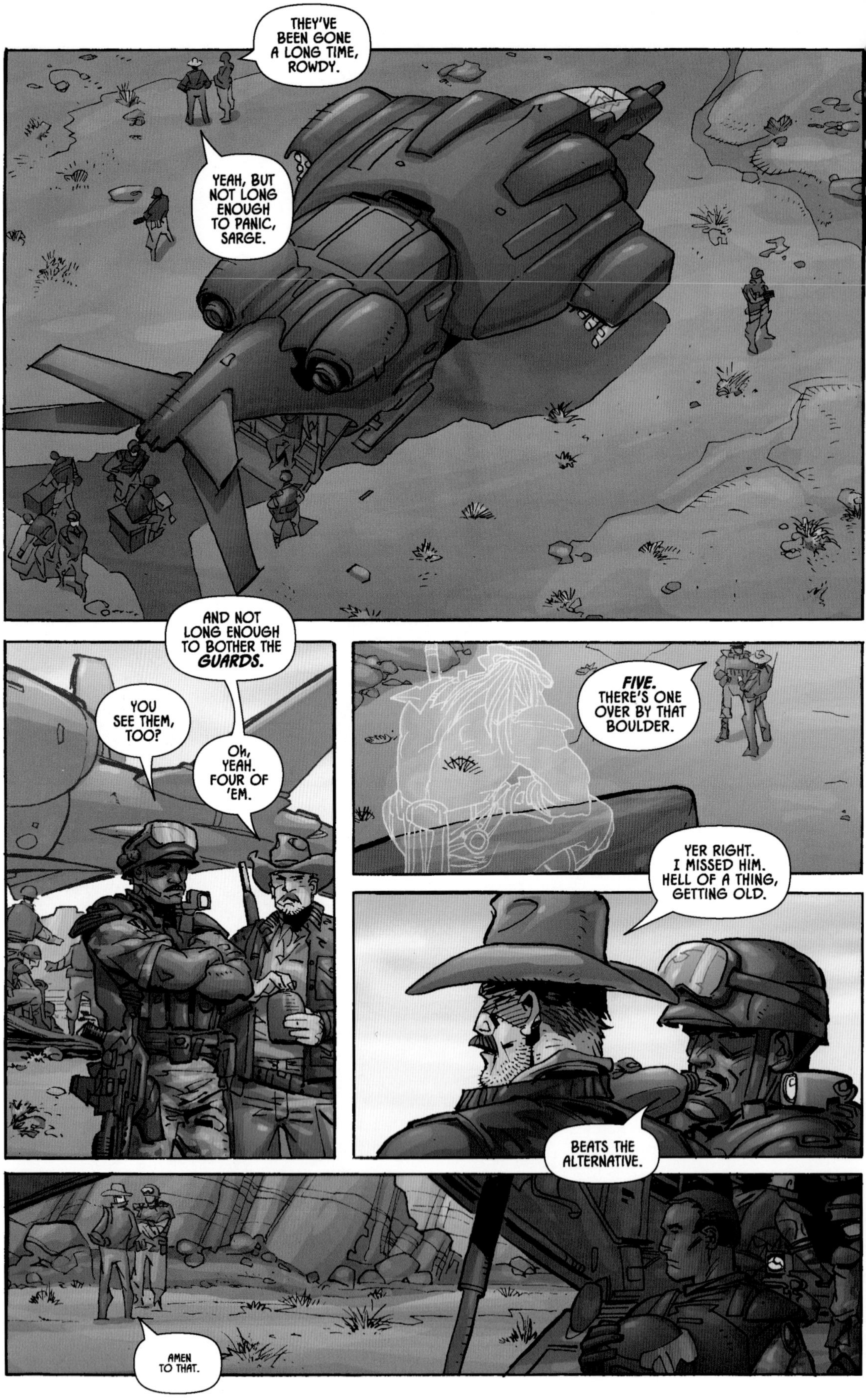
THEY'VE BEEN GONE A LONG TIME, ROWDY.
YEAH, BUT NOT LONG ENOUGH TO PANIC, SARGE.
AND NOT LONG ENOUGH TO BOTHER THE GUARDS.
YOU SEE THEM, TOO?
Oh, YEAH. FOUR OF 'EM.
FIVE. THERE'S ONE OVER BY THAT BOULDER.
YER RIGHT. I MISSED HIM. HELL OF A THING, GETTING OLD.
BEATS THE ALTERNATIVE.
AMEN TO THAT.

HOW DID MS. NOGUCHI *KNOW?*

SHE SPENT MORE THAN A YEAR WITH THE HUNTERS. SHE KNEW THEY'D RESPOND TO A SHOW OF FORCE.

THAT'S NOT WHAT I MEANT...

...I MEAN, HOW DID SHE KNOW I WAS A *SYNTHETIC?*

Oh.

WELL, IT'S JUST HOW HER MIND WORKS.

SHE SEES THE SAME THINGS EVERYBODY ELSE DOES, BUT SHE SEES WHERE THEY *LEAD* TO...

...GUESSES WHAT'S GOING TO HAPPEN *NEXT.* IT'S ALMOST IMPOSSIBLE TO HIDE ANYTHING FROM HER.

IT MAKES HER GREAT AT HER JOB, BUT IT ALSO MAKES HER HELL TO LIVE WITH SOMETIMES...THE WAY SHE PUTS THINGS TOGETHER SO FAST...

LIKE OUR FRIENDS OUT THERE. SOMETHING'S GOT THEM AGITATED--LOOK AT THEM GO!

YOU CAN *SEE* THEM--*CLEARLY,* I MEAN?

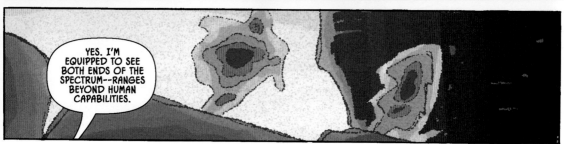

YES. I'M EQUIPPED TO SEE BOTH ENDS OF THE SPECTRUM--RANGES BEYOND HUMAN CAPABILITIES.

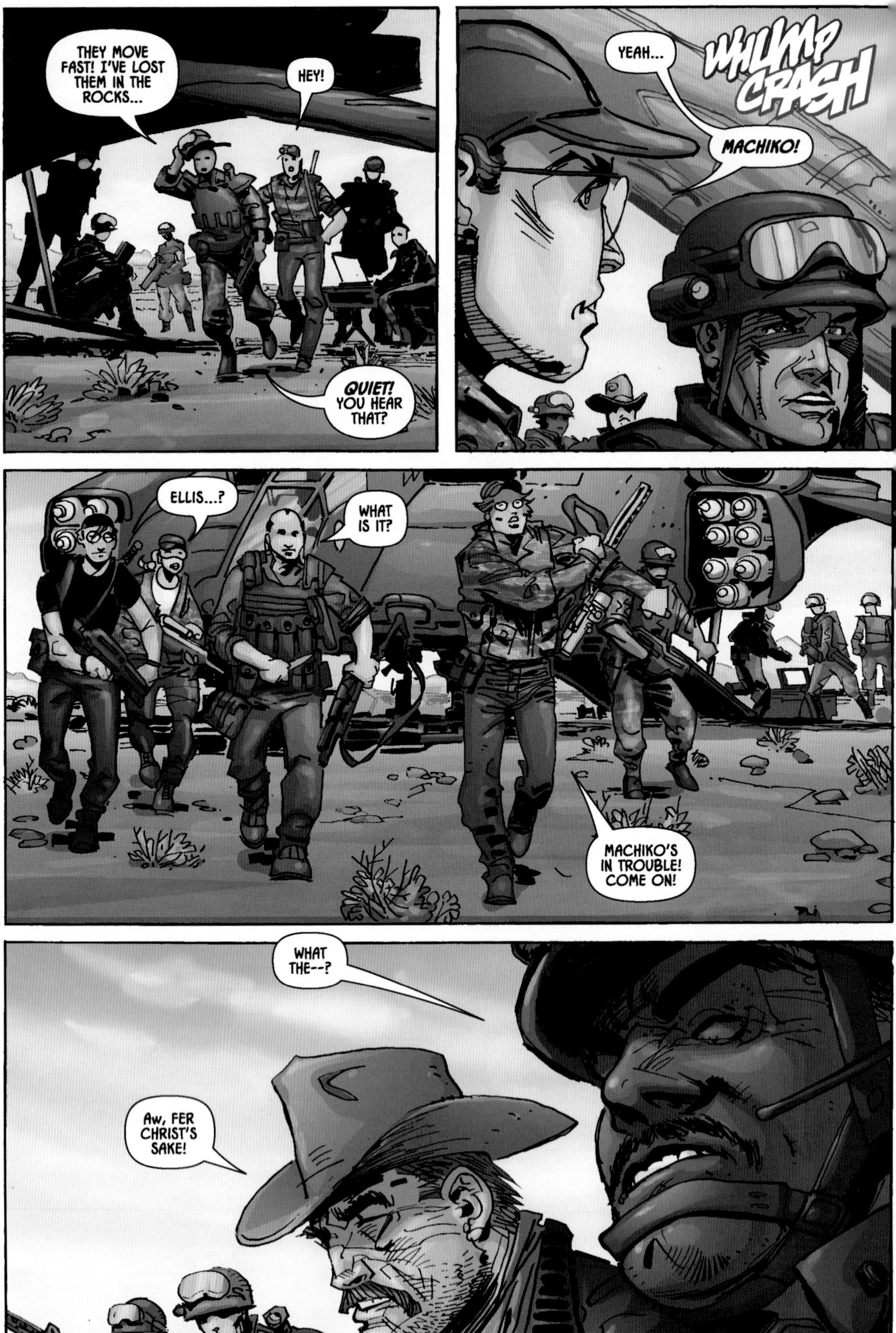
THEY MOVE FAST! I'VE LOST THEM IN THE ROCKS...
HEY!
QUIET! YOU HEAR THAT?
YEAH...
WHUMP CRASH
MACHIKO!
ELLIS...?
WHAT IS IT?
MACHIKO'S IN TROUBLE! COME ON!
WHAT THE--?
Aw, FER CHRIST'S SAKE!

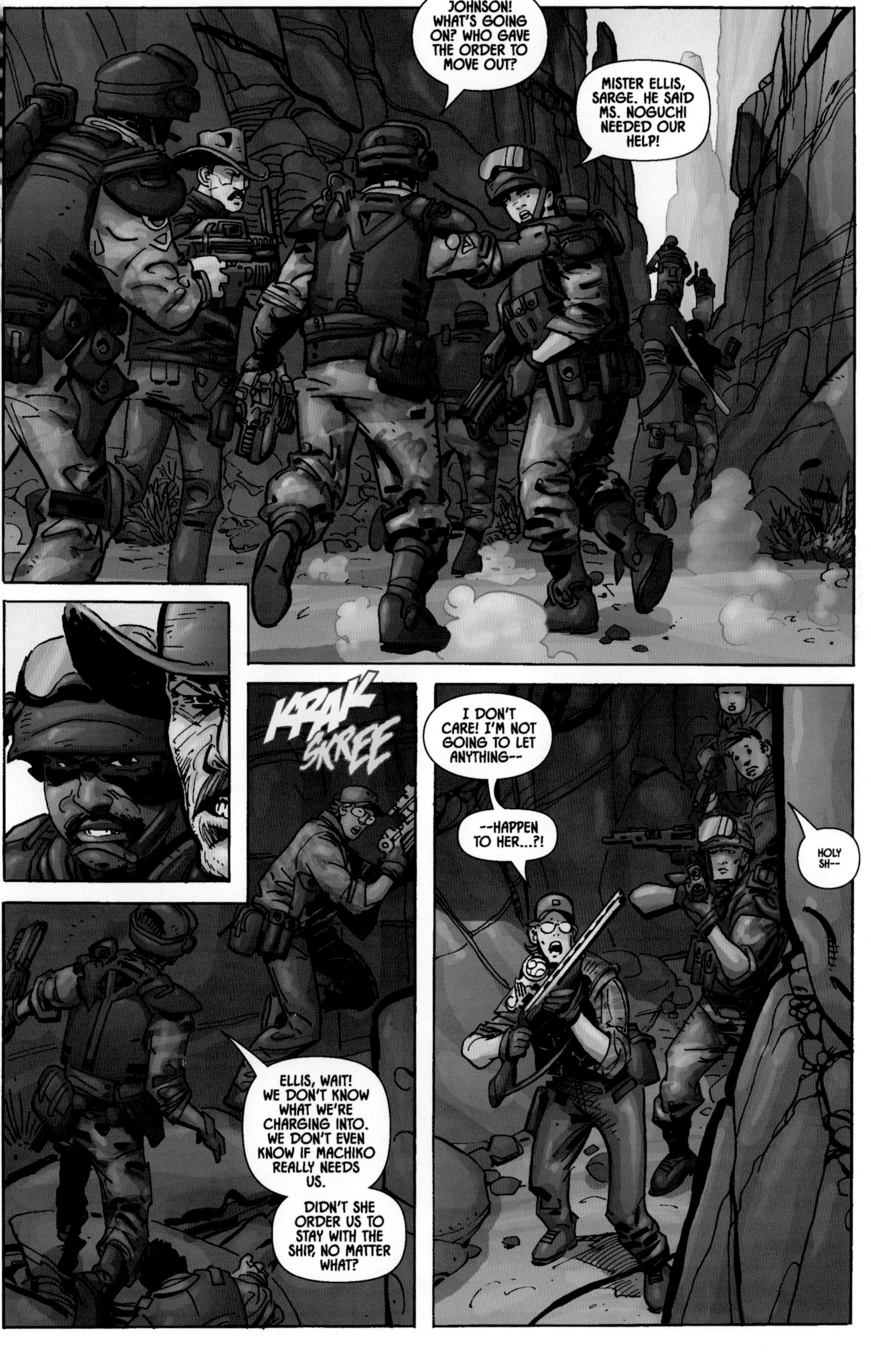

JOHNSON! WHAT'S GOING ON? WHO GAVE THE ORDER TO MOVE OUT?
MISTER ELLIS, SARGE. HE SAID MS. NOGUCHI NEEDED OUR HELP!
KRAK SKREE
ELLIS, WAIT! WE DON'T KNOW WHAT WE'RE CHARGING INTO. WE DON'T EVEN KNOW IF MACHIKO REALLY NEEDS US.
DIDN'T SHE ORDER US TO STAY WITH THE SHIP, NO MATTER WHAT?
I DON'T CARE! I'M NOT GOING TO LET ANYTHING--
--HAPPEN TO HER...?!
HOLY SH--

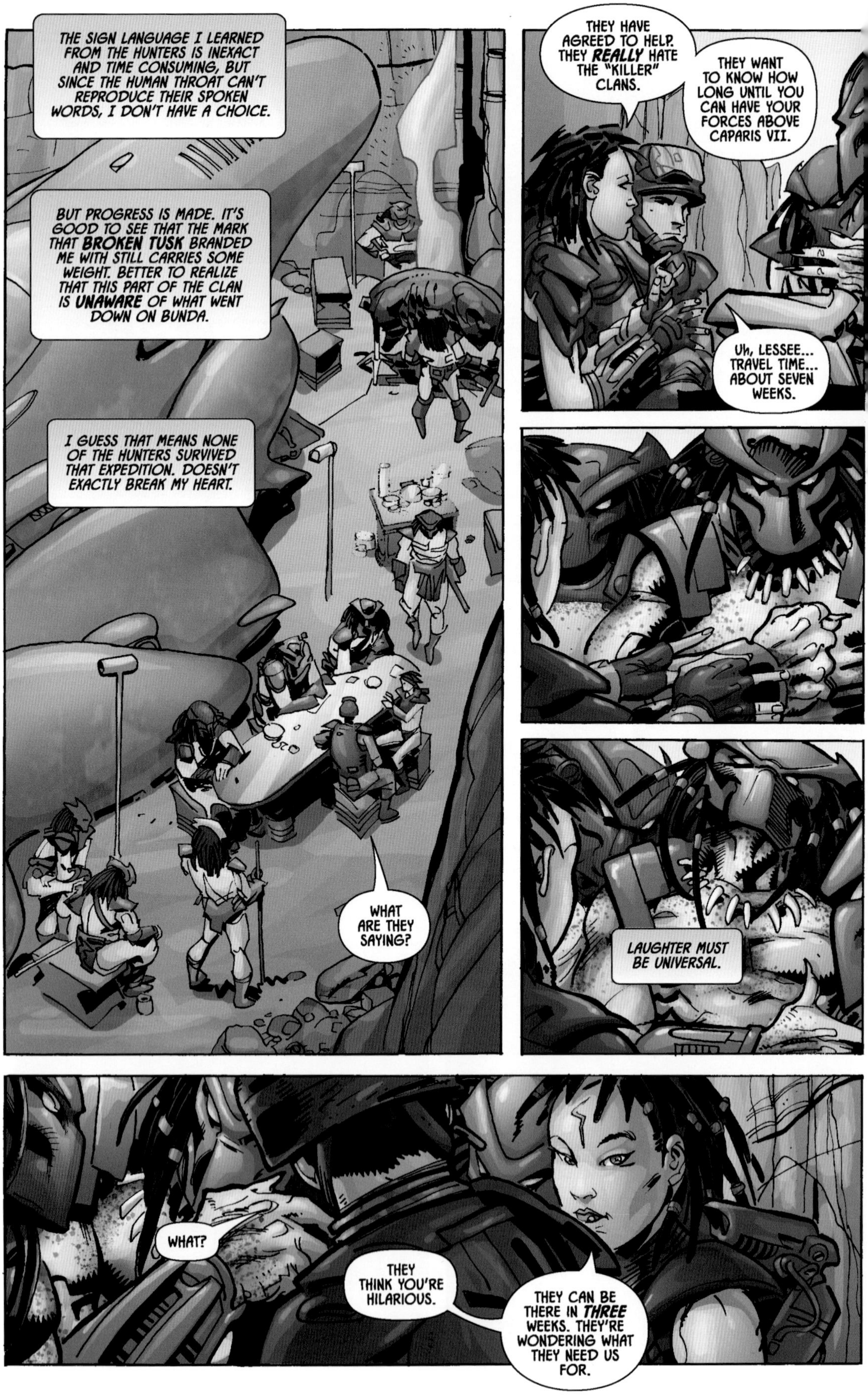
THE SIGN LANGUAGE I LEARNED FROM THE HUNTERS IS INEXACT AND TIME CONSUMING, BUT SINCE THE HUMAN THROAT CAN'T REPRODUCE THEIR SPOKEN WORDS, I DON'T HAVE A CHOICE.
BUT PROGRESS IS MADE. IT'S GOOD TO SEE THAT THE MARK THAT BROKEN TUSK BRANDED ME WITH STILL CARRIES SOME WEIGHT. BETTER TO REALIZE THAT THIS PART OF THE CLAN IS UNAWARE OF WHAT WENT DOWN ON BUNDA.
I GUESS THAT MEANS NONE OF THE HUNTERS SURVIVED THAT EXPEDITION. DOESN'T EXACTLY BREAK MY HEART.
WHAT ARE THEY SAYING?
THEY HAVE AGREED TO HELP. THEY REALLY HATE THE "KILLER" CLANS.
THEY WANT TO KNOW HOW LONG UNTIL YOU CAN HAVE YOUR FORCES ABOVE CAPARIS VII.
Uh, LESSEE... TRAVEL TIME... ABOUT SEVEN WEEKS.
LAUGHTER MUST BE UNIVERSAL.
WHAT?
THEY THINK YOU'RE HILARIOUS.
THEY CAN BE THERE IN THREE WEEKS. THEY'RE WONDERING WHAT THEY NEED US FOR.

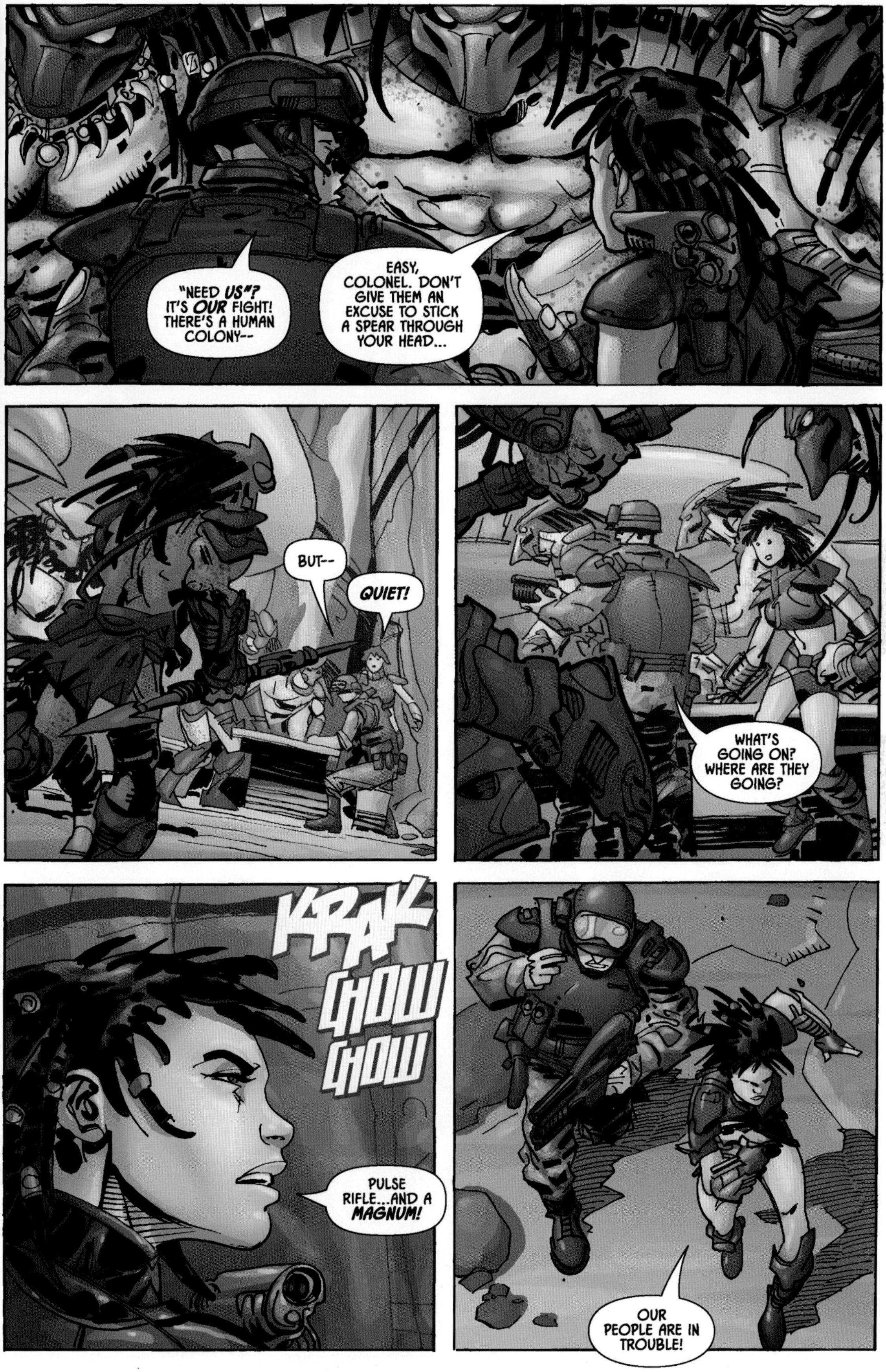
"NEED US"? IT'S OUR FIGHT! THERE'S A HUMAN COLONY--
EASY, COLONEL. DON'T GIVE THEM AN EXCUSE TO STICK A SPEAR THROUGH YOUR HEAD...
BUT--
QUIET!
WHAT'S GOING ON? WHERE ARE THEY GOING?
KRAK
CHOW
CHOW
PULSE RIFLE...AND A MAGNUM!
OUR PEOPLE ARE IN TROUBLE!

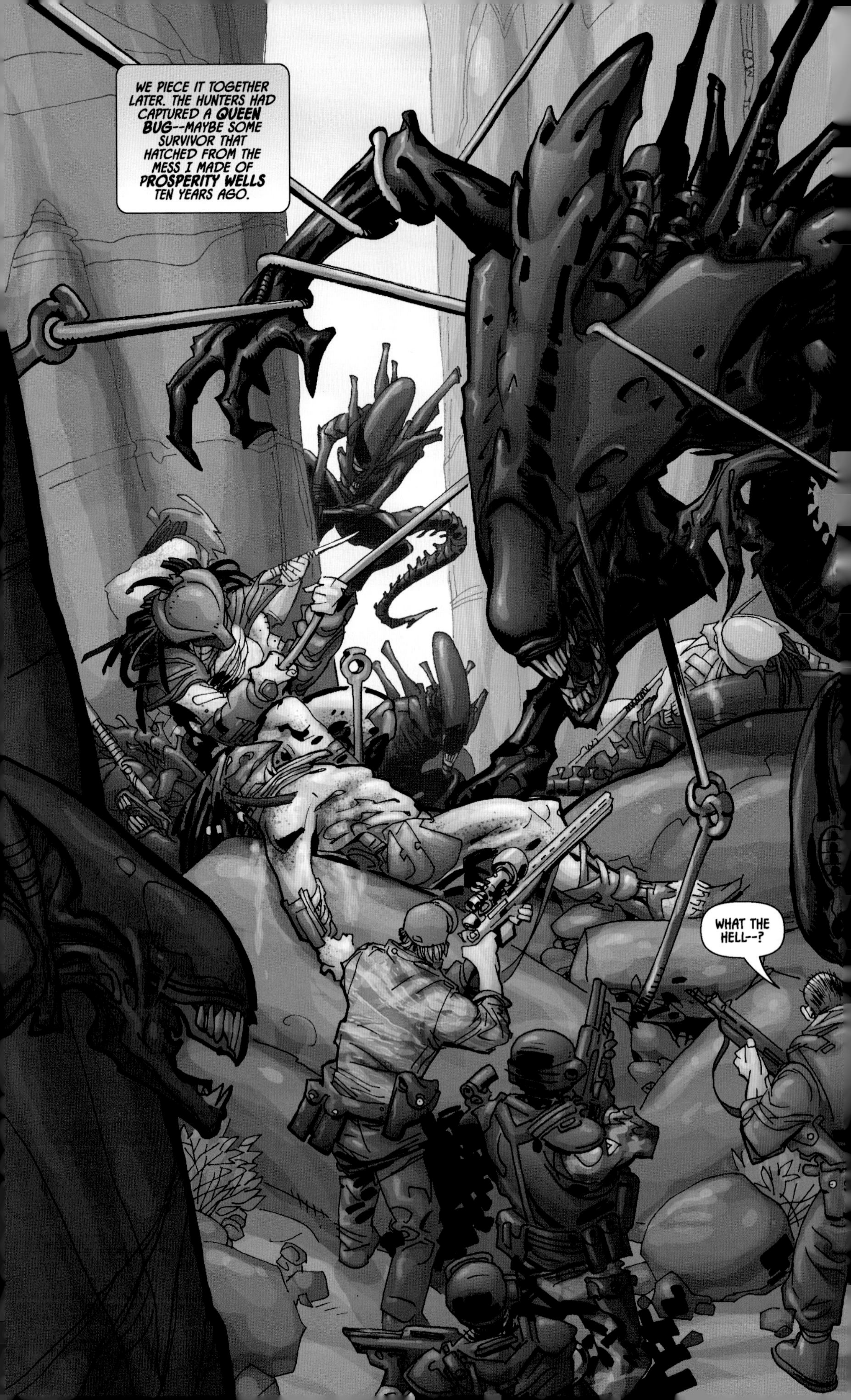
WE PIECE IT TOGETHER LATER. THE HUNTERS HAD CAPTURED A QUEEN BUG--MAYBE SOME SURVIVOR THAT HATCHED FROM THE MESS I MADE OF PROSPERITY WELLS TEN YEARS AGO.
WHAT THE HELL--?

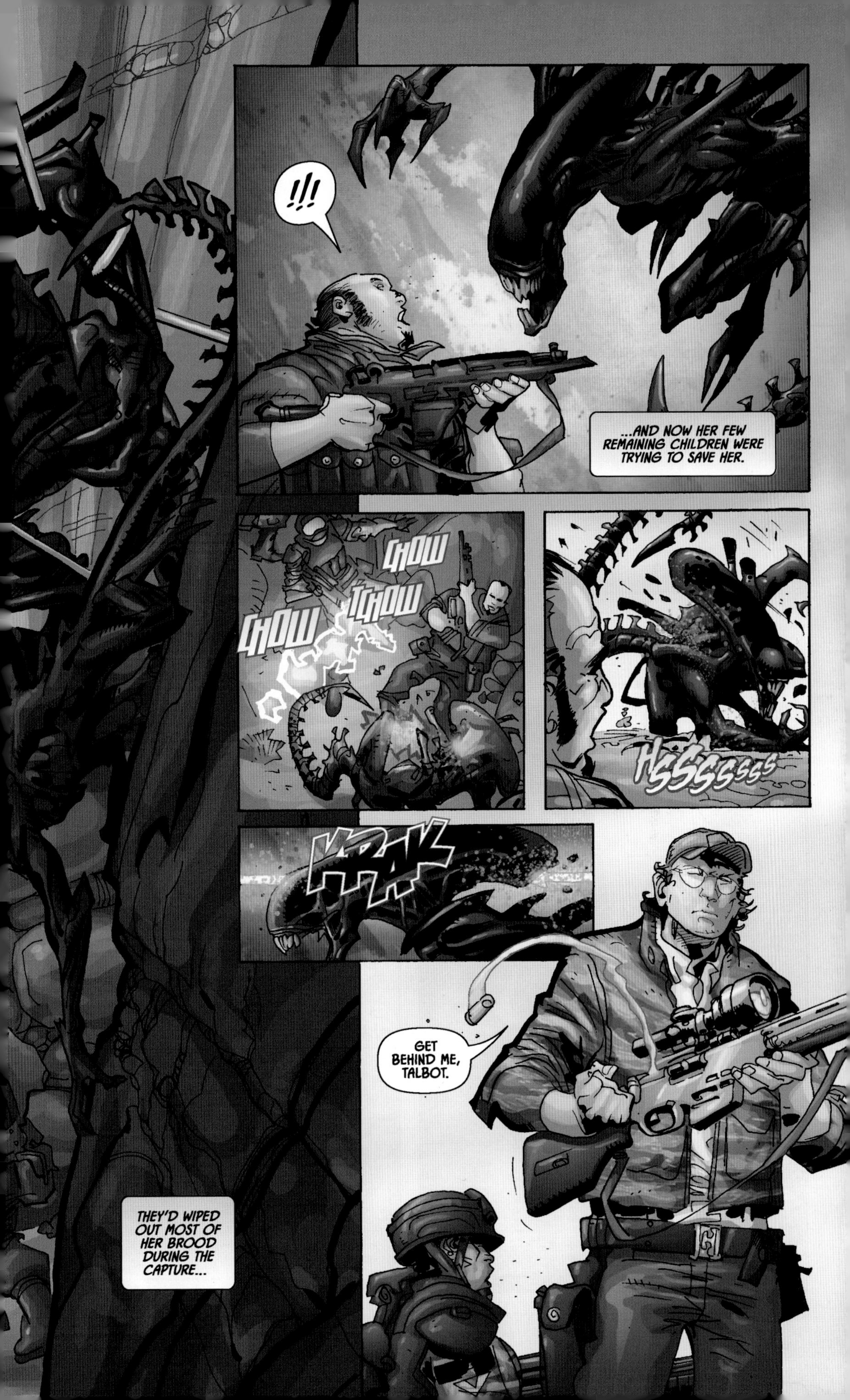
!!!
...AND NOW HER FEW REMAINING CHILDREN WERE TRYING TO SAVE HER.
CHOW
TCHOW
CHOW
HSSSSSSS
KRAK
GET BEHIND ME, TALBOT.
THEY'D WIPED OUT MOST OF HER BROOD DURING THE CAPTURE...

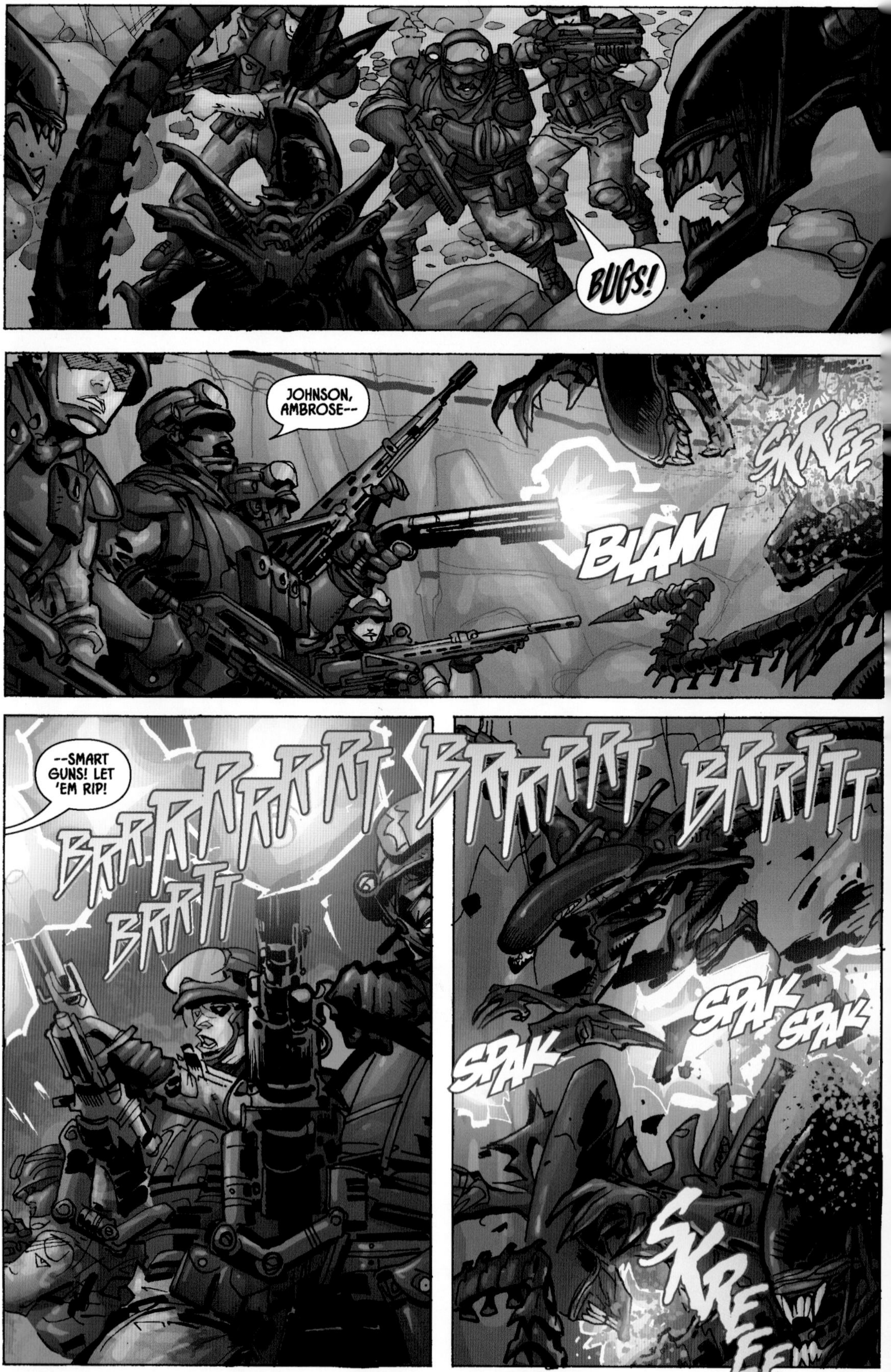
BUGS!
JOHNSON, AMBROSE--
BLAM
SKREE
--SMART GUNS! LET 'EM RIP!
BRRRRRRRRRRT
BRRTT
BRRRRRT
BRRTTT
SPAK
SPAK
SPAK
SKREEEE

AHHH! GET IT OFF M--!

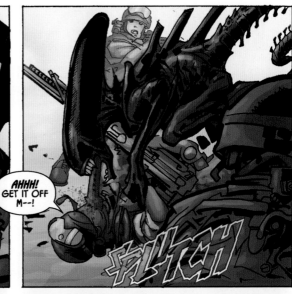

SPLTCH

CHOM CHOM

AAIEE!

THORA! OMIGOD!

TSSSSS

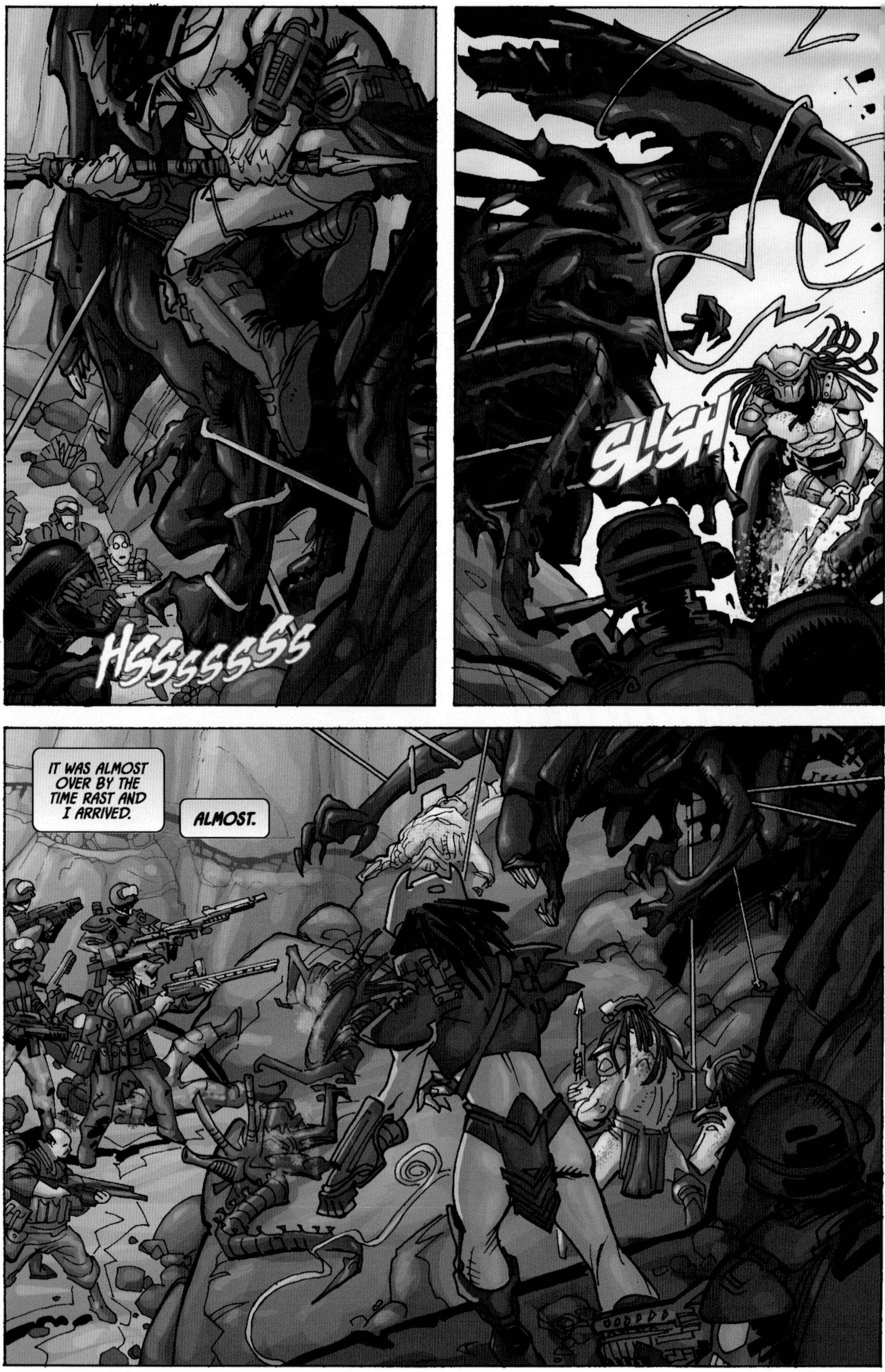
HSSSSSSSS
SLISH
IT WAS ALMOST OVER BY THE TIME RAST AND I ARRIVED.
ALMOST.

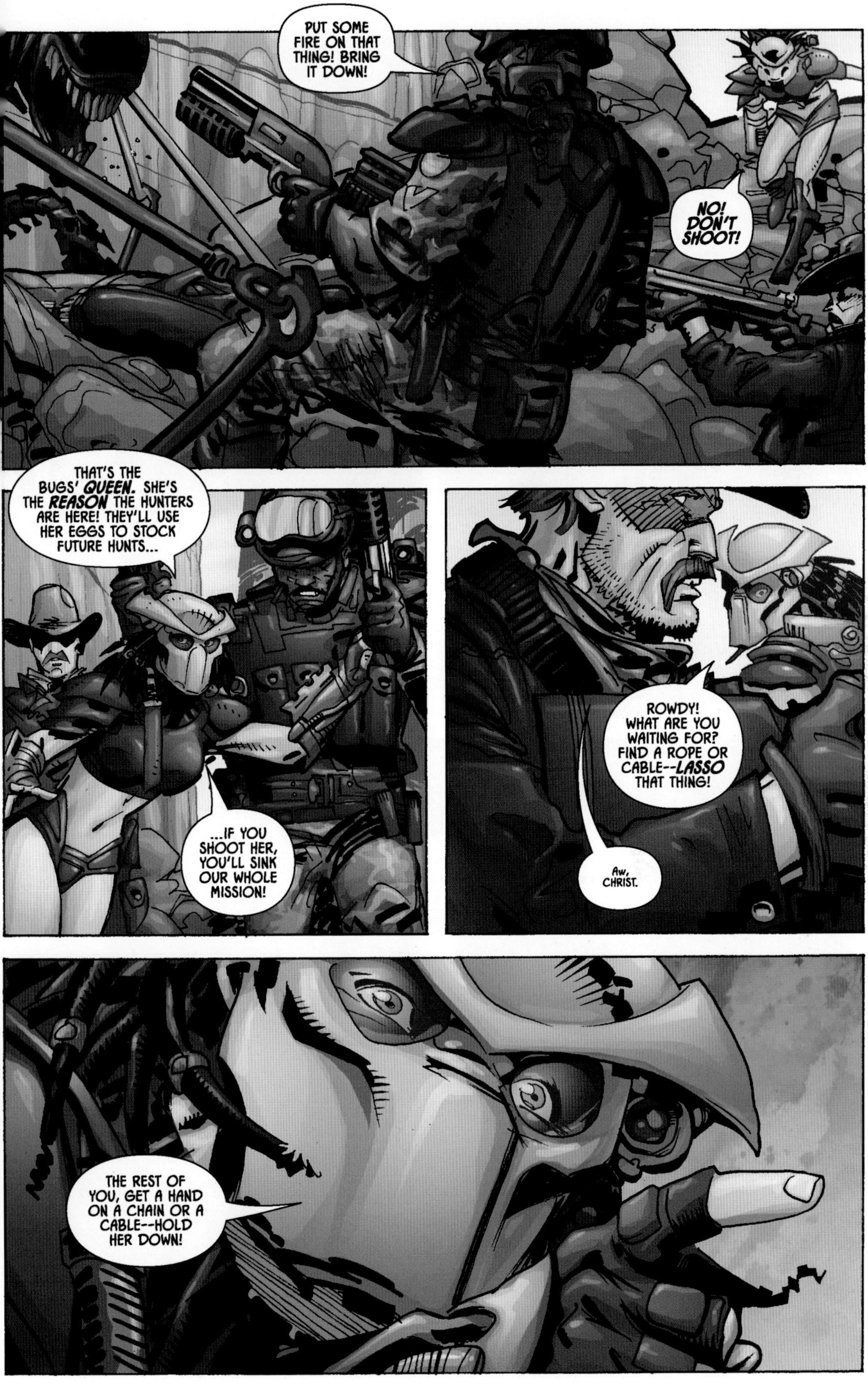

PUT SOME FIRE ON THAT THING! BRING IT DOWN!
NO! DON'T SHOOT!
THAT'S THE BUGS' QUEEN. SHE'S THE REASON THE HUNTERS ARE HERE! THEY'LL USE HER EGGS TO STOCK FUTURE HUNTS...
...IF YOU SHOOT HER, YOU'LL SINK OUR WHOLE MISSION!
ROWDY! WHAT ARE YOU WAITING FOR? FIND A ROPE OR CABLE--LASSO THAT THING!
AW, CHRIST.
THE REST OF YOU, GET A HAND ON A CHAIN OR A CABLE--HOLD HER DOWN!

SNAP

HSSsss

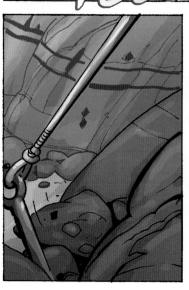

MACHIKO-- LISTEN TO ME. IF I SAY "LET GO"--YOU **HAVE** TO LET GO.

DON'T YOU SAY IT, ELLIS!

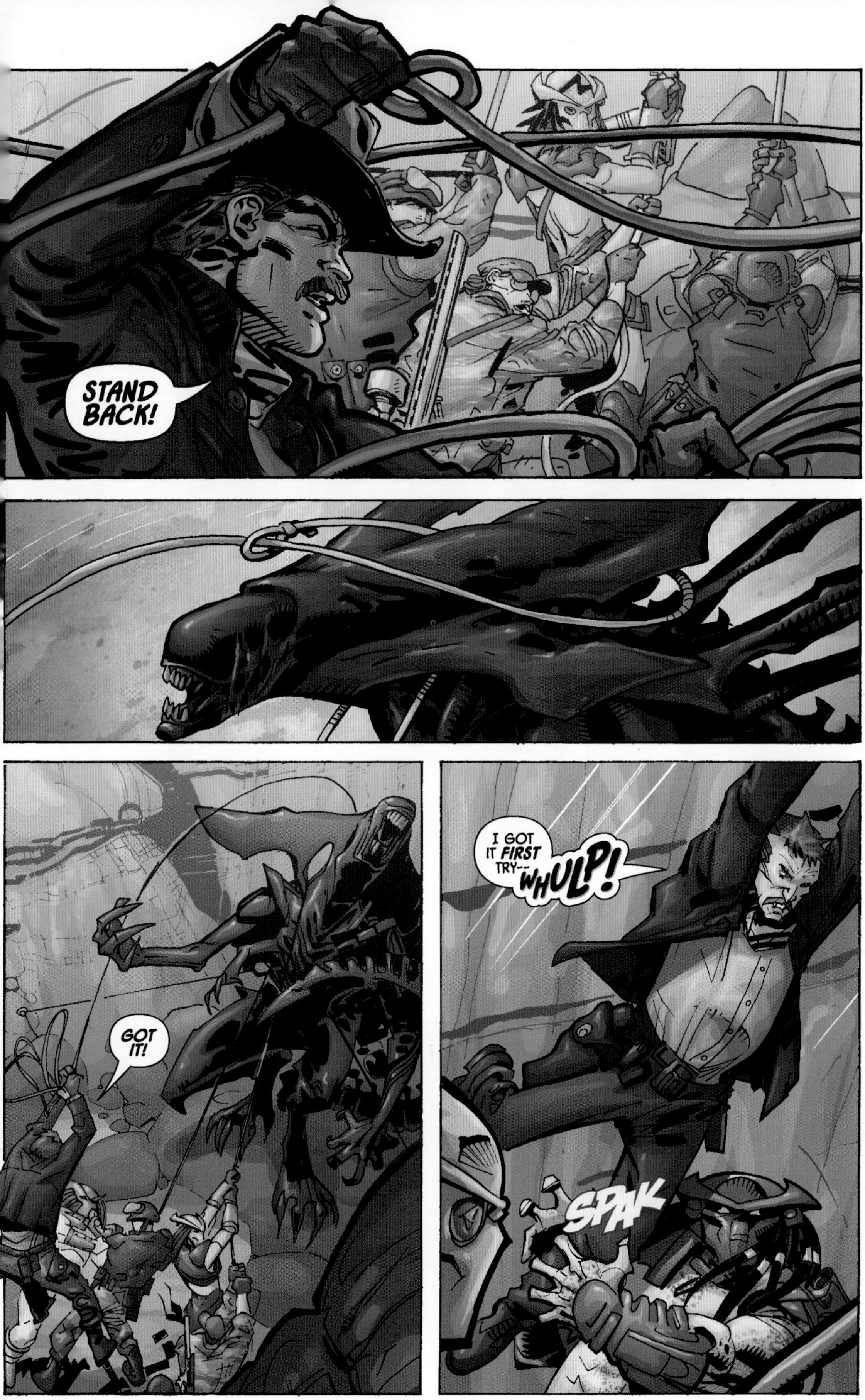
STAND BACK!
GOT IT!
I GOT IT FIRST TRY-- WHULP!
SPAK

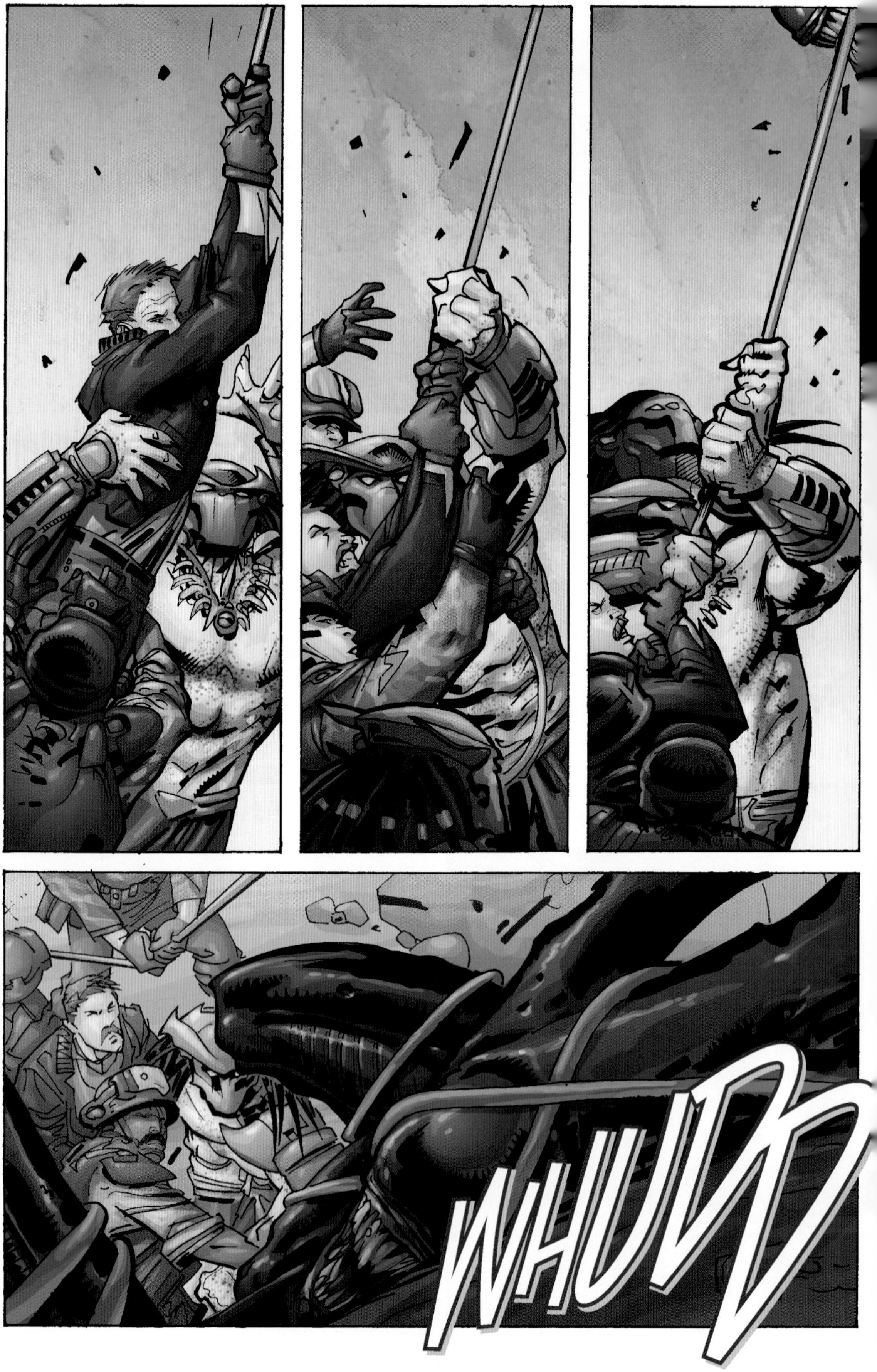
WHUD

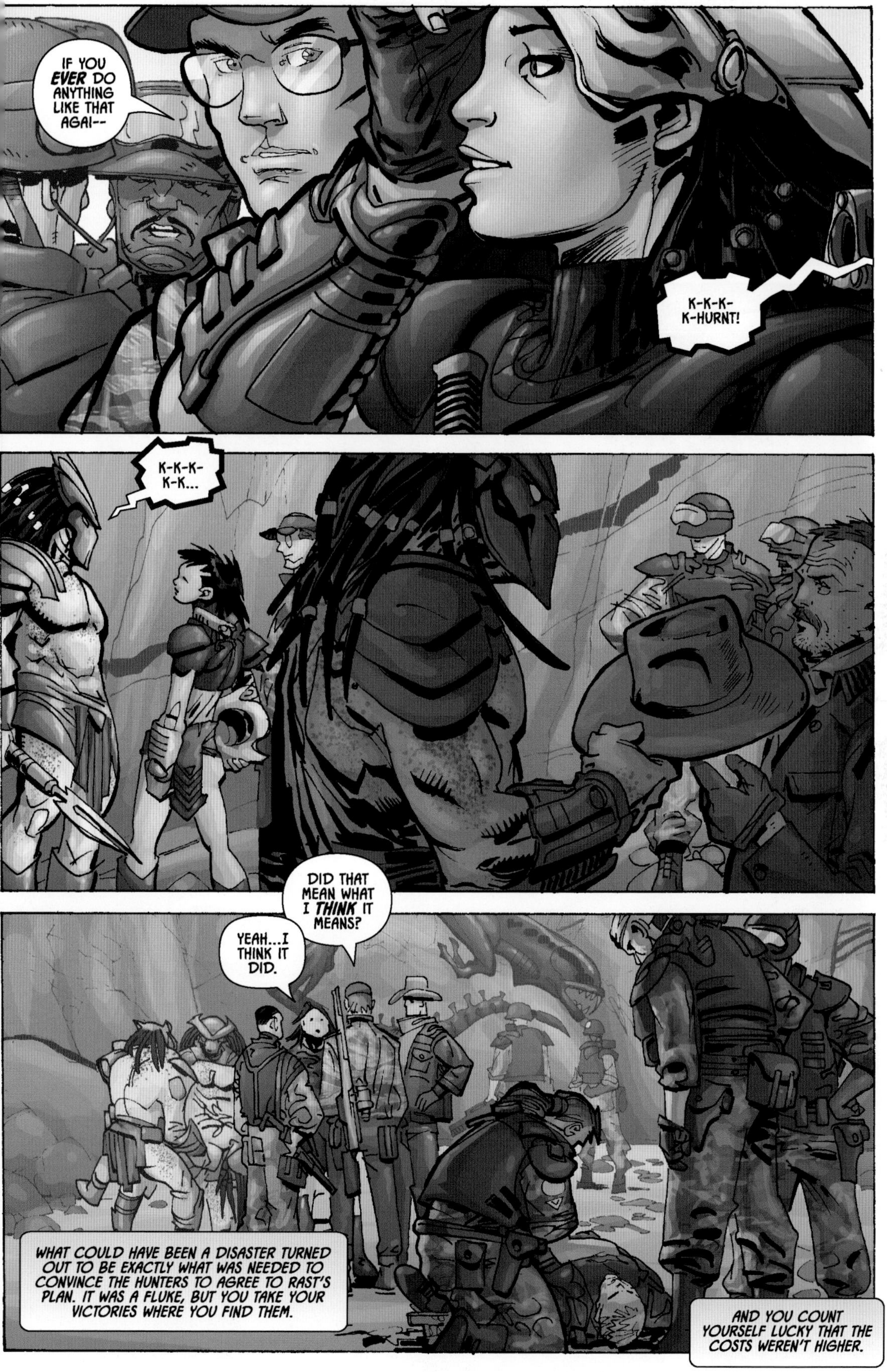
IF YOU EVER DO ANYTHING LIKE THAT AGAI--
K-K-K-K-HURNT!
K-K-K-K-K...
DID THAT MEAN WHAT I THINK IT MEANS?
YEAH...I THINK IT DID.
WHAT COULD HAVE BEEN A DISASTER TURNED OUT TO BE EXACTLY WHAT WAS NEEDED TO CONVINCE THE HUNTERS TO AGREE TO RAST'S PLAN. IT WAS A FLUKE, BUT YOU TAKE YOUR VICTORIES WHERE YOU FIND THEM.
AND YOU COUNT YOURSELF LUCKY THAT THE COSTS WEREN'T HIGHER.

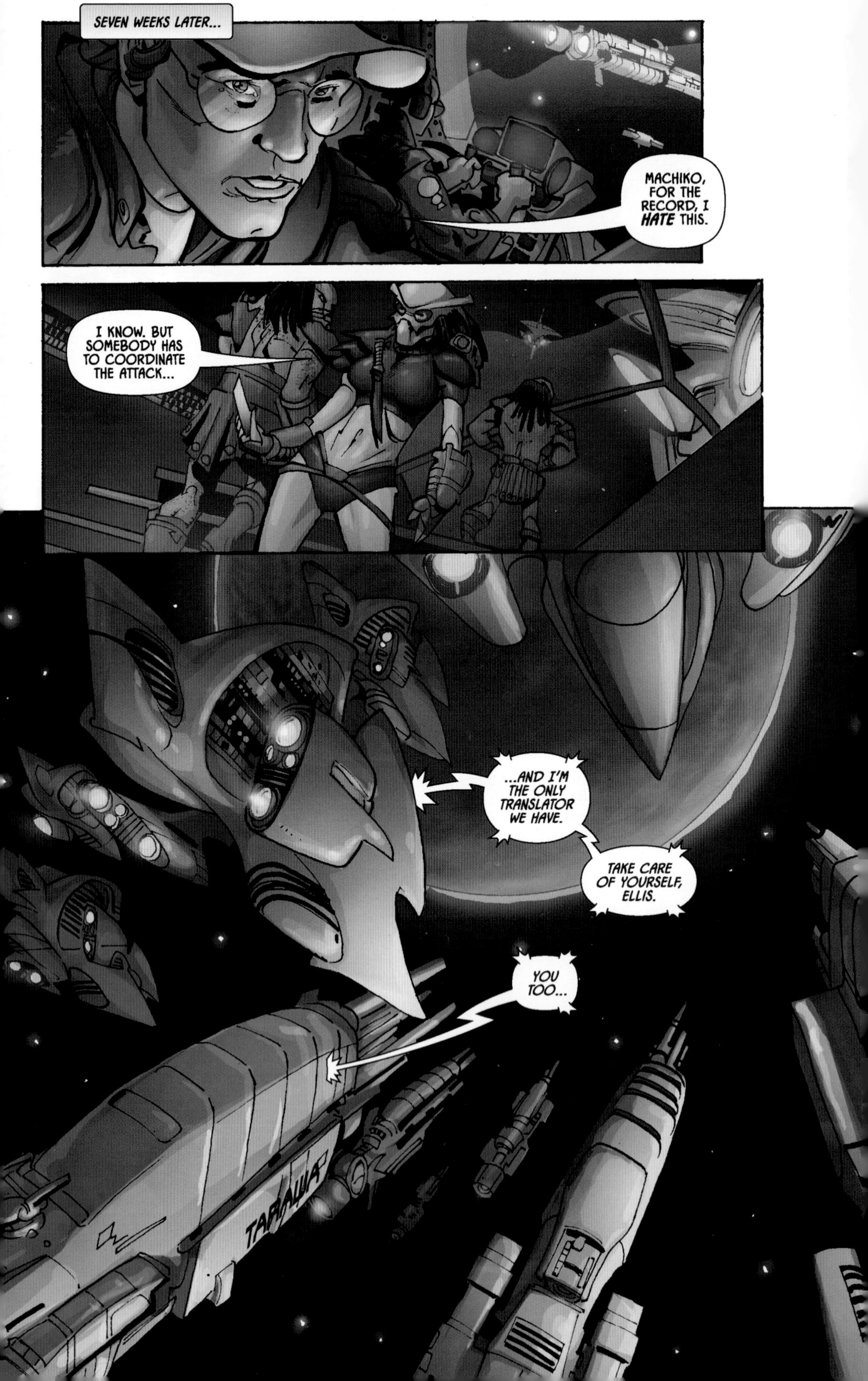
SEVEN WEEKS LATER...
MACHIKO, FOR THE RECORD, I HATE THIS.
I KNOW. BUT SOMEBODY HAS TO COORDINATE THE ATTACK...
...AND I'M THE ONLY TRANSLATOR WE HAVE.
TAKE CARE OF YOURSELF, ELLIS.
YOU TOO...

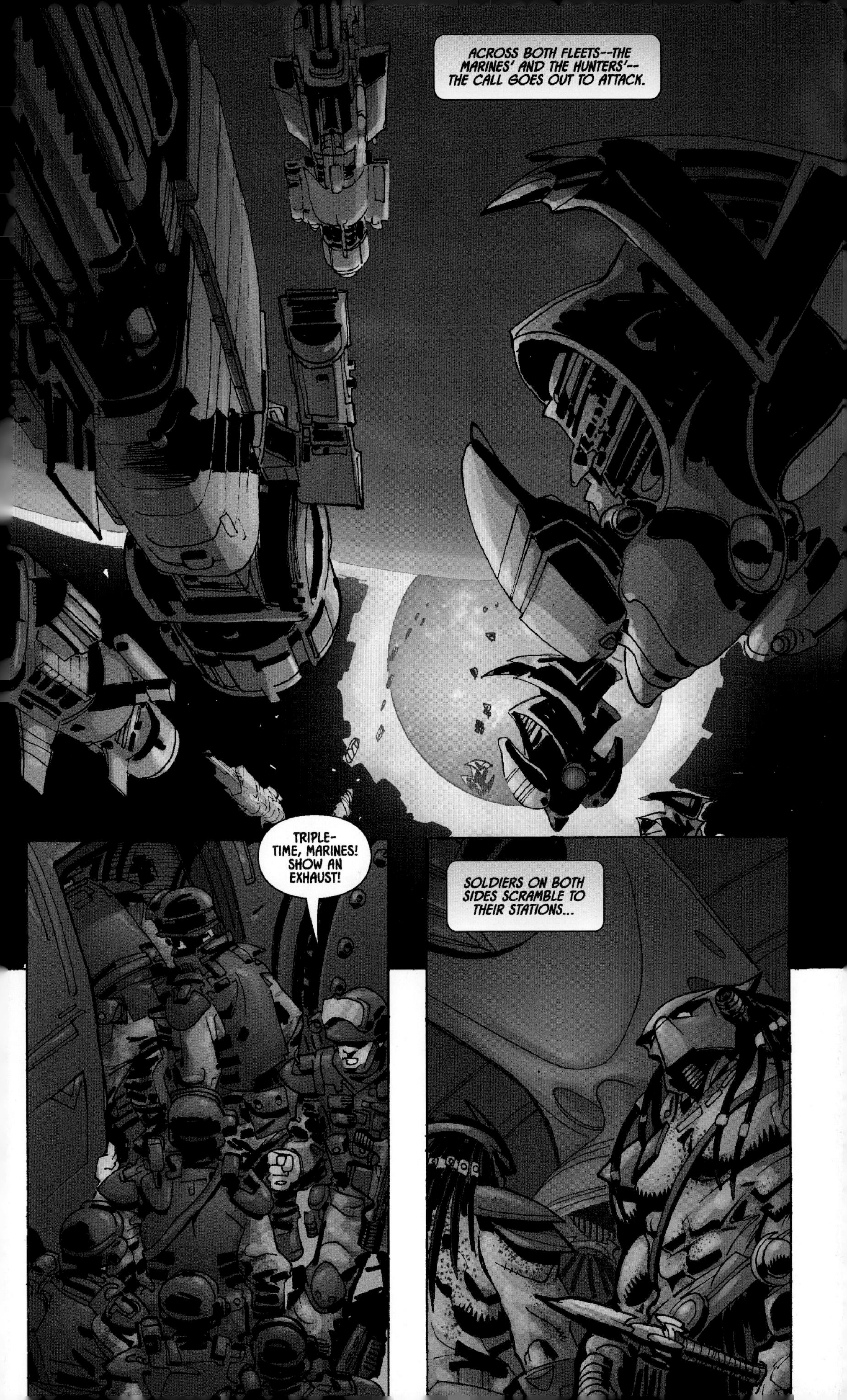
ACROSS BOTH FLEETS--THE MARINES' AND THE HUNTERS'--THE CALL GOES OUT TO ATTACK.
TRIPLE-TIME, MARINES! SHOW AN EXHAUST!
SOLDIERS ON BOTH SIDES SCRAMBLE TO THEIR STATIONS...

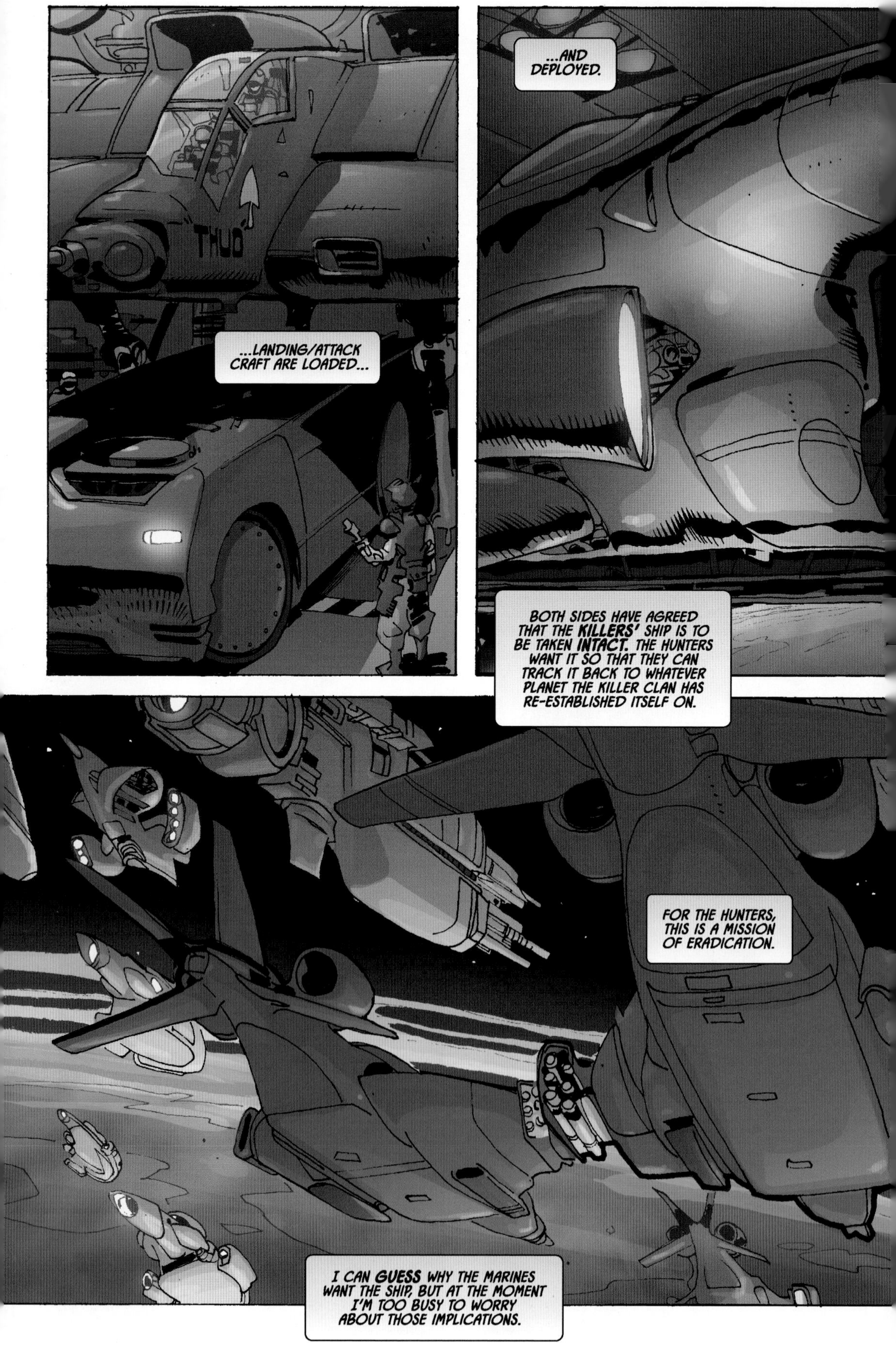
...LANDING/ATTACK CRAFT ARE LOADED...
THUD
...AND DEPLOYED.
BOTH SIDES HAVE AGREED THAT THE **KILLERS'** SHIP IS TO BE TAKEN **INTACT.** THE HUNTERS WANT IT SO THAT THEY CAN TRACK IT BACK TO WHATEVER PLANET THE KILLER CLAN HAS RE-ESTABLISHED ITSELF ON.
FOR THE HUNTERS, THIS IS A MISSION OF ERADICATION.
I CAN **GUESS** WHY THE MARINES WANT THE SHIP, BUT AT THE MOMENT I'M TOO BUSY TO WORRY ABOUT THOSE IMPLICATIONS.

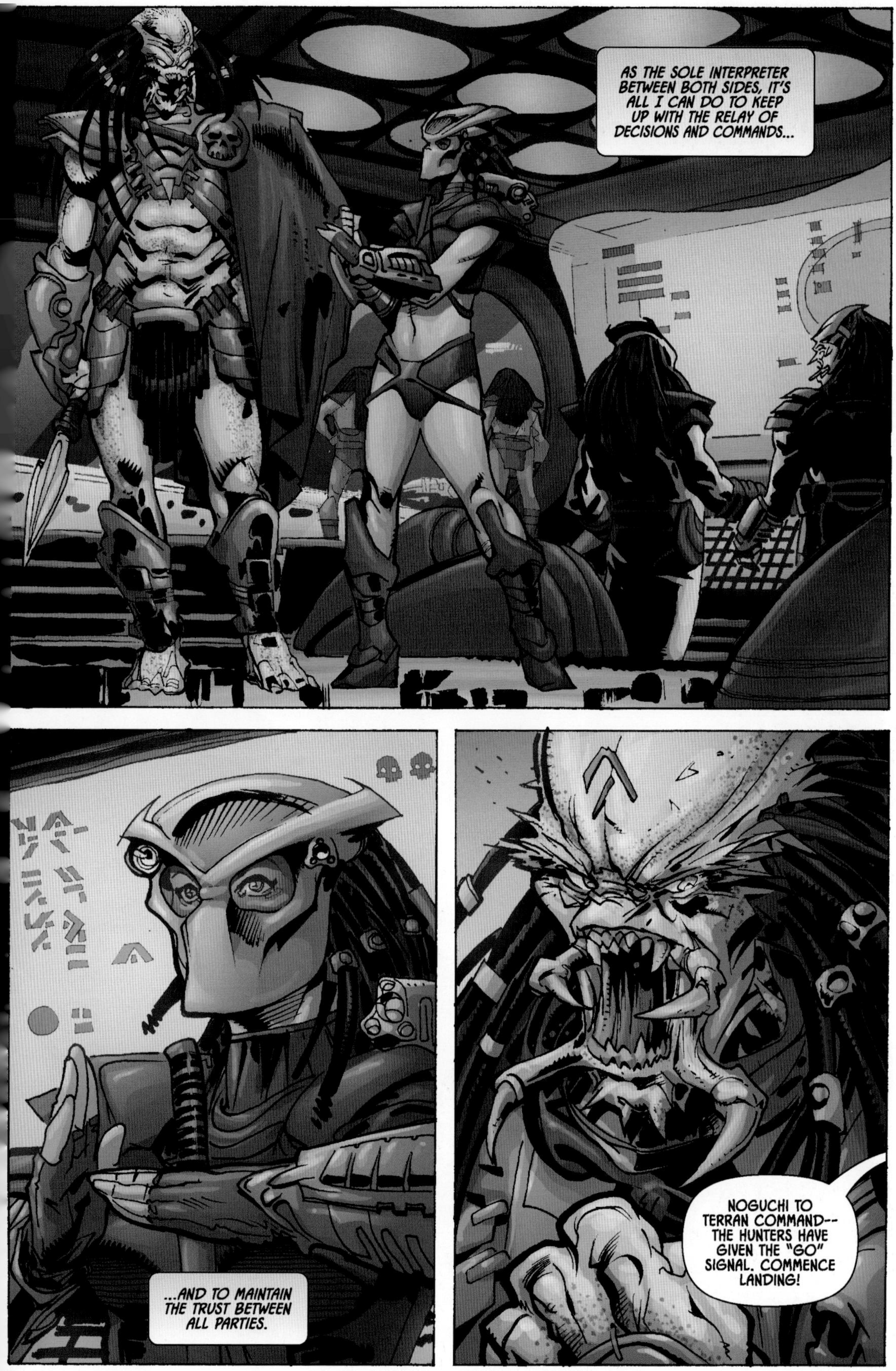
AS THE SOLE INTERPRETER BETWEEN BOTH SIDES, IT'S ALL I CAN DO TO KEEP UP WITH THE RELAY OF DECISIONS AND COMMANDS...
...AND TO MAINTAIN THE TRUST BETWEEN ALL PARTIES.
NOGUCHI TO TERRAN COMMAND-- THE HUNTERS HAVE GIVEN THE "GO" SIGNAL. COMMENCE LANDING!

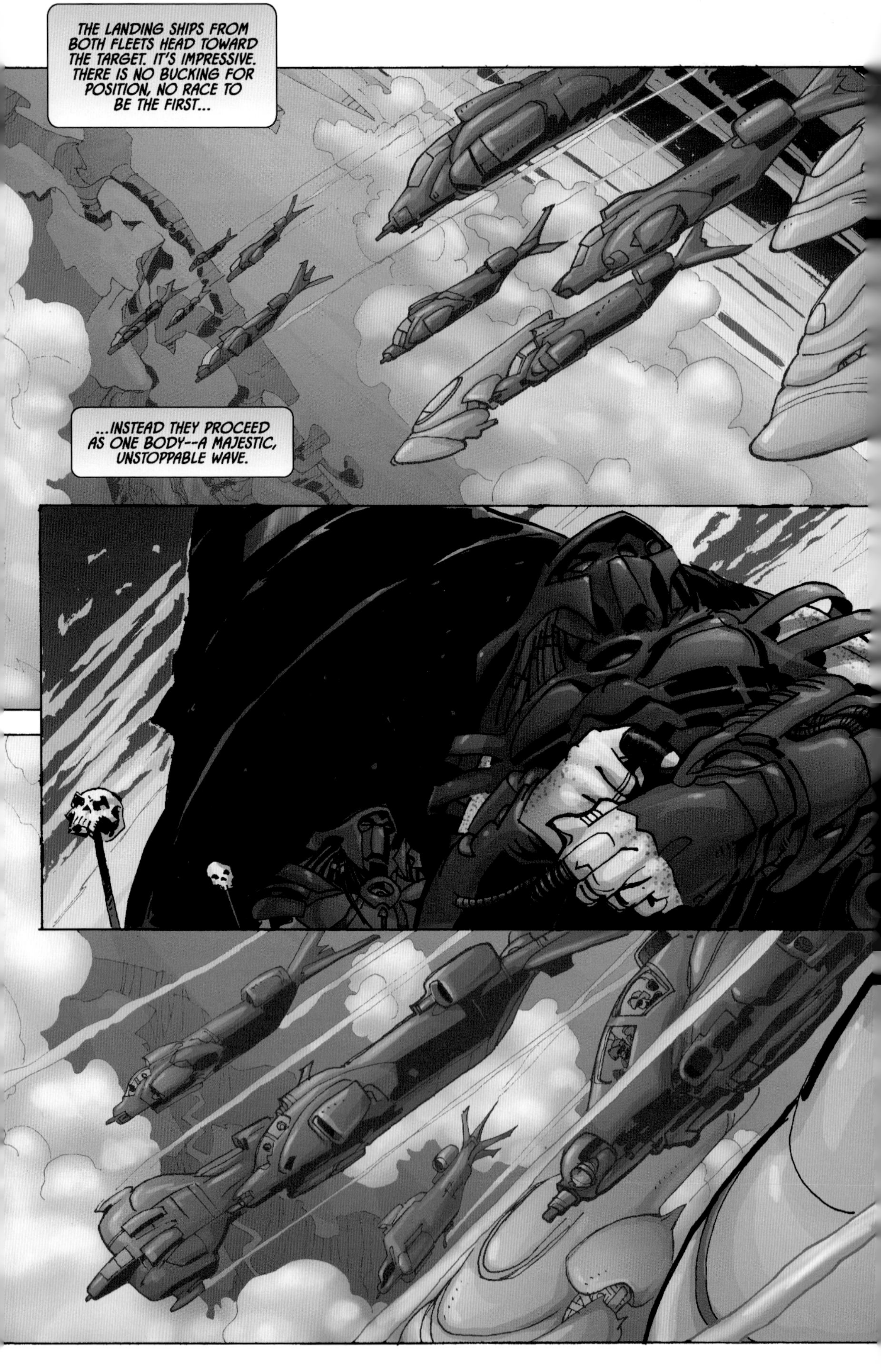
THE LANDING SHIPS FROM BOTH FLEETS HEAD TOWARD THE TARGET. IT'S IMPRESSIVE. THERE IS NO BUCKING FOR POSITION, NO RACE TO BE THE FIRST...
...INSTEAD THEY PROCEED AS ONE BODY--A MAJESTIC, UNSTOPPABLE WAVE.

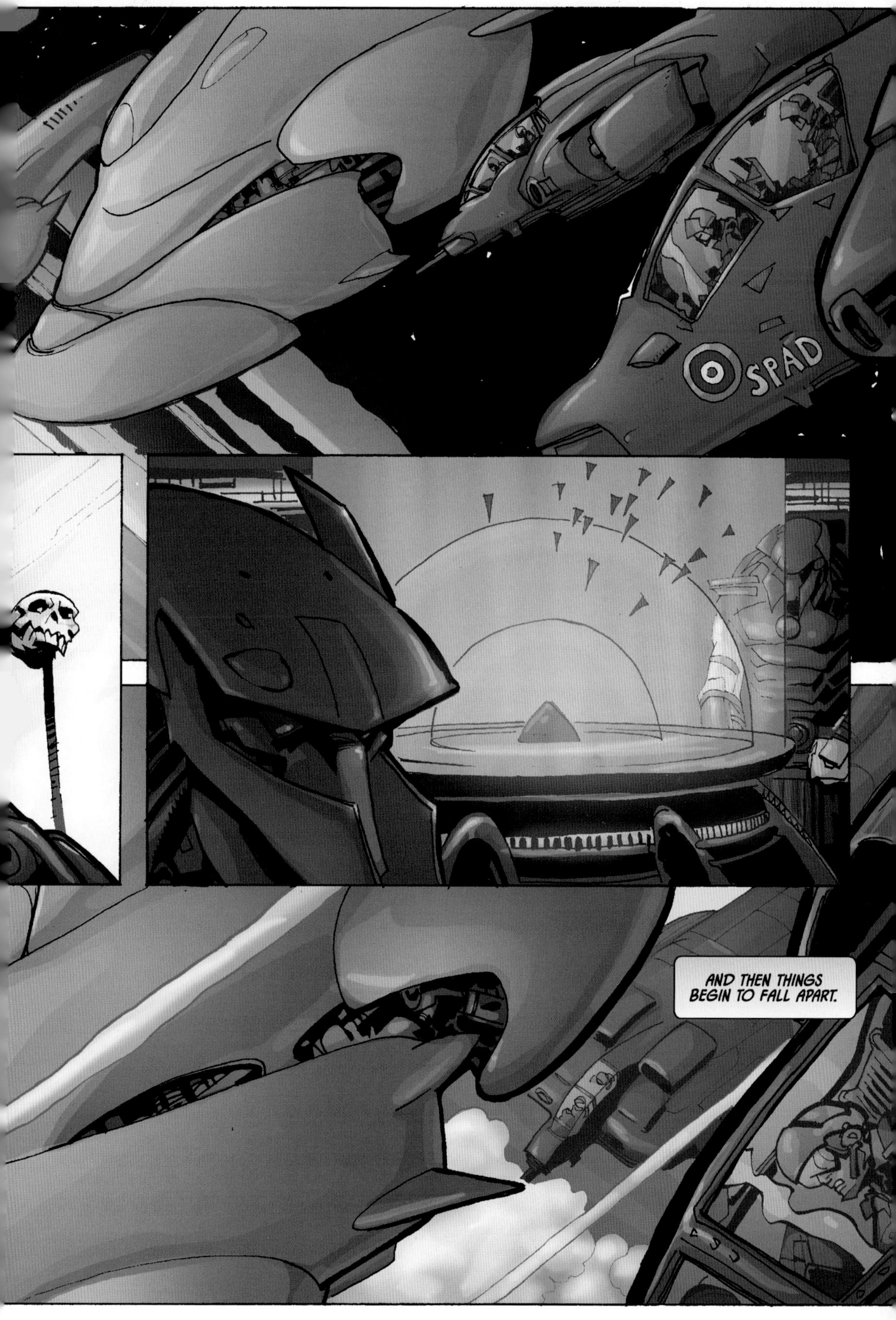
SPAD
AND THEN THINGS BEGIN TO FALL APART.

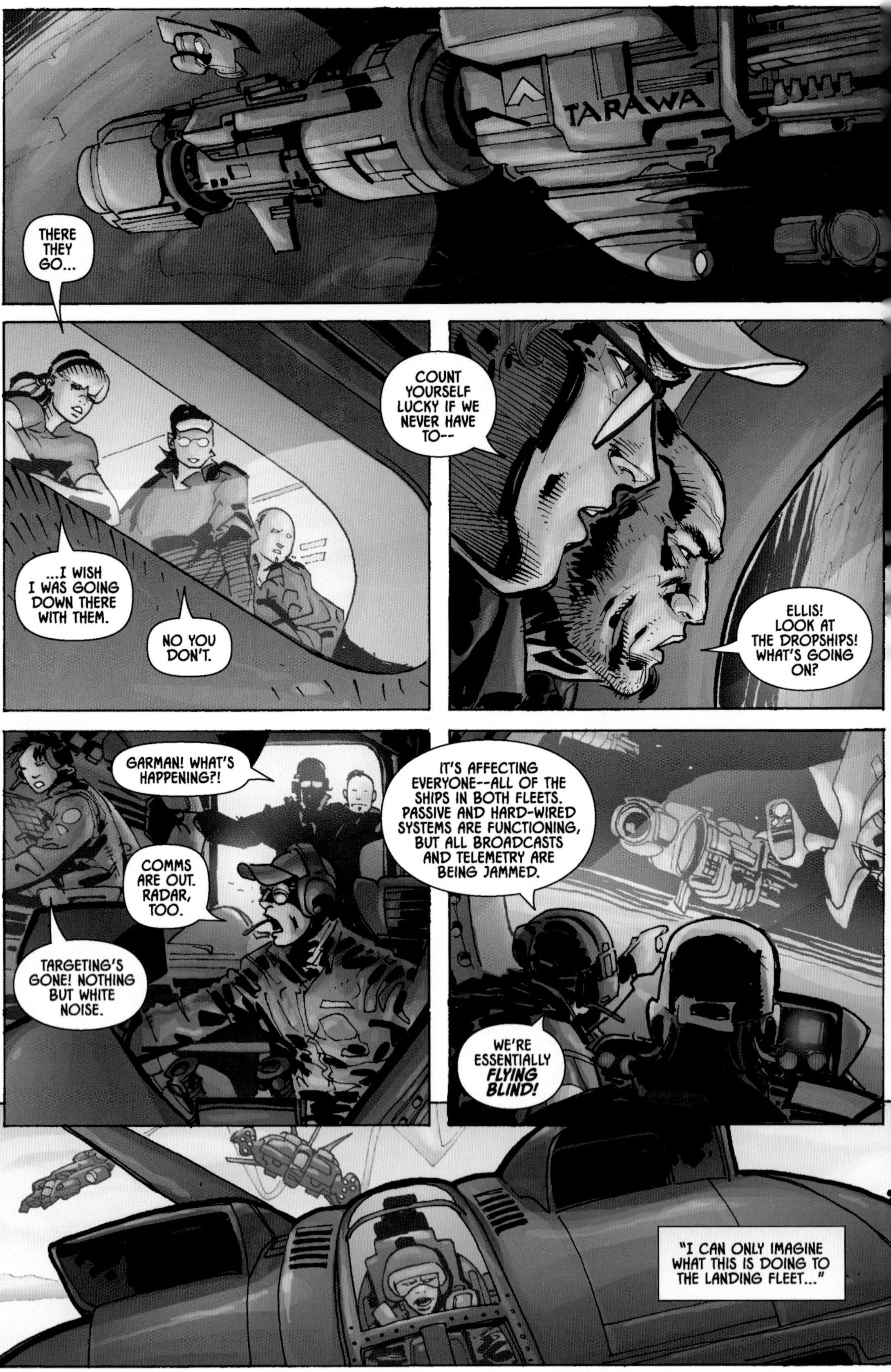
THERE THEY GO...
...I WISH I WAS GOING DOWN THERE WITH THEM.
NO YOU DON'T.
COUNT YOURSELF LUCKY IF WE NEVER HAVE TO--
ELLIS! LOOK AT THE DROPSHIPS! WHAT'S GOING ON?
GARMAN! WHAT'S HAPPENING?!
COMMS ARE OUT. RADAR, TOO.
TARGETING'S GONE! NOTHING BUT WHITE NOISE.
IT'S AFFECTING EVERYONE--ALL OF THE SHIPS IN BOTH FLEETS. PASSIVE AND HARD-WIRED SYSTEMS ARE FUNCTIONING, BUT ALL BROADCASTS AND TELEMETRY ARE BEING JAMMED.
WE'RE ESSENTIALLY *FLYING BLIND!*
"I CAN ONLY IMAGINE WHAT THIS IS DOING TO THE LANDING FLEET..."

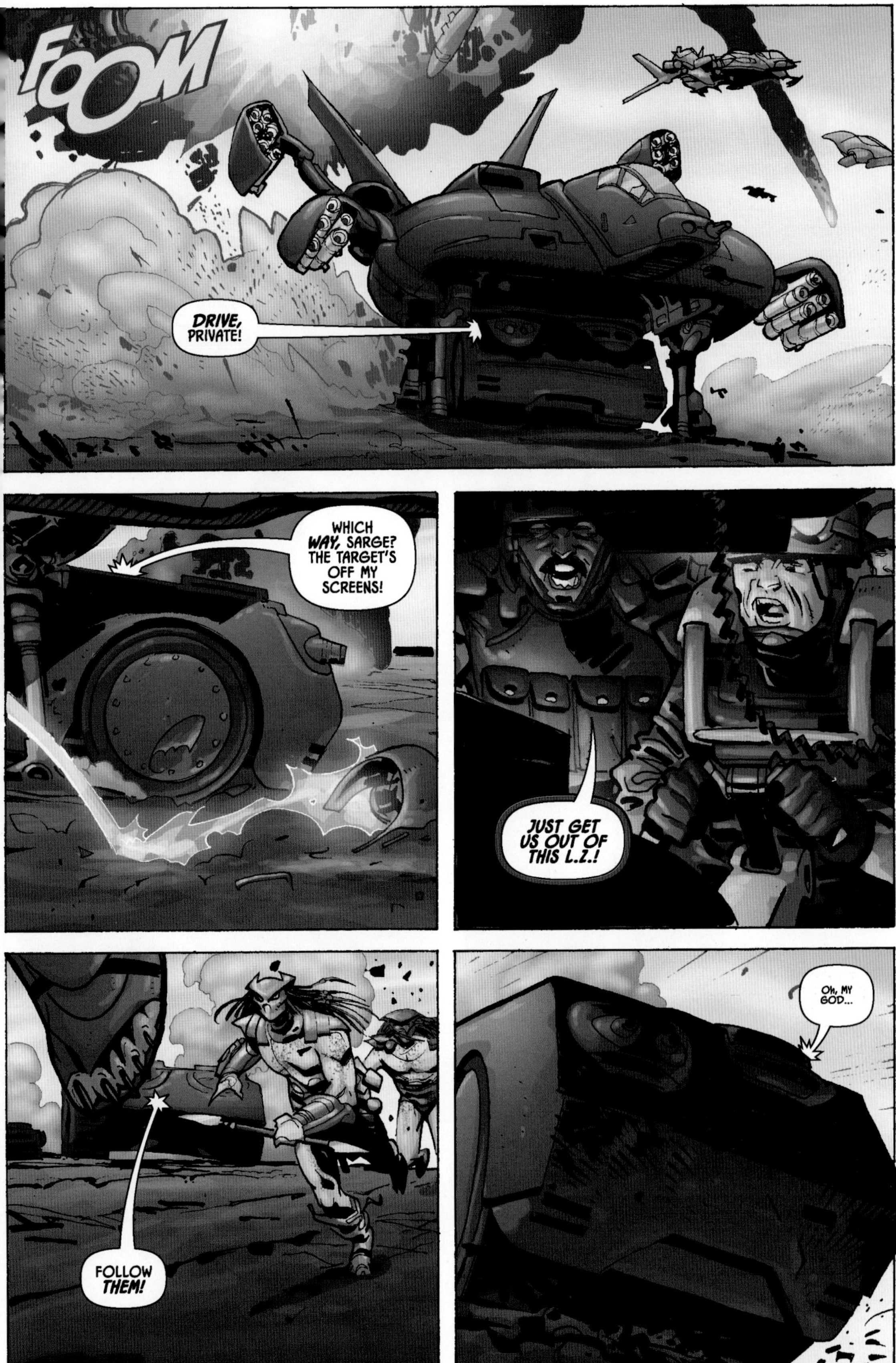
FOOM
DRIVE, PRIVATE!
WHICH WAY, SARGE? THE TARGET'S OFF MY SCREENS!
JUST GET US OUT OF THIS L.Z.!
FOLLOW THEM!
Oh, MY GOD...

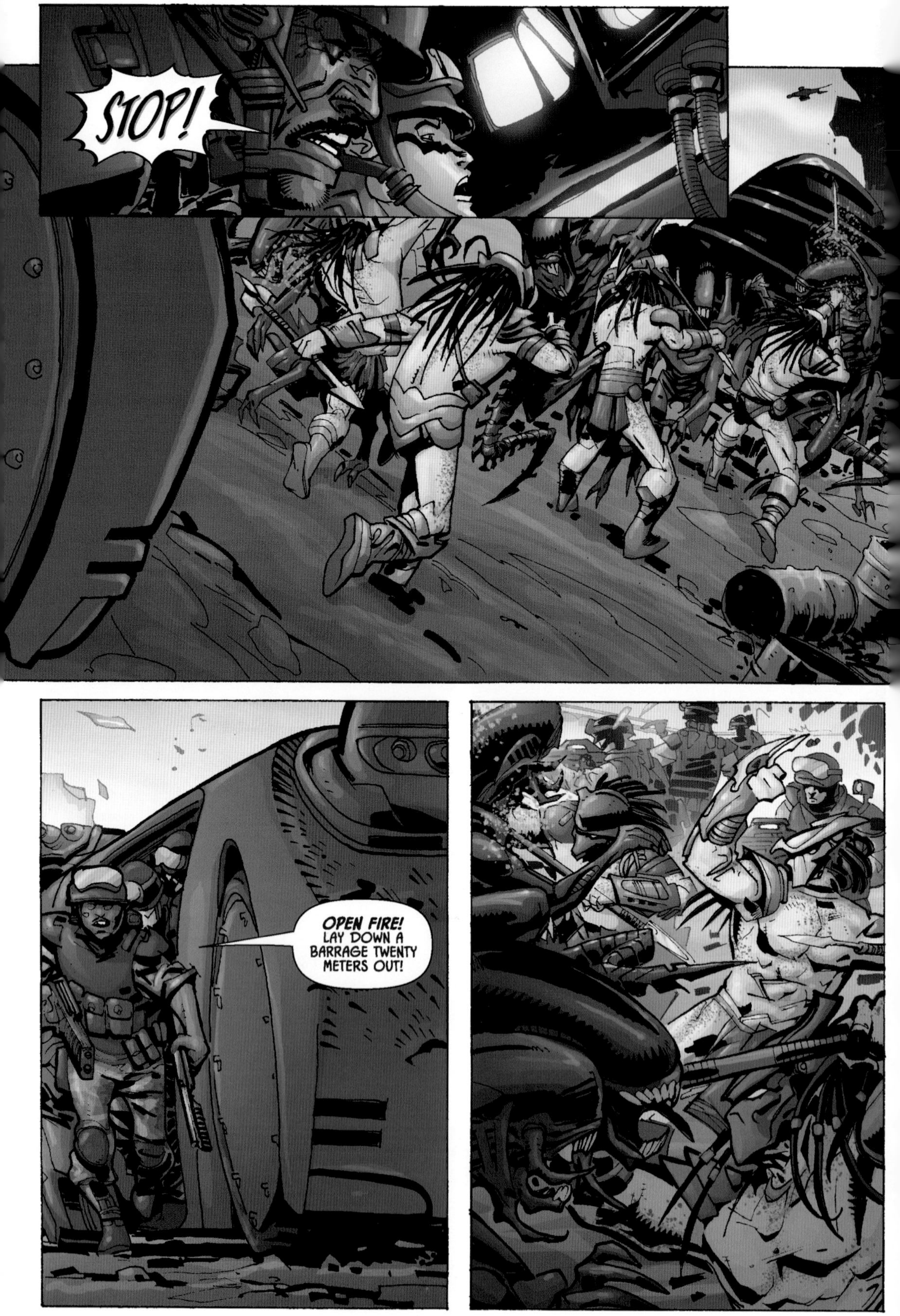
STOP!
OPEN FIRE! LAY DOWN A BARRAGE TWENTY METERS OUT!

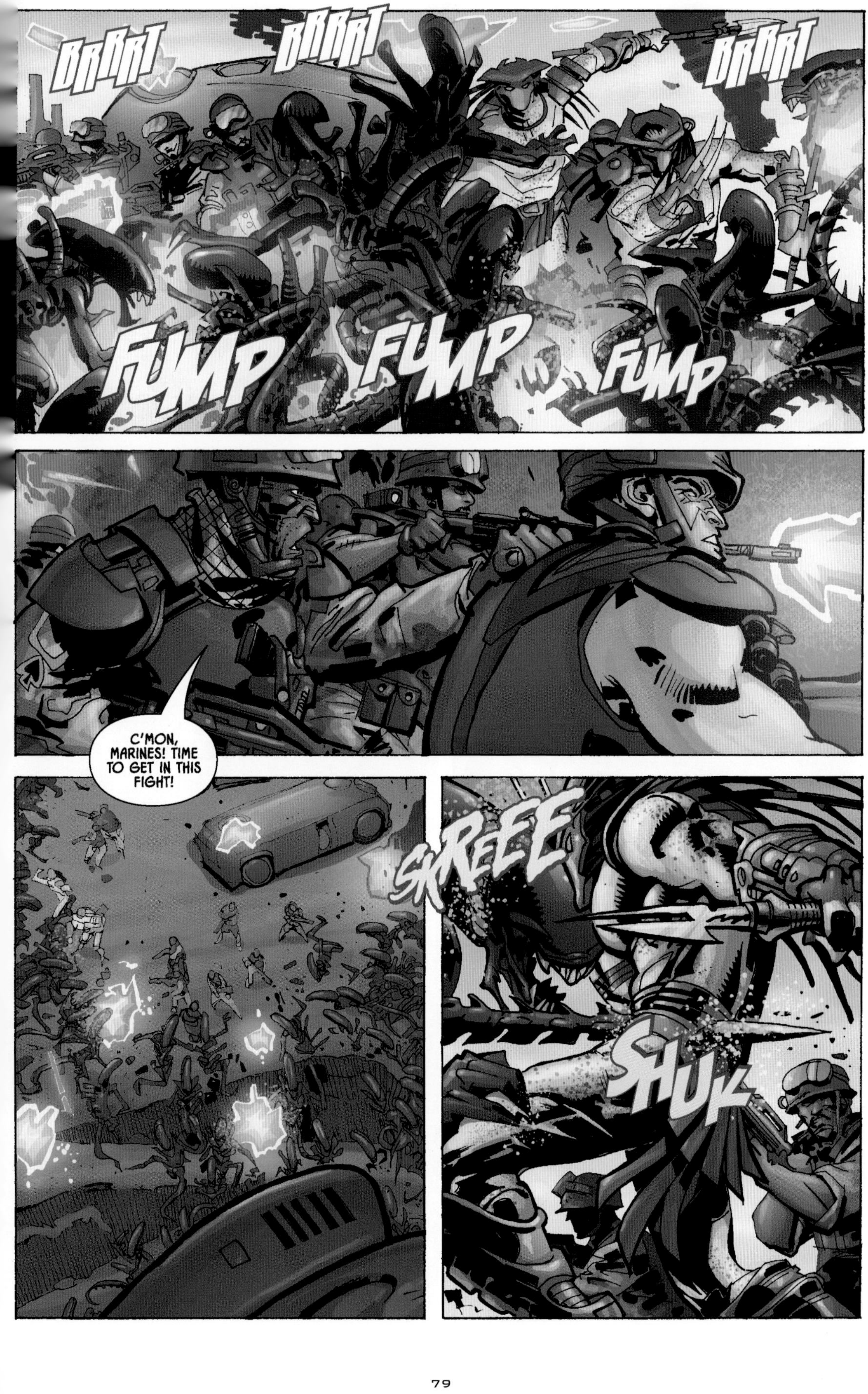
BRRRT
BRRRT
BRRRT
FUMP
FUMP
FUMP
C'MON, MARINES! TIME TO GET IN THIS FIGHT!
SKREEE
SHUK

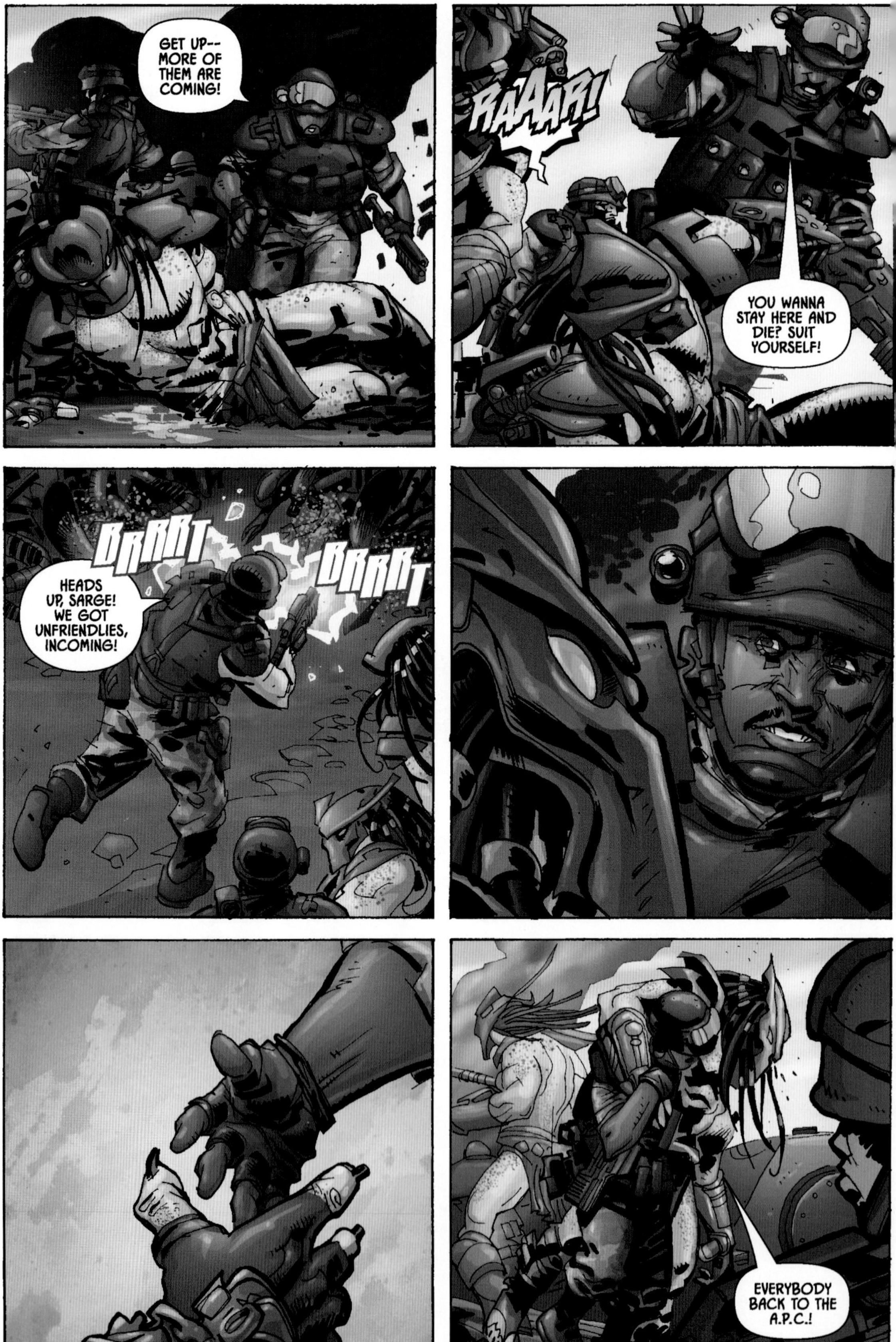
GET UP-- MORE OF THEM ARE COMING!
RAAAR!
YOU WANNA STAY HERE AND DIE? SUIT YOURSELF!
BRRRT
BRRRT
HEADS UP, SARGE! WE GOT UNFRIENDLIES, INCOMING!
EVERYBODY BACK TO THE A.P.C.!

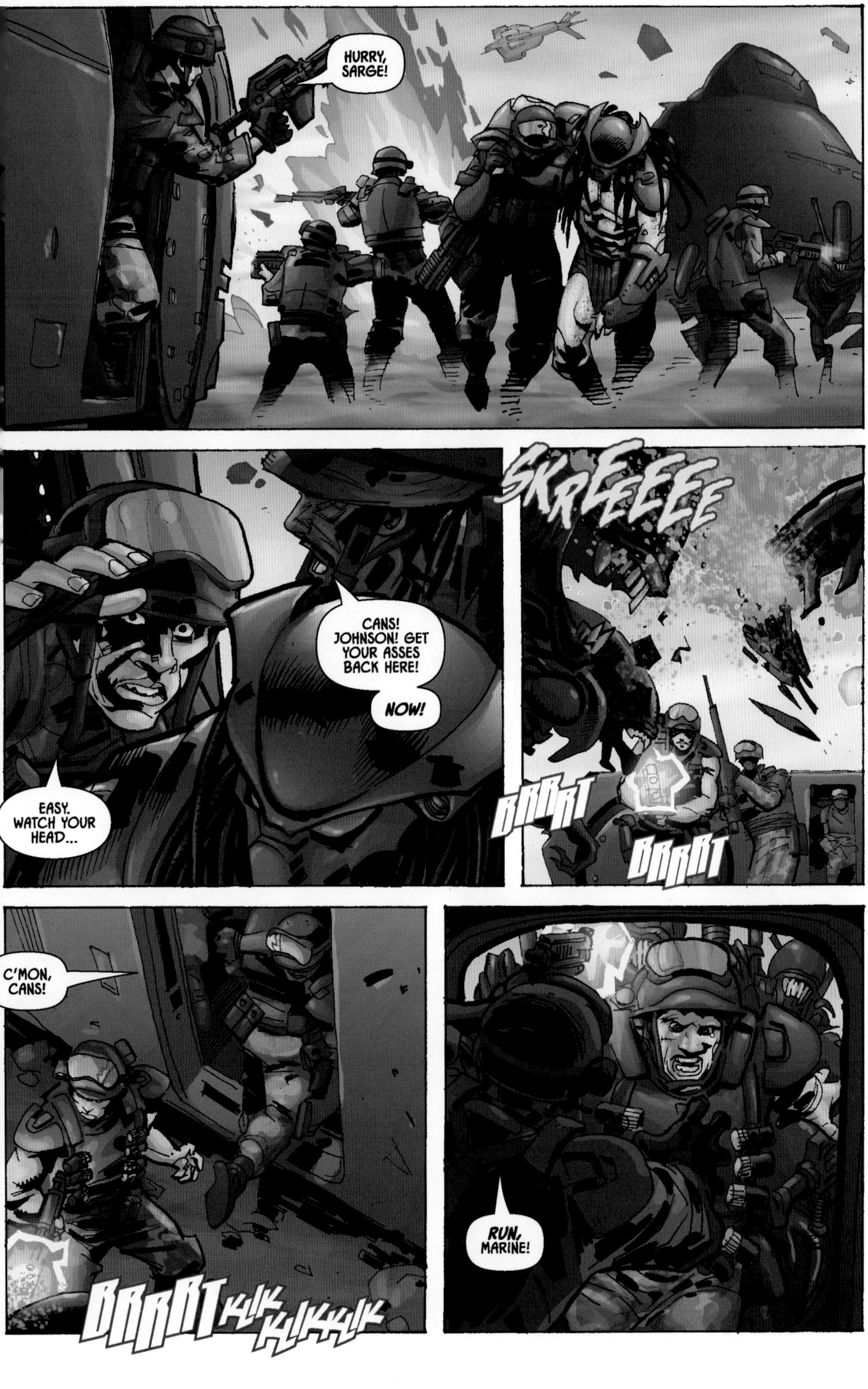
HURRY, SARGE!
EASY. WATCH YOUR HEAD...
CANS! JOHNSON! GET YOUR ASSES BACK HERE!
NOW!
SKREEEEEE
BRRRT
BRRRT
C'MON, CANS!
BRRRT KLIK KLIKKLIK
RUN, MARINE!

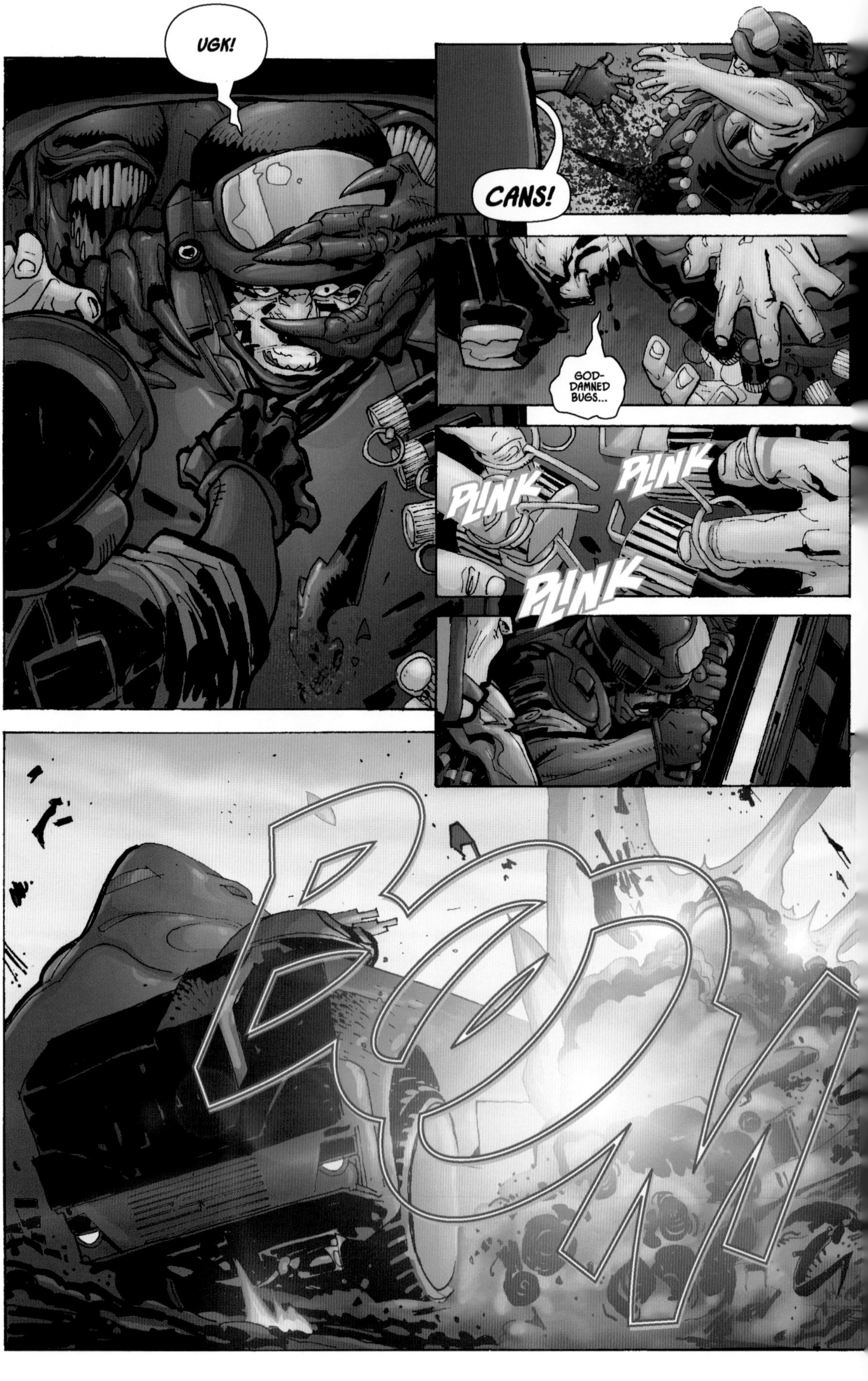

UGK!
CANS!
GOD-DAMNED BUGS...
PLINK
PLINK
PLINK
BOOM

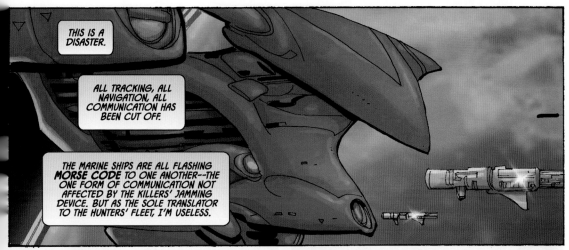

THIS IS A DISASTER.

ALL TRACKING, ALL NAVIGATION, ALL COMMUNICATION HAS BEEN CUT OFF.

THE MARINE SHIPS ARE ALL FLASHING **MORSE CODE** TO ONE ANOTHER--THE ONE FORM OF COMMUNICATION NOT AFFECTED BY THE KILLERS' JAMMING DEVICE. BUT AS THE SOLE TRANSLATOR TO THE HUNTERS' FLEET, I'M USELESS.

I DON'T **KNOW** MORSE CODE.

THE HUNTERS ARE TRYING TO RESTORE ORDER WITHIN THEIR OWN RANKS--

--BUT I CAN'T TELL THEM **WHAT** THE MARINES ARE PLANNING...

...OR IF THEY EVEN **HAVE** A PLAN.

I'M TELLING YOU, THIS **WILL** WORK, COLONEL!

83

LOOK, I WASN'T ALWAYS MACHIKO'S CHIEF OF STAFF. I USED TO BE A *MARINE*, TECHNICIAN FIRST CLASS. I SERVICED *M.A.X.* UNITS. I *KNOW* WHAT I'M TALKING ABOUT--

--AND I *KNOW* THIS WILL WORK!

I THINK MR. ELLIS IS RIGHT, SIR...

...AND WE'VE GOT TO DO *SOMETHING* TO HELP THOSE MARINES ON THE GROUND.

ALL RIGHT. GO.

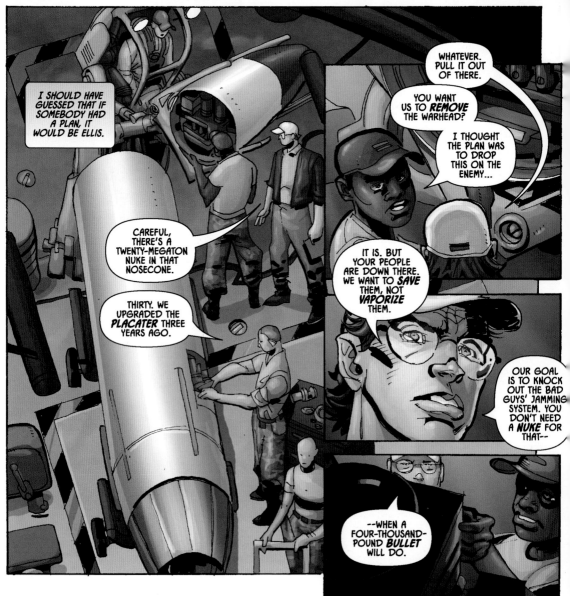

I SHOULD HAVE GUESSED THAT IF SOMEBODY HAD A PLAN, IT WOULD BE ELLIS.

CAREFUL, THERE'S A TWENTY-MEGATON NUKE IN THAT NOSECONE.

THIRTY. WE UPGRADED THE *PLACATER* THREE YEARS AGO.

WHATEVER. PULL IT OUT OF THERE.

YOU WANT US TO *REMOVE* THE WARHEAD?

I THOUGHT THE PLAN WAS TO DROP THIS ON THE ENEMY...

IT IS. BUT YOUR PEOPLE ARE DOWN THERE. WE WANT TO *SAVE* THEM, NOT *VAPORIZE* THEM.

OUR GOAL IS TO KNOCK OUT THE BAD GUYS' JAMMING SYSTEM. YOU DON'T NEED A *NUKE* FOR THAT--

--WHEN A FOUR-THOUSAND-POUND *BULLET* WILL DO.

ANYTHING I CAN DO, ELLIS?

YES, *TALBOT.* I NEED YOU TO BUILD A PLASTIC BOX--A NEW NOSECONE FOR THE MISSILE. I'LL GIVE YOU THE DIMENSIONS.

SEE, WE'RE GOING TO BUILD AN *ELECTROSCOPE*--A DEVICE THAT WAS FIRST BUILT IN THE SEVENTEEN HUNDREDS.

THE ELECTROSCOPE'S ONE MOVING PART IS A *NONCONDUCTIVE* BALL, WHICH WILL BE ATTRACTED TOWARD ANY ELECTROMAGNETIC SOURCE--SUCH AS THE KILLERS' JAMMING SIGNAL.

MY PLAN IS TO SURROUND THAT BALL WITH A SERIES OF EQUALLY NON-CONDUCTIVE RODS. WHEN THE BALL TOUCHES A ROD, THAT PURELY *MECHANICAL* ACTION--

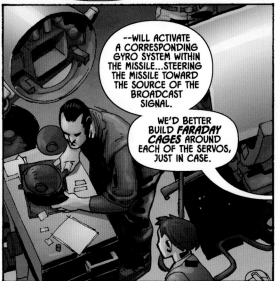

--WILL ACTIVATE A CORRESPONDING GYRO SYSTEM WITHIN THE MISSILE...STEERING THE MISSILE TOWARD THE SOURCE OF THE BROADCAST SIGNAL.

WE'D BETTER BUILD *FARADAY CAGES* AROUND EACH OF THE SERVOS, JUST IN CASE.

IT WON'T BE THE MOST ACCURATE GUIDANCE SYSTEM EVER MADE, BUT THERE'S ONLY *ONE* TARGET IT CAN POSSIBLY BE ATTRACTED TO.

HEAV

I HAVE TO HAND IT TO YOU, MR. ELLIS--NOBODY ELSE WOULD HAVE THOUGHT TO USE SEVEN-HUNDRED-YEAR-OLD TECHNOLOGY...

...BUT THIS THING WE'VE BUILT IS *DELICATE.* TOO MUCH TURBULENCE, AND--

I KNOW. WE'LL NEED TO GET CLOSE. THAT'S WHY I NEED SOMEONE TO *VOLUNTEER* TO BE MY PILOT.

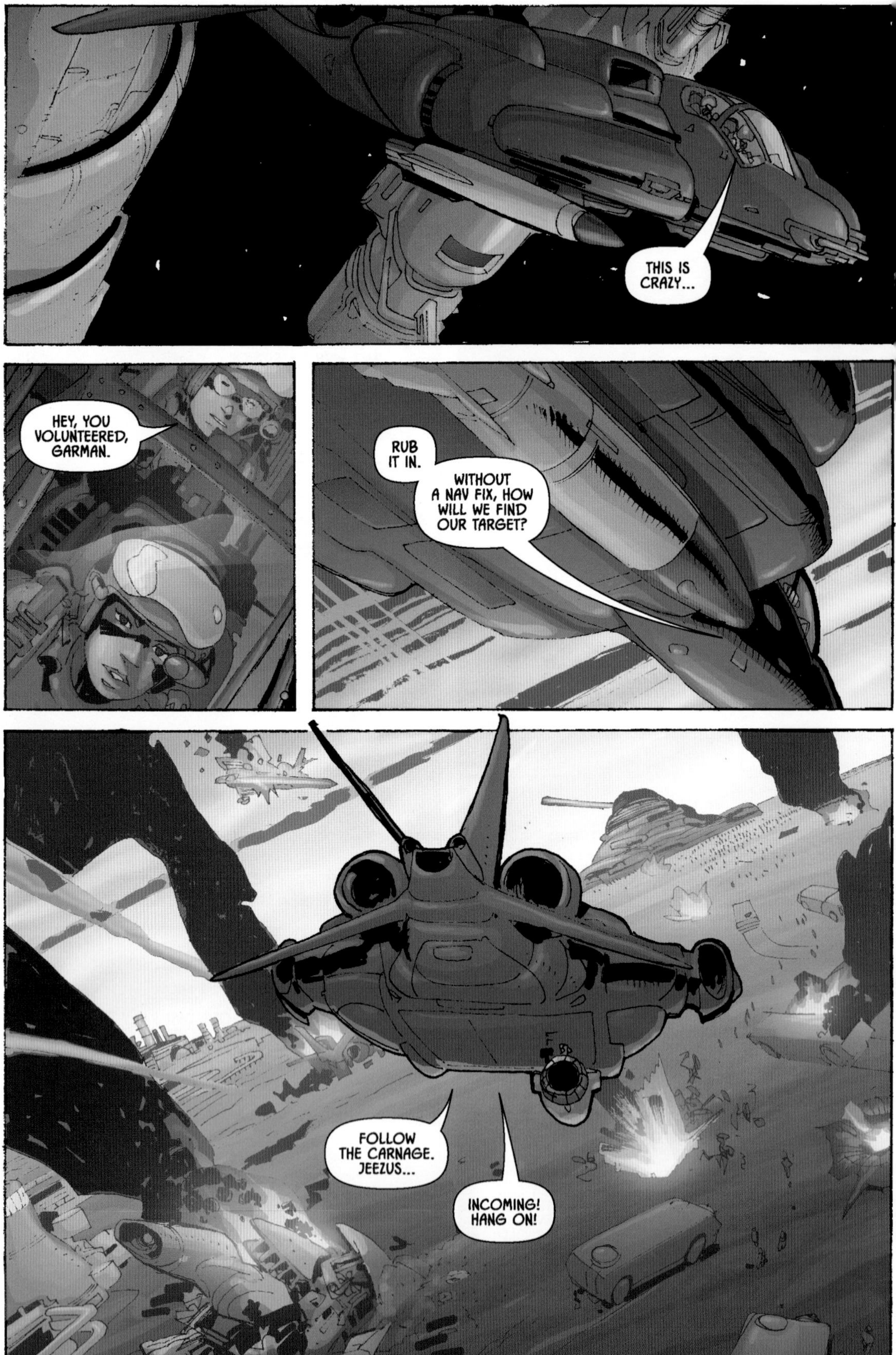
THIS IS CRAZY...
HEY, YOU VOLUNTEERED, GARMAN.
RUB IT IN.
WITHOUT A NAV FIX, HOW WILL WE FIND OUR TARGET?
FOLLOW THE CARNAGE. JEEZUS...
INCOMING! HANG ON!

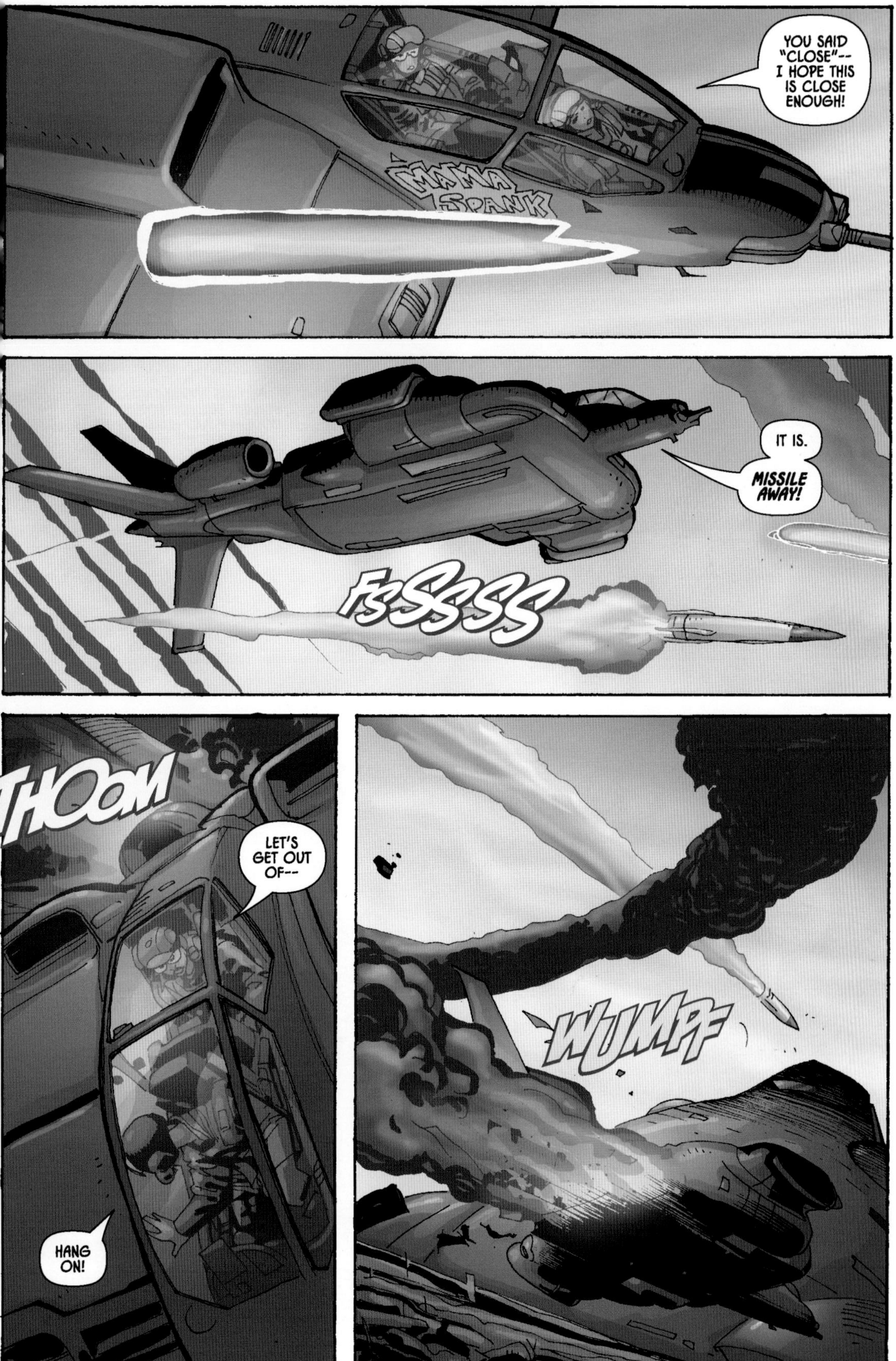
YOU SAID "CLOSE"-- I HOPE THIS IS CLOSE ENOUGH!
MAMA SPANK
IT IS.
MISSILE AWAY!
FSSSSS
THOOM
LET'S GET OUT OF--
HANG ON!
WUMPF

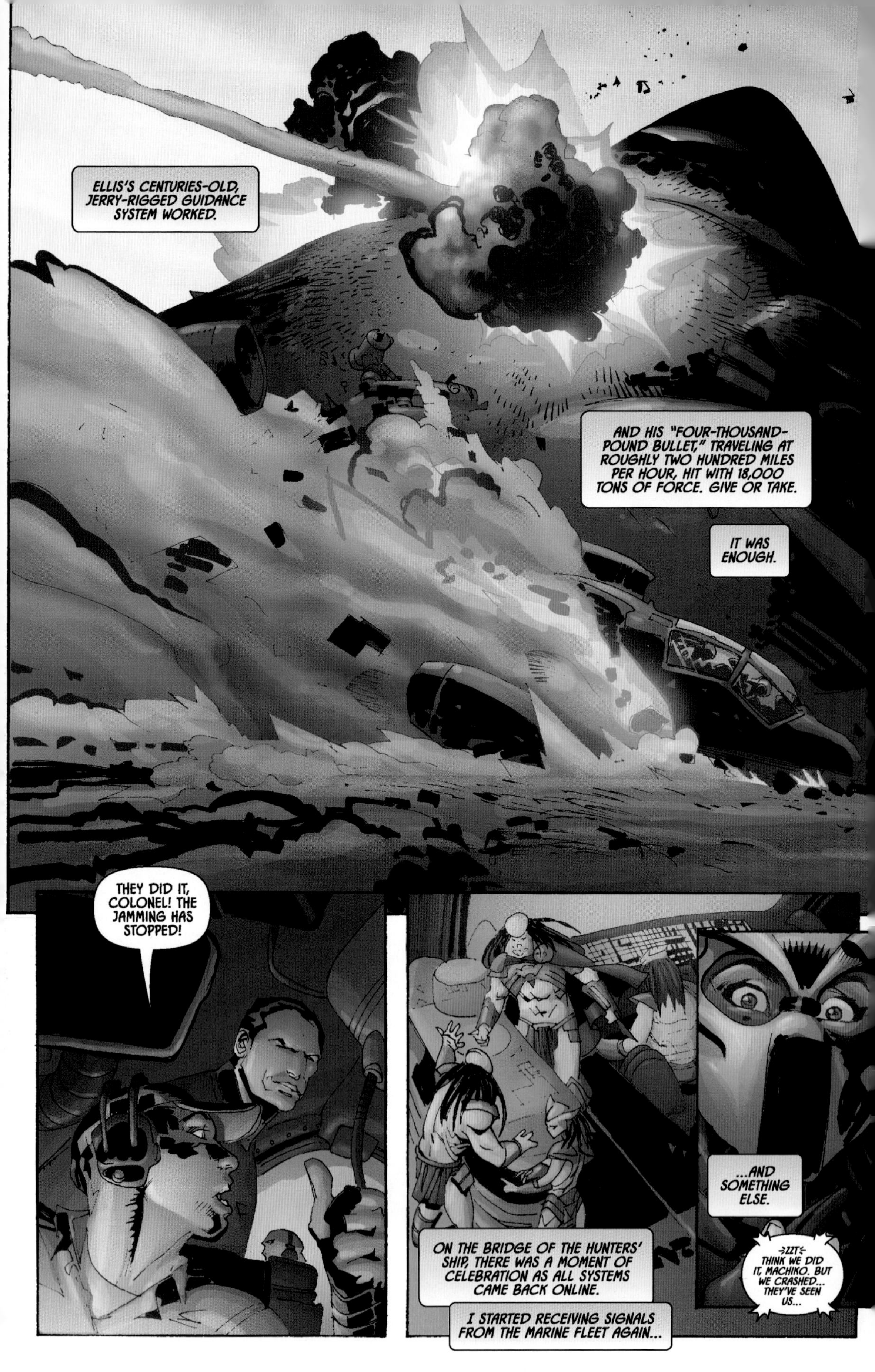
ELLIS'S CENTURIES-OLD, JERRY-RIGGED GUIDANCE SYSTEM WORKED.
AND HIS "FOUR-THOUSAND-POUND BULLET," TRAVELING AT ROUGHLY TWO HUNDRED MILES PER HOUR, HIT WITH 18,000 TONS OF FORCE. GIVE OR TAKE.
IT WAS ENOUGH.
THEY DID IT, COLONEL! THE JAMMING HAS STOPPED!
ON THE BRIDGE OF THE HUNTERS' SHIP, THERE WAS A MOMENT OF CELEBRATION AS ALL SYSTEMS CAME BACK ONLINE.
I STARTED RECEIVING SIGNALS FROM THE MARINE FLEET AGAIN...
...AND SOMETHING ELSE.
-ZZT- THINK WE DID IT, MACHIKO. BUT WE CRASHED... THEY'VE SEEN US...

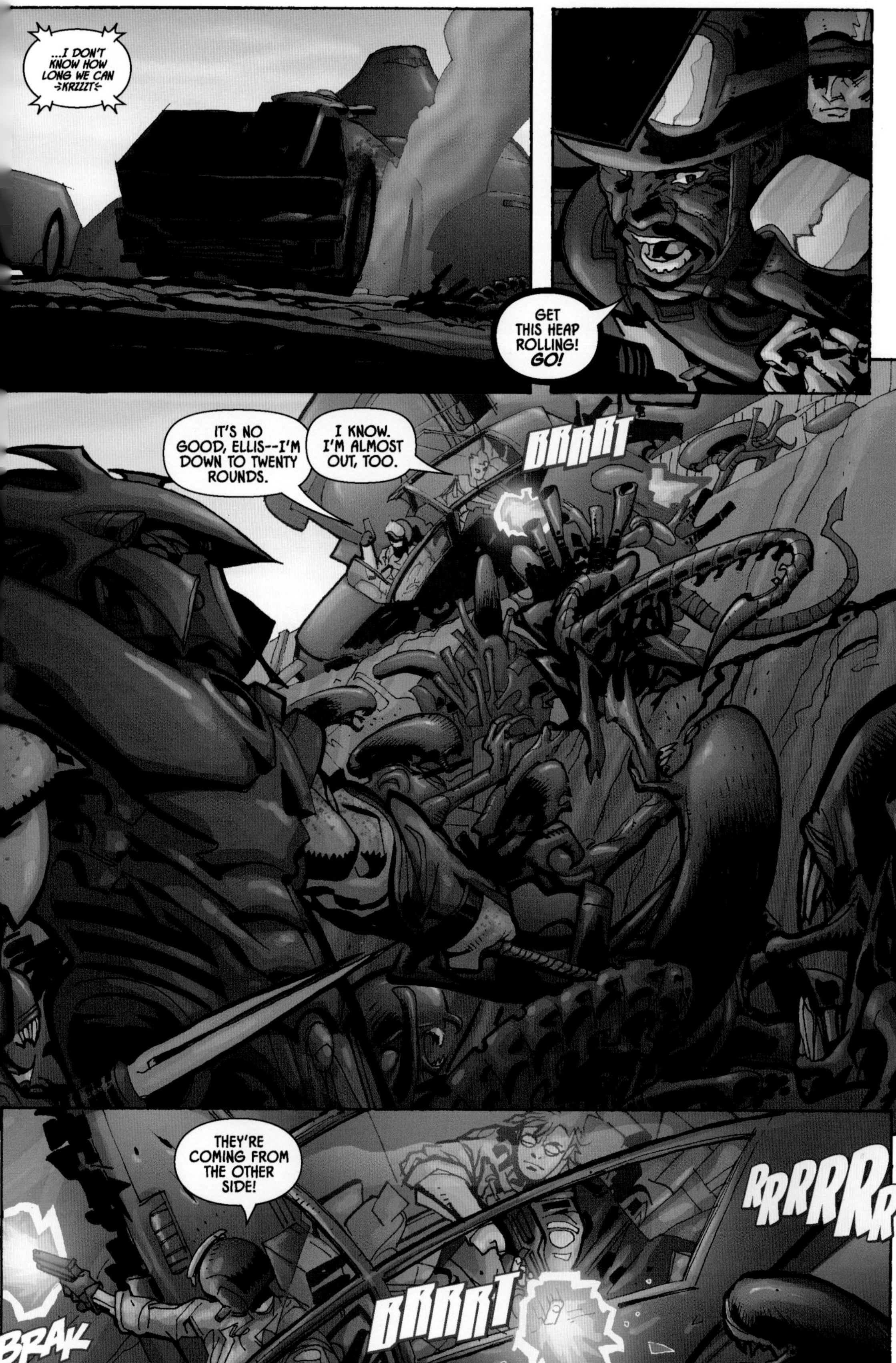
...I DON'T KNOW HOW LONG WE CAN
-KRZZZT-
GET THIS HEAP ROLLING! GO!
IT'S NO GOOD, ELLIS--I'M DOWN TO TWENTY ROUNDS.
I KNOW. I'M ALMOST OUT, TOO.
BRRRT
THEY'RE COMING FROM THE OTHER SIDE!
RRRRRR
BRAK
BRRRT

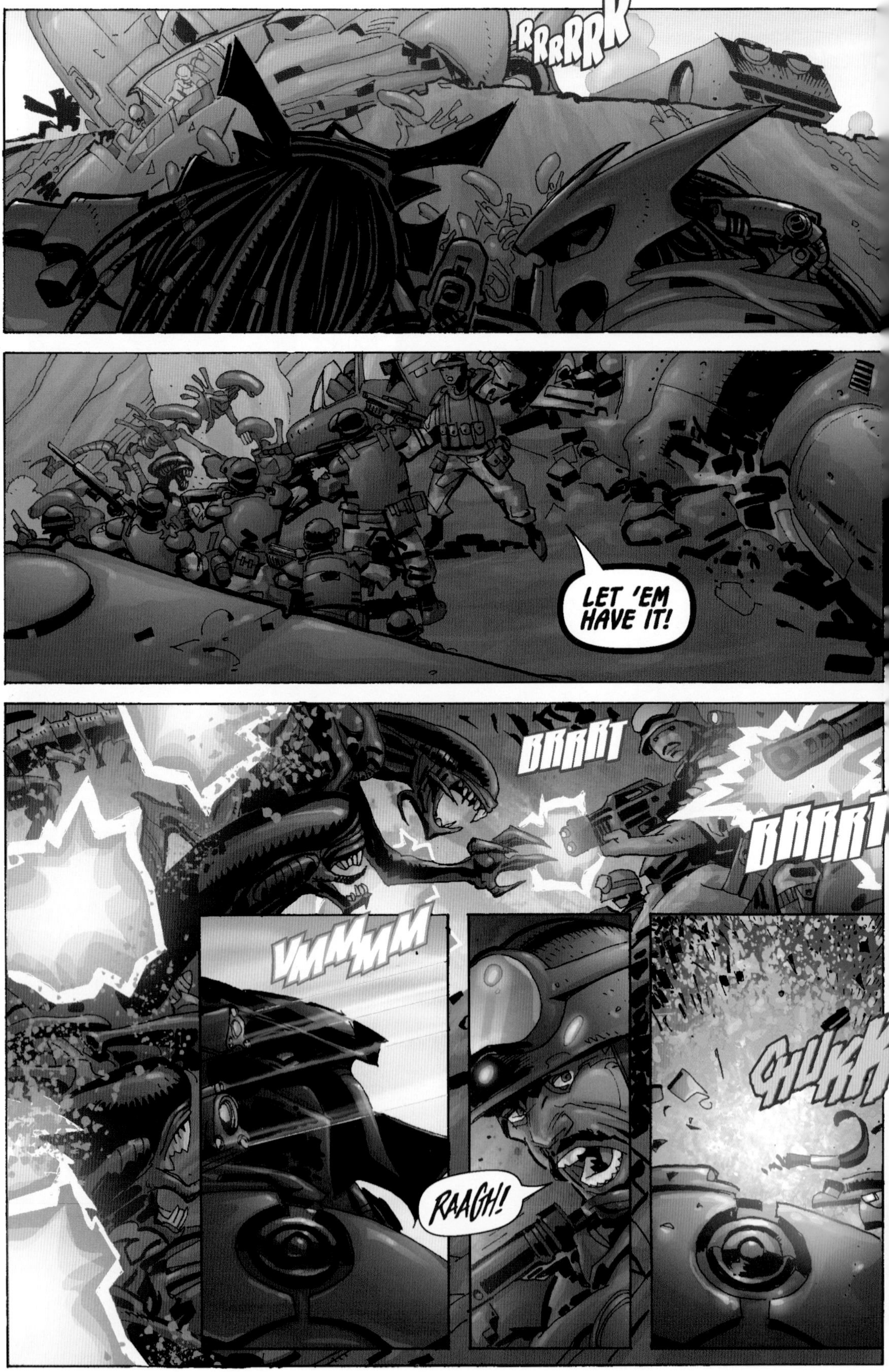
RRRRRR
LET 'EM HAVE IT!
BRRRT
BRRR
VMMMM
RAAGH!
CHUK

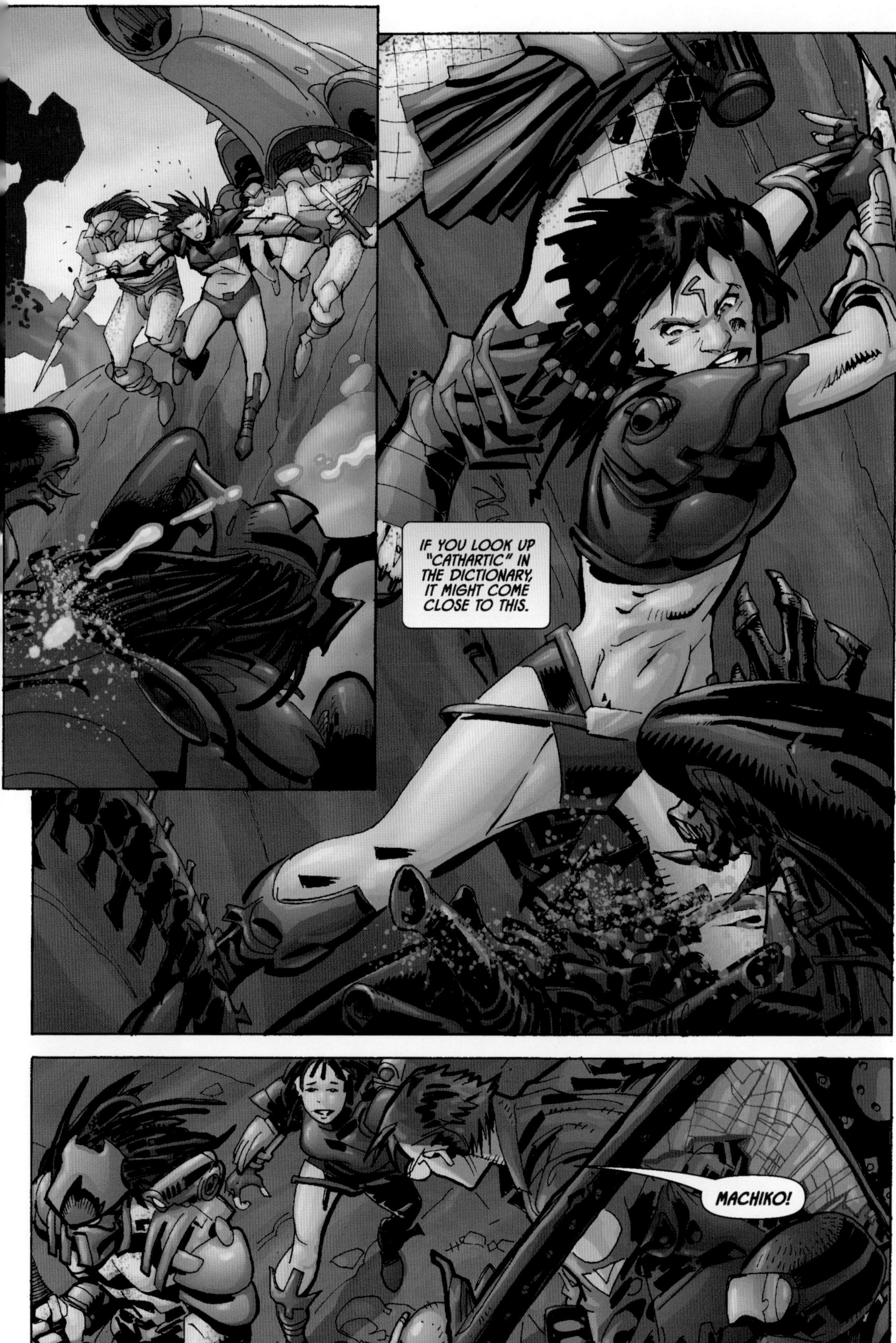
IF YOU LOOK UP "CATHARTIC" IN THE DICTIONARY, IT MIGHT COME CLOSE TO THIS.
MACHIKO!

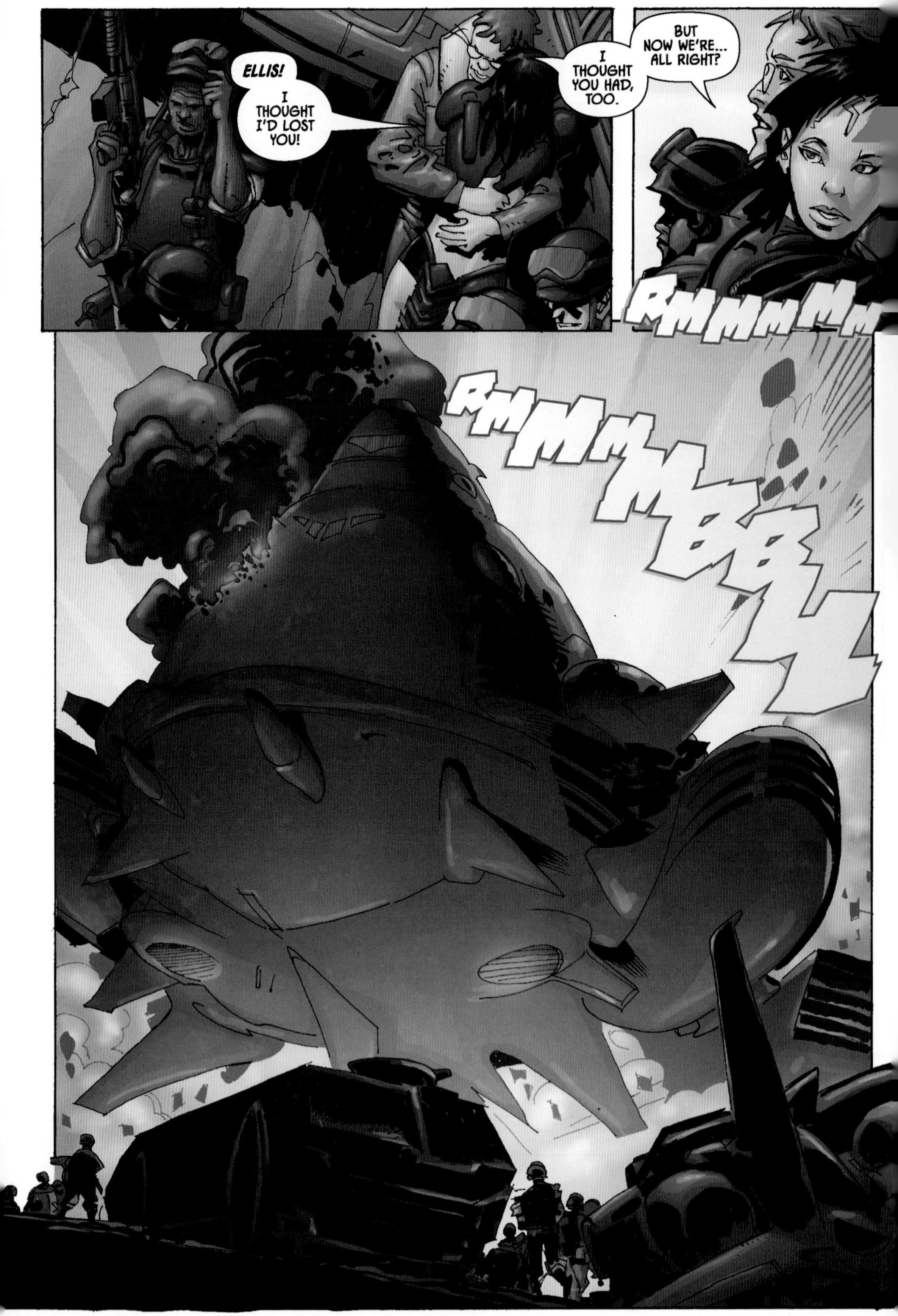
ELLIS!
I THOUGHT I'D LOST YOU!
I THOUGHT YOU HAD, TOO.
BUT NOW WE'RE... ALL RIGHT?
RMMMMMM
RMMMMMBBL

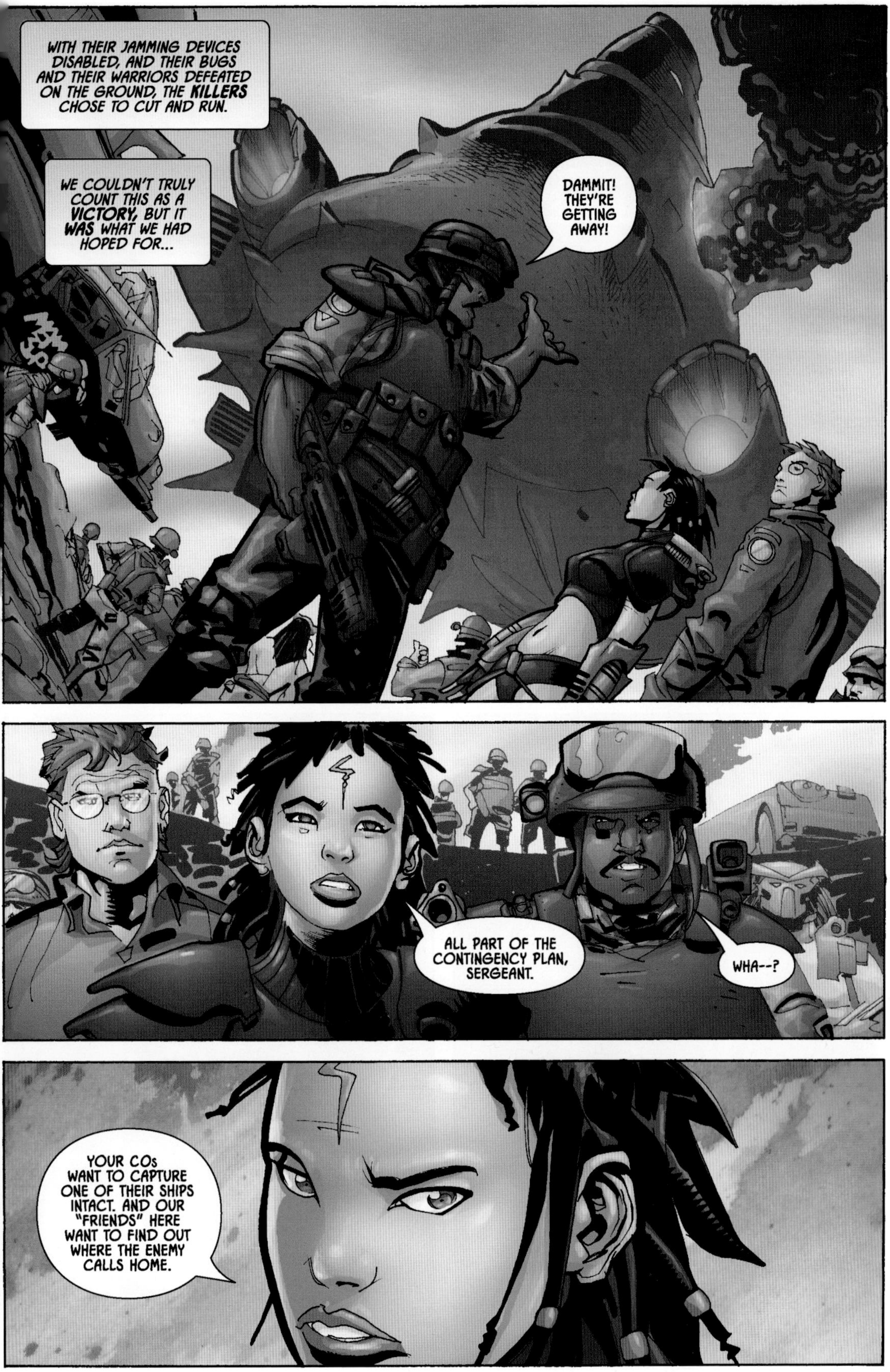
WITH THEIR JAMMING DEVICES DISABLED, AND THEIR BUGS AND THEIR WARRIORS DEFEATED ON THE GROUND, THE KILLERS CHOSE TO CUT AND RUN.
WE COULDN'T TRULY COUNT THIS AS A VICTORY, BUT IT WAS WHAT WE HAD HOPED FOR...
DAMMIT! THEY'RE GETTING AWAY!
ALL PART OF THE CONTINGENCY PLAN, SERGEANT.
WHA--?
YOUR COs WANT TO CAPTURE ONE OF THEIR SHIPS INTACT. AND OUR "FRIENDS" HERE WANT TO FIND OUT WHERE THE ENEMY CALLS HOME.

EVEN AS I EXPLAINED THE SITUATION TO RIOS, ONE OF THE **HUNTERS'** SHIPS WAS ENSURING THAT WE COULD LOCATE THAT "HOME"...

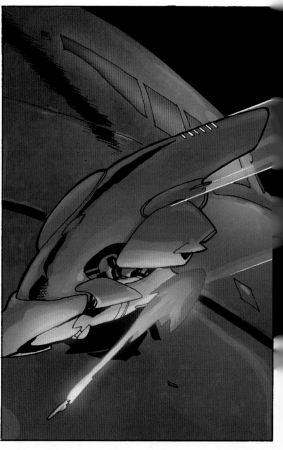

...BY TAGGING THE ESCAPING SHIP WITH A TRACKING DEVICE.

A SUCCESSFUL MANEUVER, BUT A FATAL ONE.

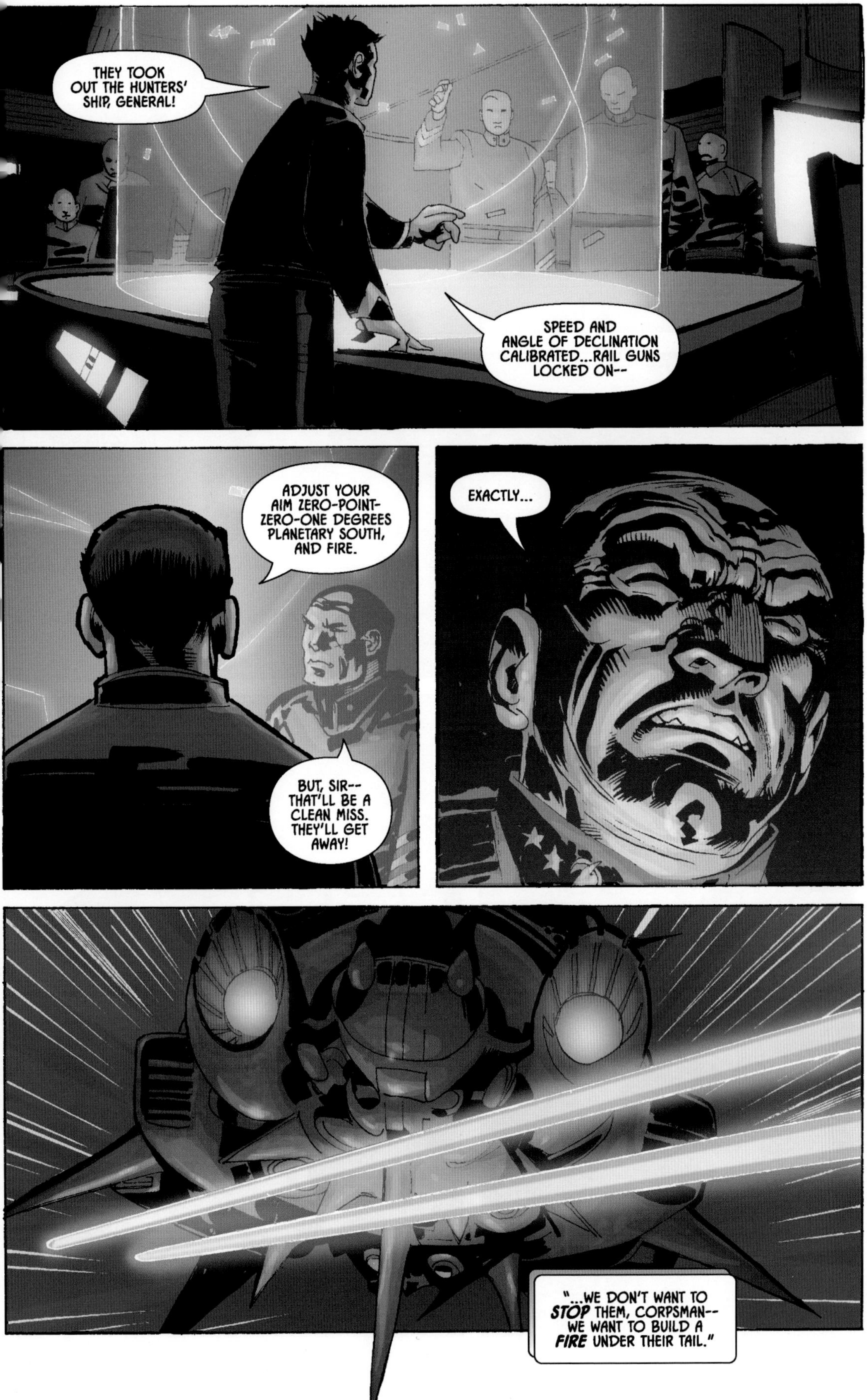
THEY TOOK OUT THE HUNTERS' SHIP, GENERAL!
SPEED AND ANGLE OF DECLINATION CALIBRATED...RAIL GUNS LOCKED ON--
ADJUST YOUR AIM ZERO-POINT-ZERO-ONE DEGREES PLANETARY SOUTH, AND FIRE.
BUT, SIR-- THAT'LL BE A CLEAN MISS. THEY'LL GET AWAY!
EXACTLY...
"...WE DON'T WANT TO STOP THEM, CORPSMAN-- WE WANT TO BUILD A FIRE UNDER THEIR TAIL."

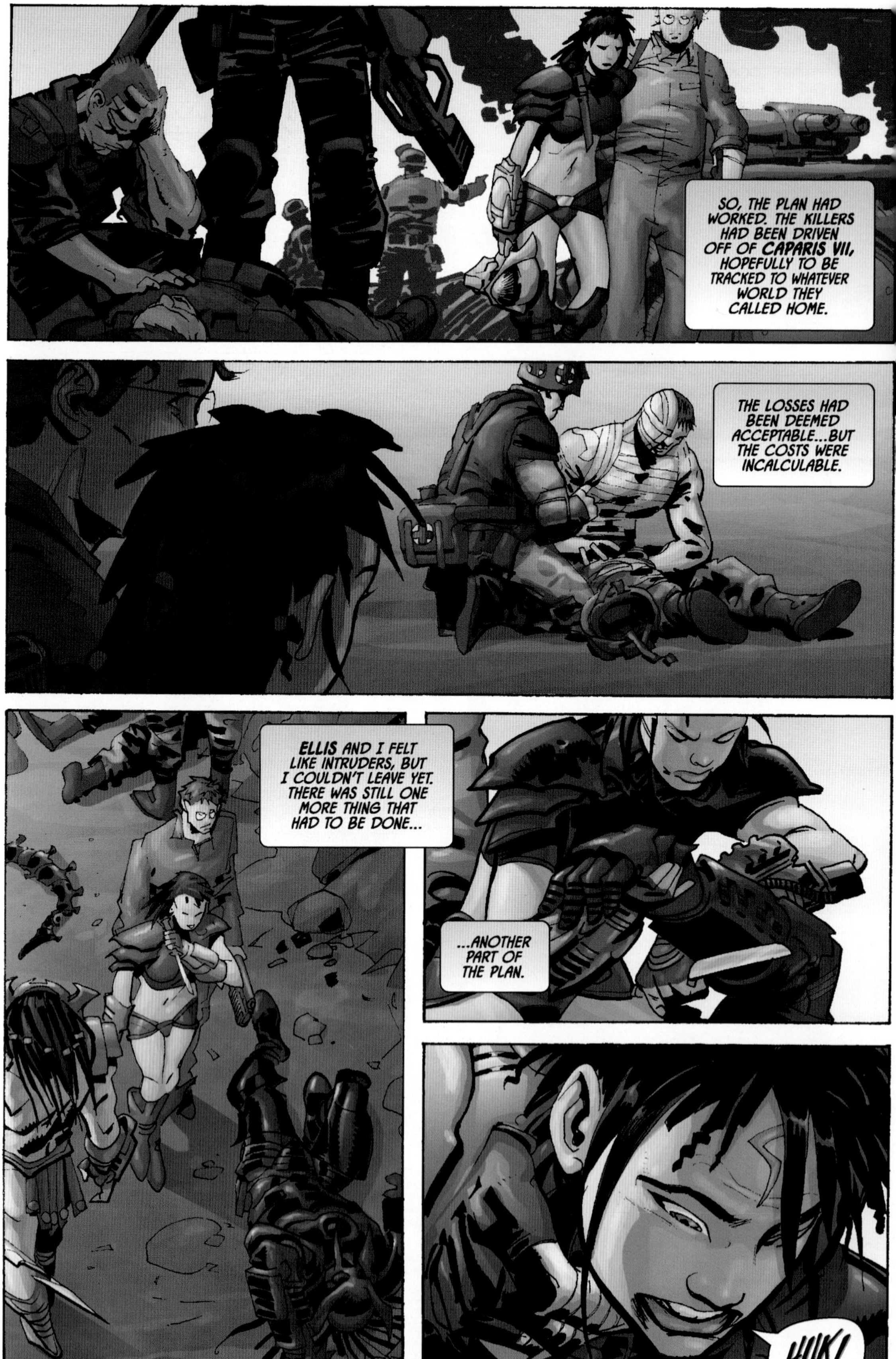
SO, THE PLAN HAD WORKED. THE KILLERS HAD BEEN DRIVEN OFF OF CAPARIS VII, HOPEFULLY TO BE TRACKED TO WHATEVER WORLD THEY CALLED HOME.
THE LOSSES HAD BEEN DEEMED ACCEPTABLE...BUT THE COSTS WERE INCALCULABLE.
ELLIS AND I FELT LIKE INTRUDERS, BUT I COULDN'T LEAVE YET. THERE WAS STILL ONE MORE THING THAT HAD TO BE DONE...
...ANOTHER PART OF THE PLAN.
HUK!

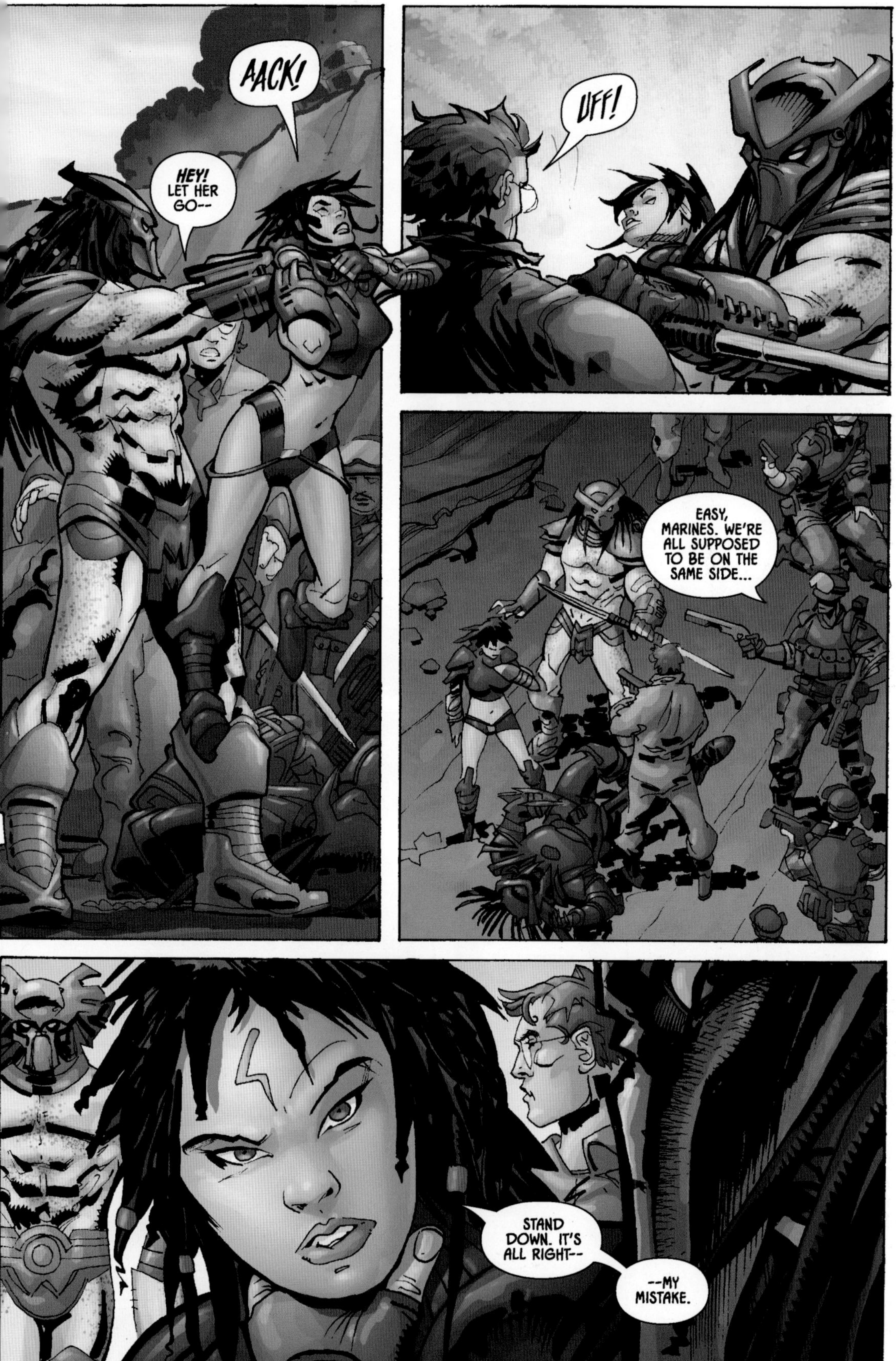

AACK!
HEY! LET HER GO--
UFF!
EASY, MARINES. WE'RE ALL SUPPOSED TO BE ON THE SAME SIDE...
STAND DOWN. IT'S ALL RIGHT--
--MY MISTAKE.

SO MUCH FOR THAT PART OF THE PLAN.

MS. NOGUCHI!

SEREDA...?

YOU DON'T HAVE TO WORRY--

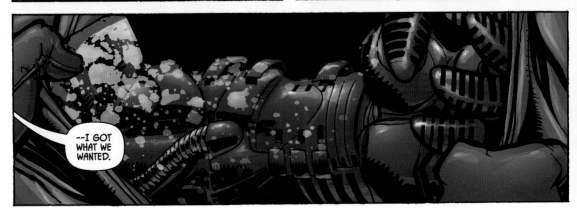

--I GOT WHAT WE WANTED.

WITH THE DEAD AND WOUNDED ACCOUNTED FOR--AND AT LEAST ONE OF THE MARINE COMMAND'S OBJECTIVES ACCOMPLISHED--IT WAS TIME TO RESUME THE HUNT.

I WENT BACK TO THE HUNTERS' FLAGSHIP TO ASSIST IN THE COORDINATION BETWEEN THE FLEETS...

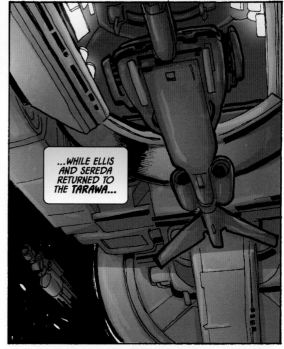

...WHILE ELLIS AND SEREDA RETURNED TO THE *TARAWA*...

...WITH SEREDA'S PRIZE.

FOR THE NEXT THREE WEEKS, WE TRACKED THE SIGNAL FROM THE KILLERS' SHIP.

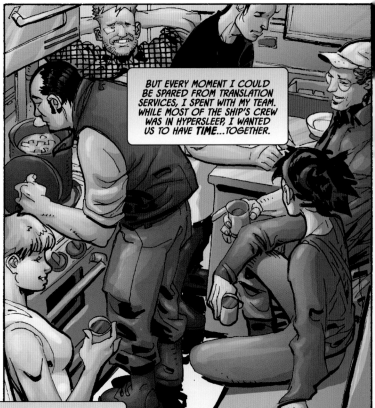

BUT EVERY MOMENT I COULD BE SPARED FROM TRANSLATION SERVICES, I SPENT WITH MY TEAM. WHILE MOST OF THE SHIP'S CREW WAS IN HYPERSLEEP, I WANTED US TO HAVE *TIME*...TOGETHER.

I'D SIGNED UP FOR THIS MISSION OUT OF SOME FEELING--HOWEVER MISGUIDED--OF LOYALTY TO *BROKEN TUSK*. BUT ELLIS AND THE OTHERS HAD COME ALONG FOR *ME*...

I GET IT, MACHIKO--YOU FEEL GUILTY. STOP. WE KNEW WHAT WE WERE SIGNING UP FOR.

BUT THAT'S JUST IT--YOU *DIDN'T*. HELL, *I* DON'T EVEN KNOW WHAT TO EXPECT. I DRAGGED YOU ALL INTO THIS--

NO ONE "DRAGGED" US. WE CAME BECAUSE WE *LOVE* YOU.

BUT WHILE I WAS PONDERING THE MYSTERIES OF THE HUMAN HEART, ELSEWHERE IN THE FLEET OTHERS WERE CONCERNED WITH *ALIEN TECHNOLOGY.*

SOMEBODY HAD GUESSED THAT THE *GAUNTLETS* WORN BY THE KILLERS HELD THE SECRET TO HOW THEY *CONTROLLED THE BUGS.*

THE PRIZE SEREDA BROUGHT BACK PROVED THEM RIGHT, BUT FROM THERE THINGS GOT COMPLICATED.

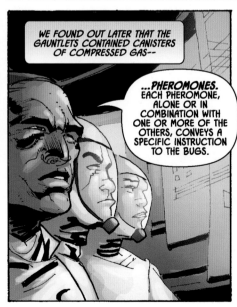

WE FOUND OUT LATER THAT THE GAUNTLETS CONTAINED CANISTERS OF COMPRESSED GAS--

...*PHEROMONES.* EACH PHEROMONE, ALONE OR IN COMBINATION WITH ONE OR MORE OF THE OTHERS, CONVEYS A SPECIFIC INSTRUCTION TO THE BUGS.

CAN WE SYNTHESIZE THESE PHEROMONES?

NO, SIR. NOT WITH THE EQUIPMENT WE HAVE AVAILABLE TO US.

BACK ON EARTH, OR ALPHA CENTAURI, I'M CERTAIN WE COULD--

--BUT EVEN THEN, WE'D BE WORKING BLIND, GENERAL. UNLESS WE HAD BUGS ON WHICH TO TEST THEM...

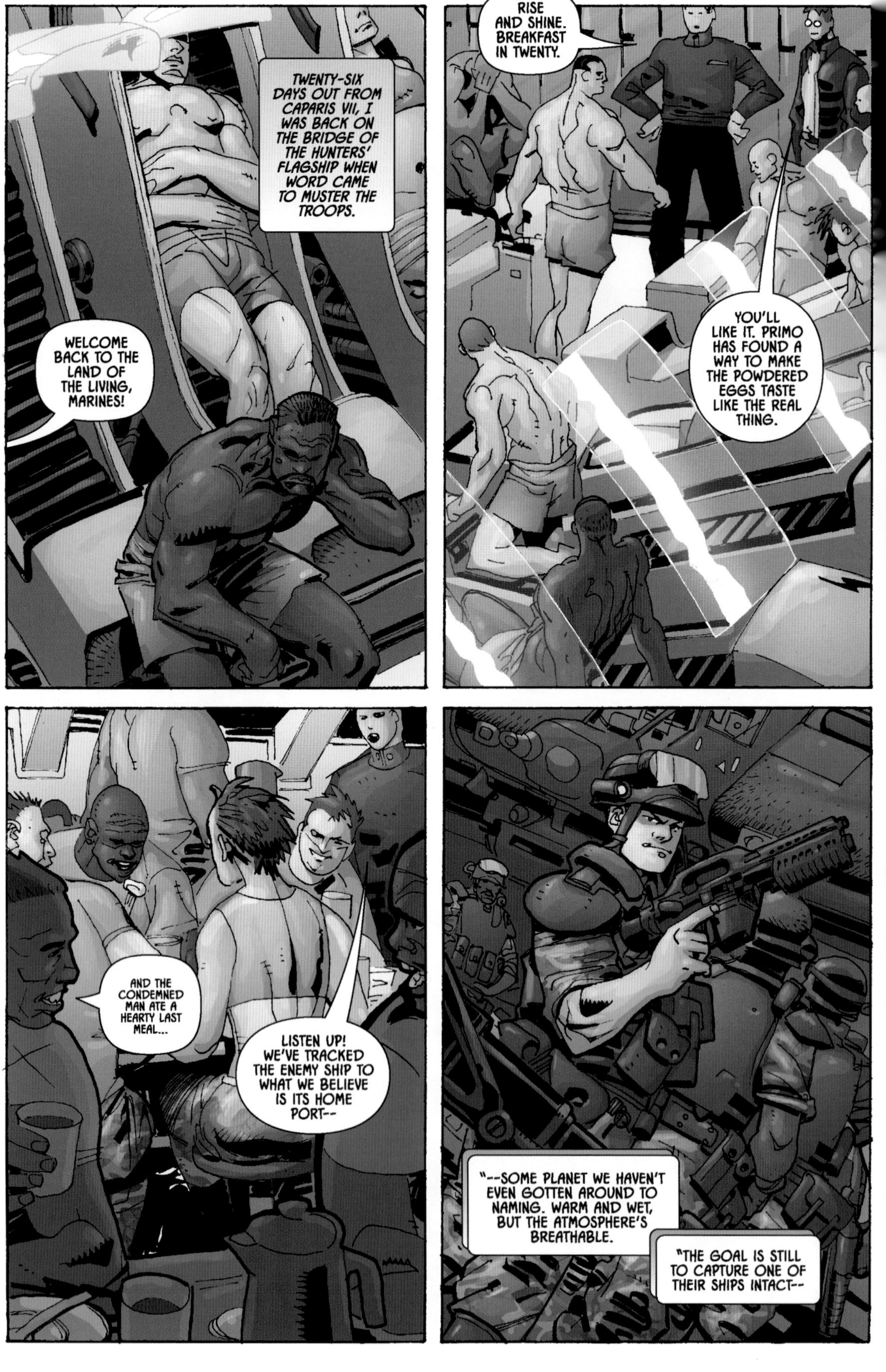
TWENTY-SIX DAYS OUT FROM CAPARIS VII, I WAS BACK ON THE BRIDGE OF THE HUNTERS' FLAGSHIP WHEN WORD CAME TO MUSTER THE TROOPS.
WELCOME BACK TO THE LAND OF THE LIVING, MARINES!
RISE AND SHINE. BREAKFAST IN TWENTY.
YOU'LL LIKE IT. PRIMO HAS FOUND A WAY TO MAKE THE POWDERED EGGS TASTE LIKE THE REAL THING.
AND THE CONDEMNED MAN ATE A HEARTY LAST MEAL...
LISTEN UP! WE'VE TRACKED THE ENEMY SHIP TO WHAT WE BELIEVE IS ITS HOME PORT--
"--SOME PLANET WE HAVEN'T EVEN GOTTEN AROUND TO NAMING. WARM AND WET, BUT THE ATMOSPHERE'S BREATHABLE.
"THE GOAL IS STILL TO CAPTURE ONE OF THEIR SHIPS INTACT--

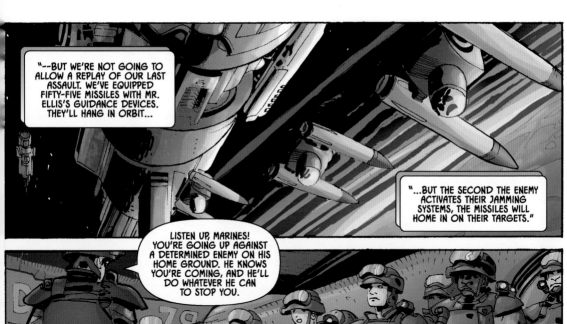

"--BUT WE'RE NOT GOING TO ALLOW A REPLAY OF OUR LAST ASSAULT. WE'VE EQUIPPED FIFTY-FIVE MISSILES WITH MR. ELLIS'S GUIDANCE DEVICES. THEY'LL HANG IN ORBIT...

"...BUT THE SECOND THE ENEMY ACTIVATES THEIR JAMMING SYSTEMS, THE MISSILES WILL HOME IN ON THEIR TARGETS."

LISTEN UP, MARINES! YOU'RE GOING UP AGAINST A DETERMINED ENEMY ON HIS HOME GROUND. HE KNOWS YOU'RE COMING, AND HE'LL DO WHATEVER HE CAN TO STOP YOU.

BUT YOU KICKED HIS ASS LAST TIME, AND YOU'LL DO IT AGAIN. YOU'RE NOT GOING *INTO* HELL, MARINES--

--YOU'RE *BRINGING HELL* TO THE ENEMY!

AM I RIGHT?!

OOO-RAH!

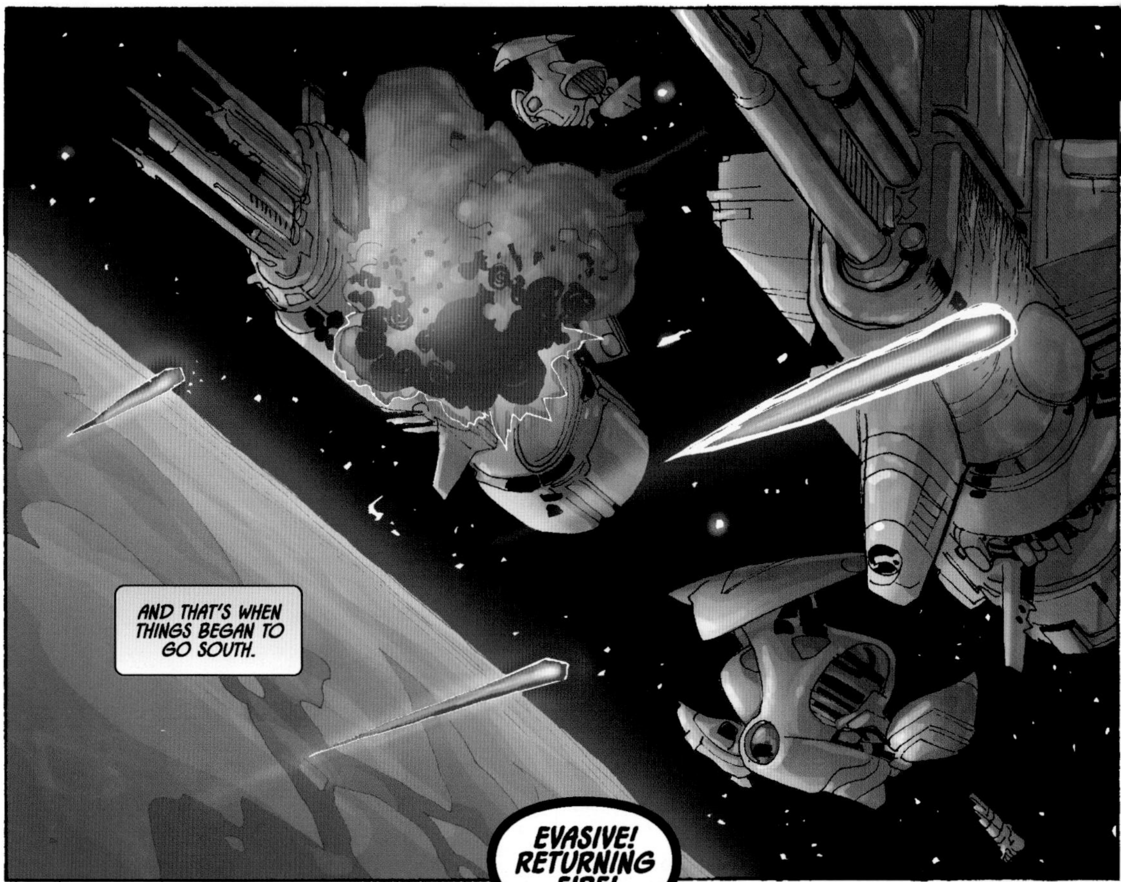
AND THAT'S WHEN THINGS BEGAN TO GO SOUTH.

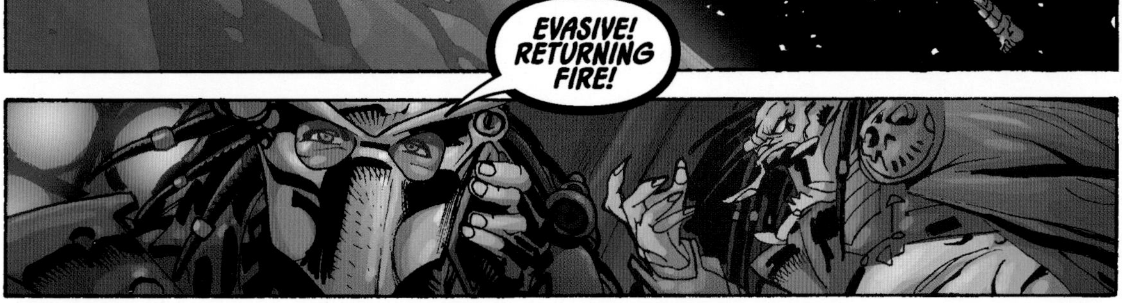
EVASIVE! RETURNING FIRE!

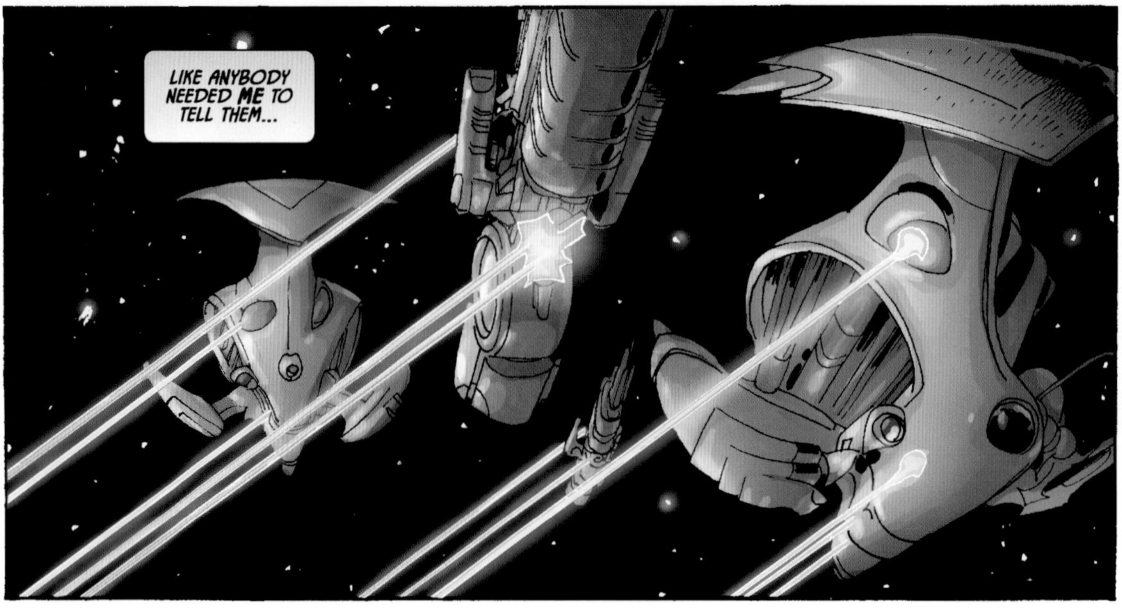
LIKE ANYBODY NEEDED **ME** TO TELL THEM...

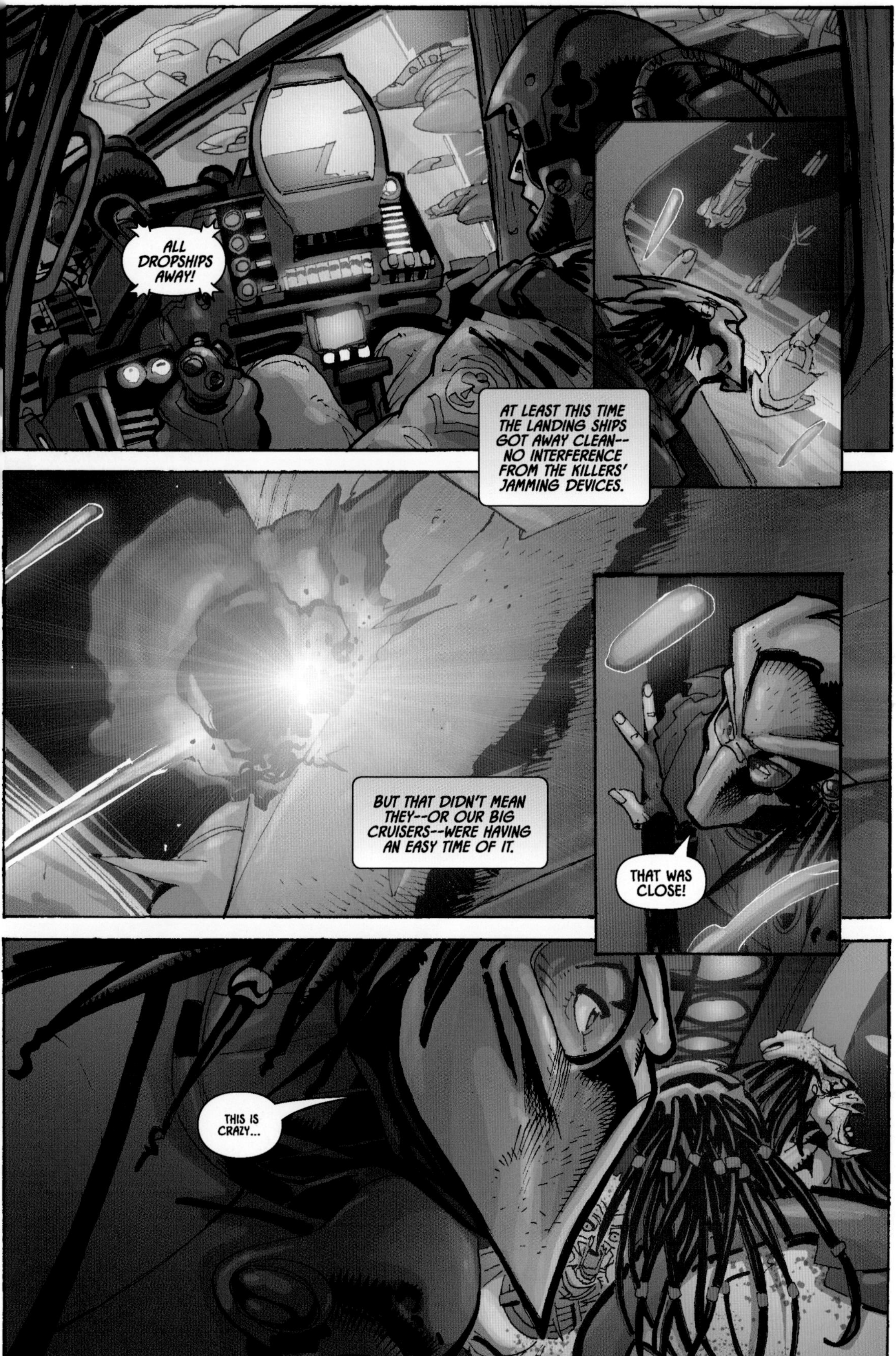
ALL DROPSHIPS AWAY!
AT LEAST THIS TIME THE LANDING SHIPS GOT AWAY CLEAN--NO INTERFERENCE FROM THE KILLERS' JAMMING DEVICES.
BUT THAT DIDN'T MEAN THEY--OR OUR BIG CRUISERS--WERE HAVING AN EASY TIME OF IT.
THAT WAS CLOSE!
THIS IS CRAZY...

ELLIS, ARE YOU THERE? CAN YOU HEAR ME?

I READ YOU, MACHIKO. WHAT'S HAPPENING? WE'VE BEEN ORDERED TO OUR BUNKS--

GET EVERYONE TOGETHER AND *GET OFF THE SHIP!*

THE ENEMY IS IGNORING THE LANDING CRAFT THIS TIME. I DON'T KNOW WHAT KIND OF RECEPTION THEY HAVE PLANNED ON THE GROUND--

--BUT THEY'RE THROWING EVERYTHING THEY'VE GOT AT US UP HERE. THE SAFEST PLACE FOR YOU IS PLANETSIDE, AWAY FROM THE FIGHTING.

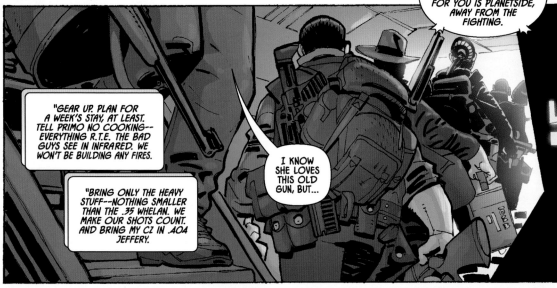

"GEAR UP. PLAN FOR A WEEK'S STAY, AT LEAST. TELL PRIMO NO COOKING-- EVERYTHING R.T.E. THE BAD GUYS SEE IN INFRARED. WE WON'T BE BUILDING ANY FIRES.

"BRING ONLY THE HEAVY STUFF--NOTHING SMALLER THAN THE .35 WHELAN. WE MAKE OUR SHOTS COUNT. AND BRING MY CZ IN .404 JEFFERY.

I KNOW SHE LOVES THIS OLD GUN, BUT...

"I'LL SEE YOU ON THE GROUND."

DROPSHIP VH-322, THIS IS THE TARAWA. WHAT IS YOUR DESTINATION, AND UNDER WHAT AUTHORIZATION--

TARAWA, THIS IS VH-322. WE'RE ON A RESCUE MISSION...

...WE'RE SAVING *OURSELVES.*

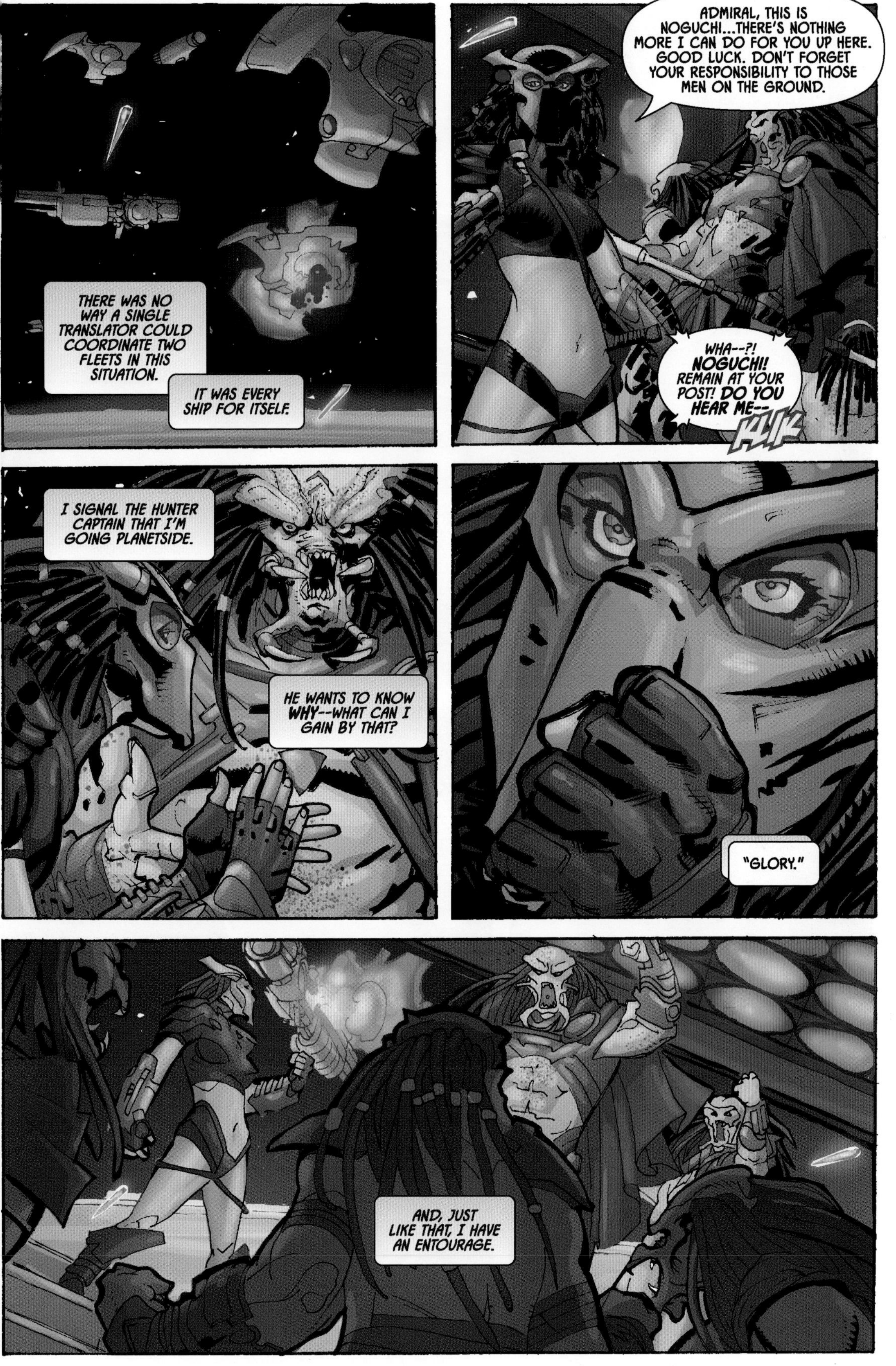
THERE WAS NO WAY A SINGLE TRANSLATOR COULD COORDINATE TWO FLEETS IN THIS SITUATION.
IT WAS EVERY SHIP FOR ITSELF.
ADMIRAL, THIS IS NOGUCHI...THERE'S NOTHING MORE I CAN DO FOR YOU UP HERE. GOOD LUCK. DON'T FORGET YOUR RESPONSIBILITY TO THOSE MEN ON THE GROUND.
WHA--?! NOGUCHI! REMAIN AT YOUR POST! DO YOU HEAR ME--
KLIK
I SIGNAL THE HUNTER CAPTAIN THAT I'M GOING PLANETSIDE.
HE WANTS TO KNOW WHY--WHAT CAN I GAIN BY THAT?
"GLORY."
AND, JUST LIKE THAT, I HAVE AN ENTOURAGE.

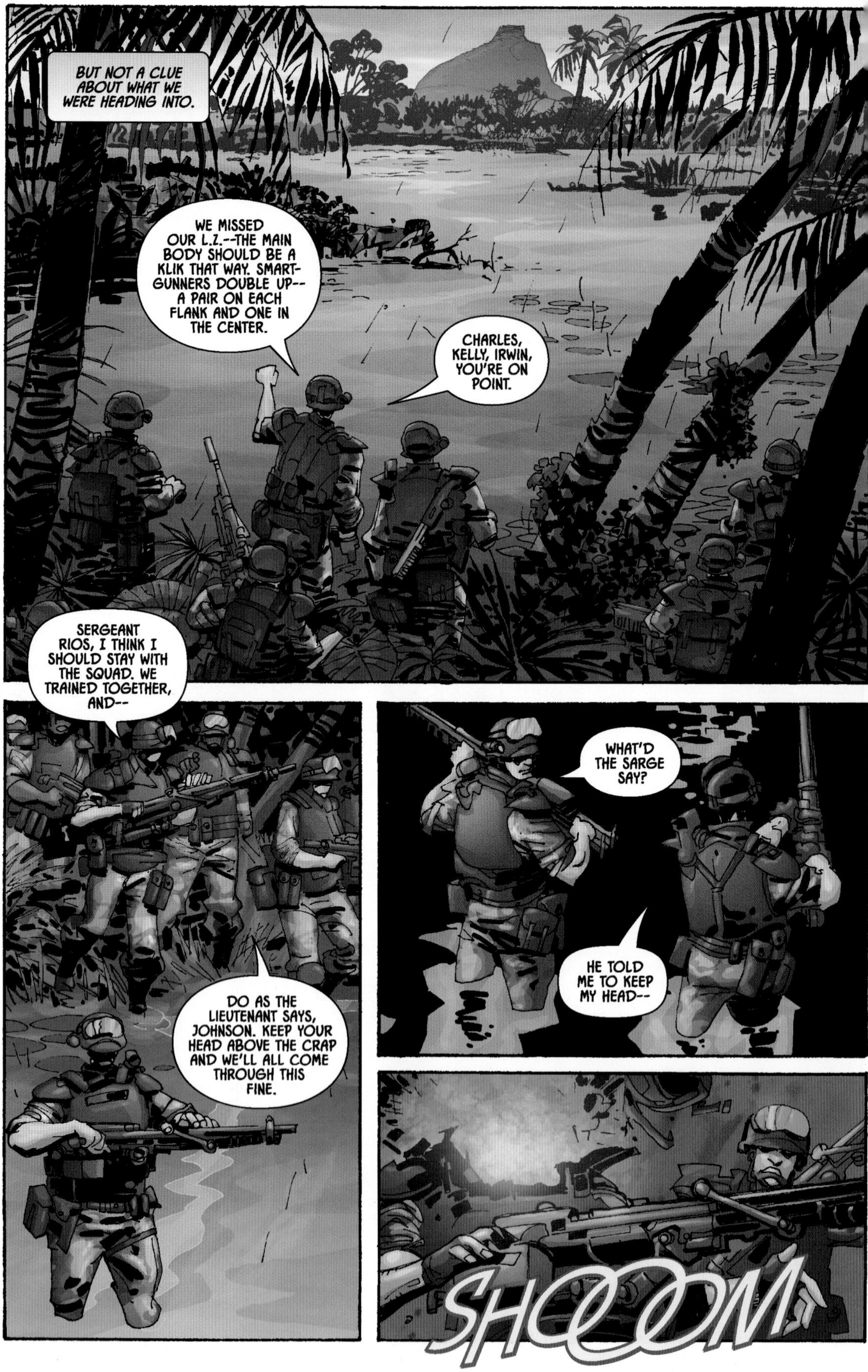
BUT NOT A CLUE ABOUT WHAT WE WERE HEADING INTO.
WE MISSED OUR L.Z.--THE MAIN BODY SHOULD BE A KLIK THAT WAY. SMART-GUNNERS DOUBLE UP--A PAIR ON EACH FLANK AND ONE IN THE CENTER.
CHARLES, KELLY, IRWIN, YOU'RE ON POINT.
SERGEANT RIOS, I THINK I SHOULD STAY WITH THE SQUAD. WE TRAINED TOGETHER, AND--
DO AS THE LIEUTENANT SAYS, JOHNSON. KEEP YOUR HEAD ABOVE THE CRAP AND WE'LL ALL COME THROUGH THIS FINE.
WHAT'D THE SARGE SAY?
HE TOLD ME TO KEEP MY HEAD--
SHOOOM

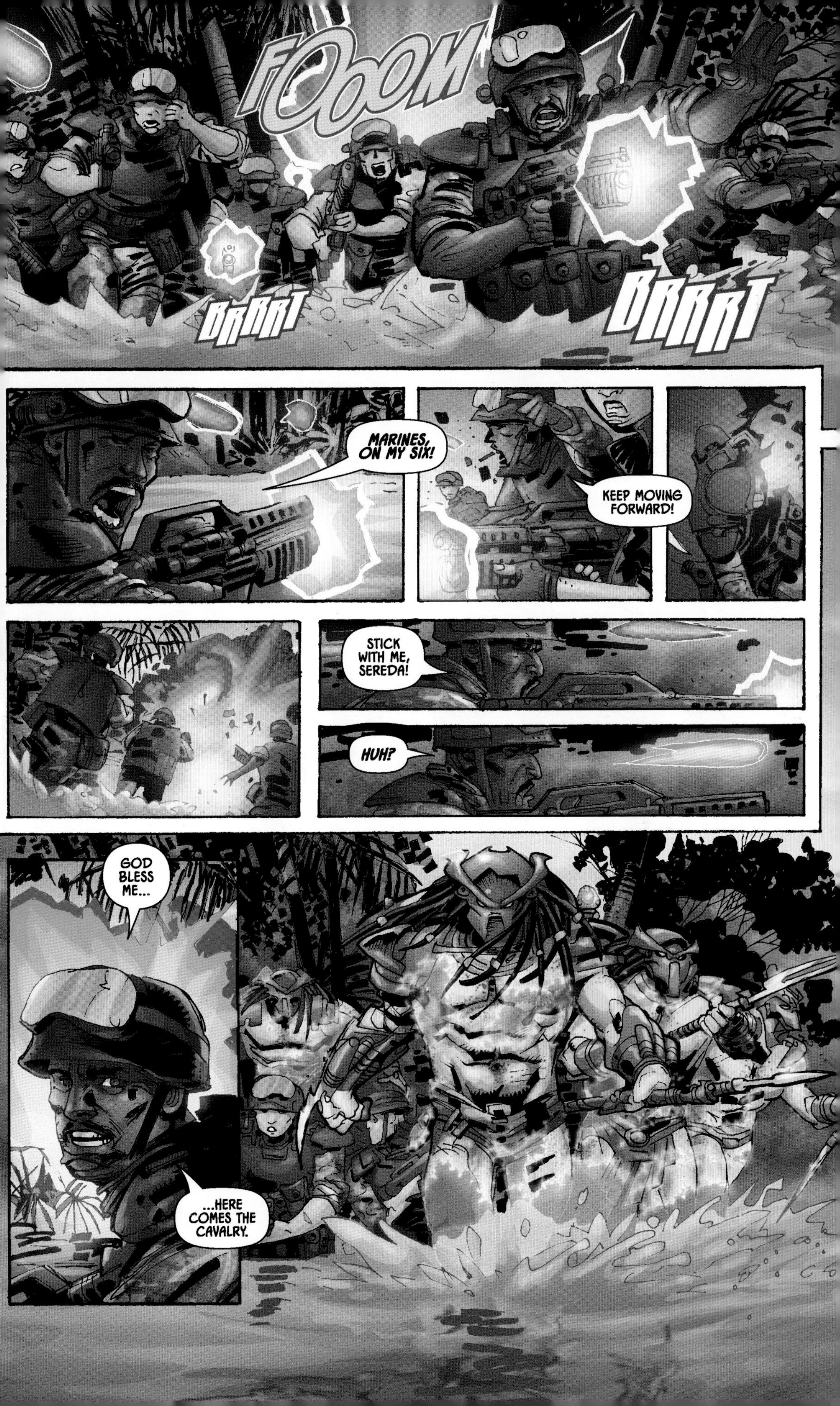
FOOOM
BRRRT
BRRRT
MARINES, ON MY SIX!
KEEP MOVING FORWARD!
STICK WITH ME, SEREDA!
HUH?
GOD BLESS ME...
...HERE COMES THE CAVALRY.

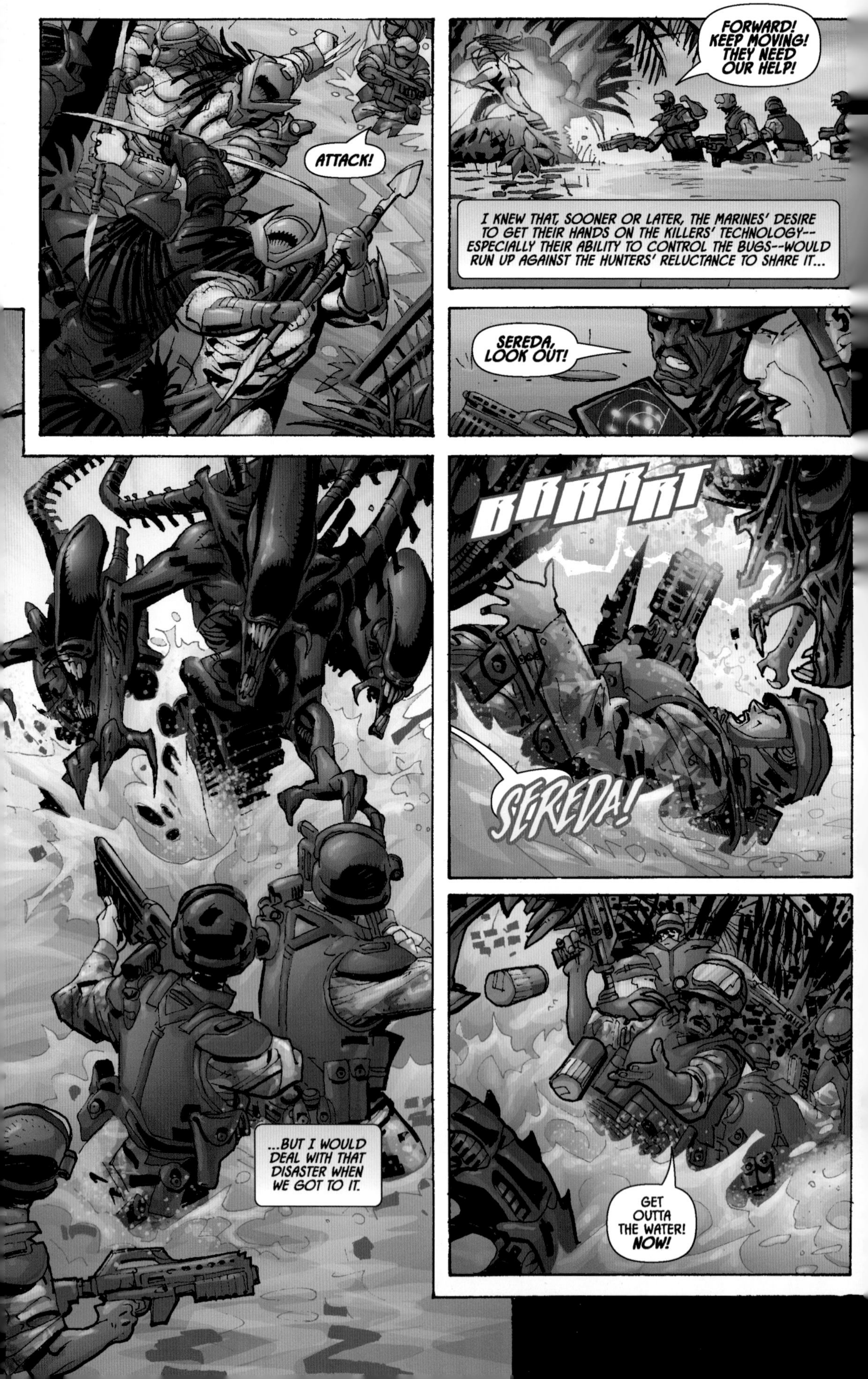
ATTACK!
FORWARD! KEEP MOVING! THEY NEED OUR HELP!
I KNEW THAT, SOONER OR LATER, THE MARINES' DESIRE TO GET THEIR HANDS ON THE KILLERS' TECHNOLOGY--ESPECIALLY THEIR ABILITY TO CONTROL THE BUGS--WOULD RUN UP AGAINST THE HUNTERS' RELUCTANCE TO SHARE IT...
SEREDA, LOOK OUT!
...BUT I WOULD DEAL WITH THAT DISASTER WHEN WE GOT TO IT.
BRRRRT
SEREDA!
GET OUTTA THE WATER! NOW!

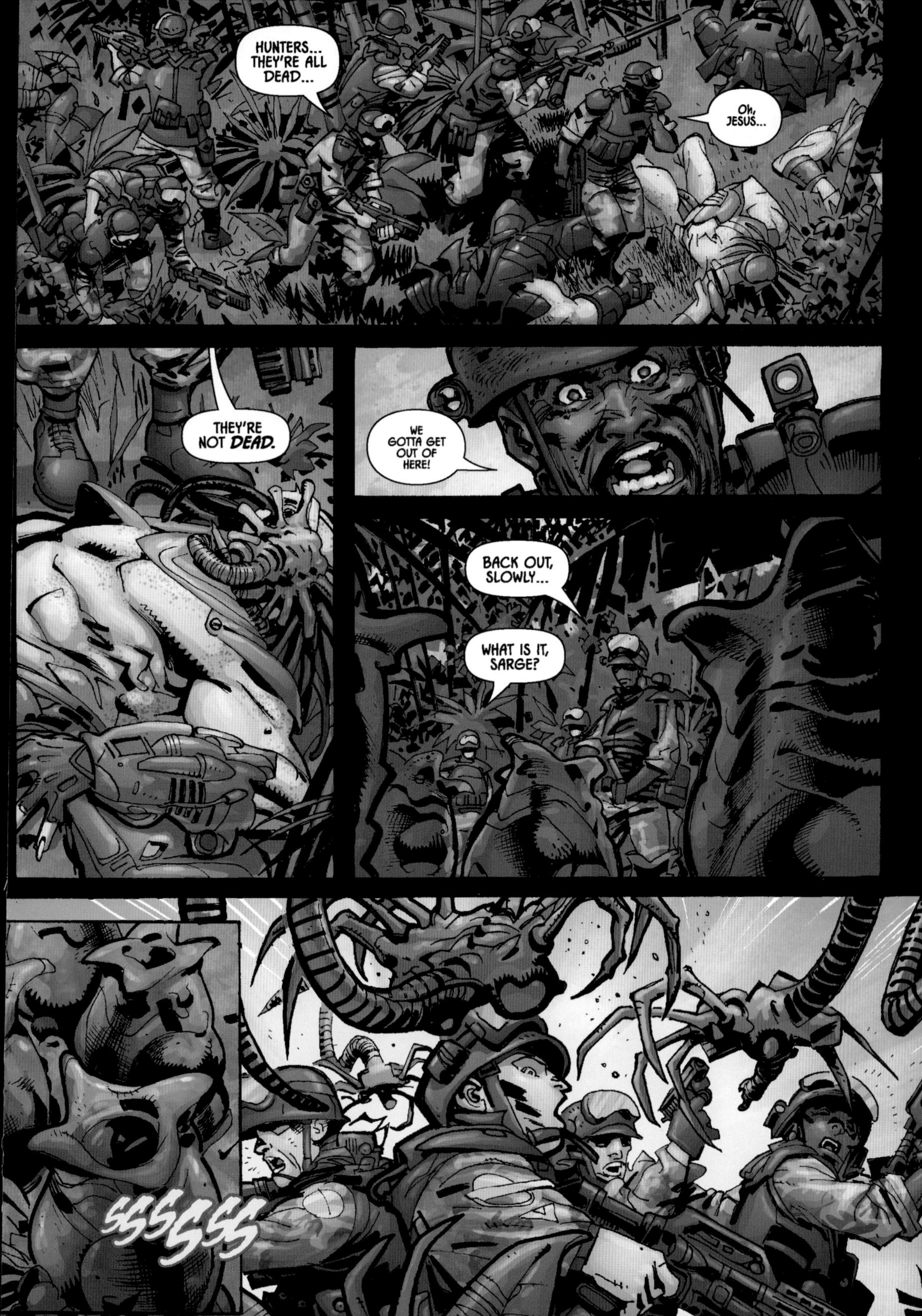
HUNTERS... THEY'RE ALL DEAD...
Oh, JESUS...
THEY'RE NOT DEAD.
WE GOTTA GET OUT OF HERE!
BACK OUT, SLOWLY...
WHAT IS IT, SARGE?
SSSSSS

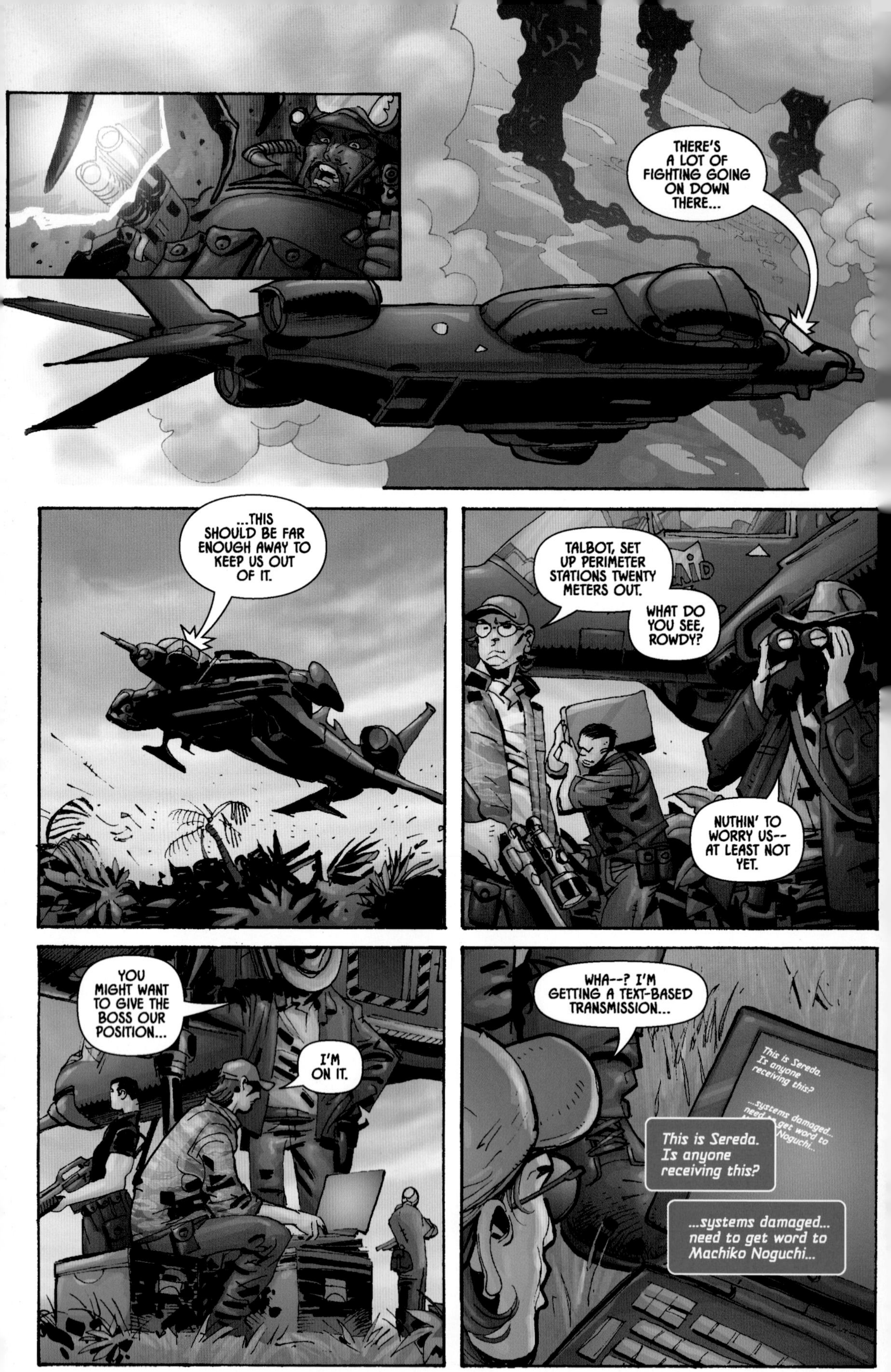
THERE'S A LOT OF FIGHTING GOING ON DOWN THERE...
...THIS SHOULD BE FAR ENOUGH AWAY TO KEEP US OUT OF IT.
TALBOT, SET UP PERIMETER STATIONS TWENTY METERS OUT.
WHAT DO YOU SEE, ROWDY?
NUTHIN' TO WORRY US--AT LEAST NOT YET.
YOU MIGHT WANT TO GIVE THE BOSS OUR POSITION...
I'M ON IT.
WHA--? I'M GETTING A TEXT-BASED TRANSMISSION...
This is Sereda. Is anyone receiving this?
...systems damaged... need to get word to Machiko Noguchi...

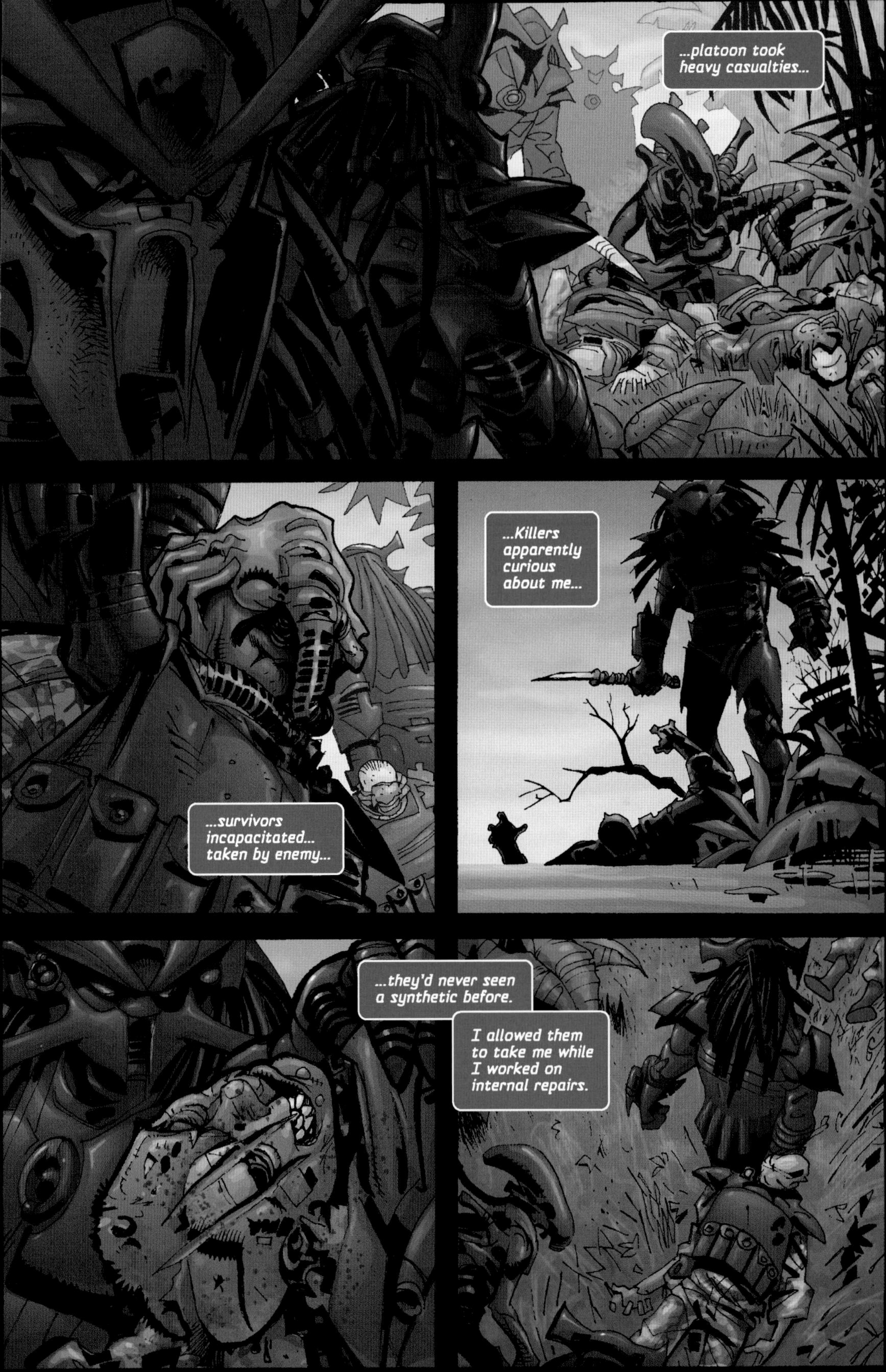
...platoon took heavy casualties...
...survivors incapacitated... taken by enemy...
...Killers apparently curious about me...
...they'd never seen a synthetic before.
I allowed them to take me while I worked on internal repairs.

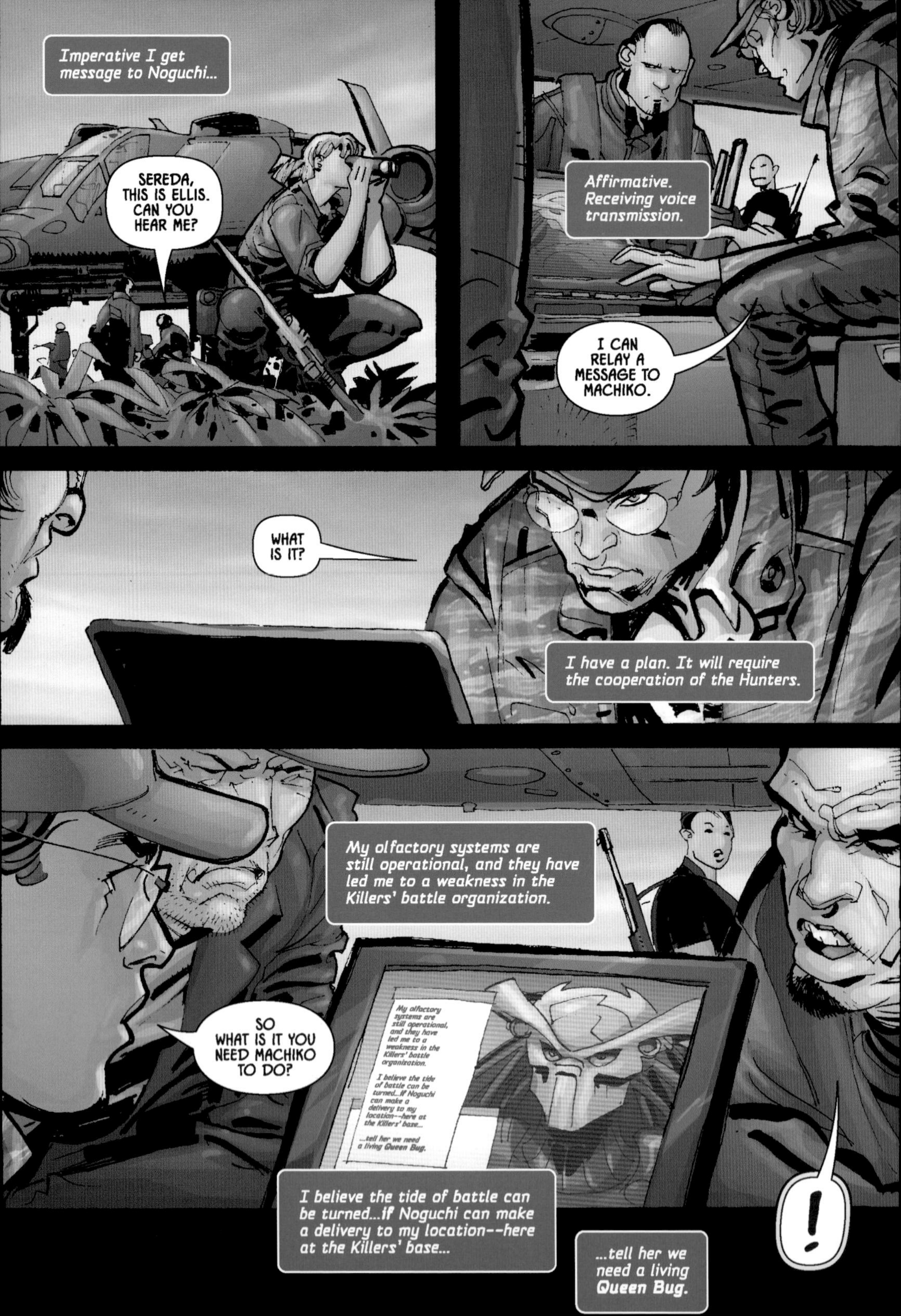

Imperative I get message to Noguchi...
SEREDA, THIS IS ELLIS. CAN YOU HEAR ME?
Affirmative. Receiving voice transmission.
I CAN RELAY A MESSAGE TO MACHIKO.
WHAT IS IT?
I have a plan. It will require the cooperation of the Hunters.
My olfactory systems are still operational, and they have led me to a weakness in the Killers' battle organization.
SO WHAT IS IT YOU NEED MACHIKO TO DO?
My olfactory systems are still operational, and they have led me to a weakness in the Killers' battle organization.
I believe the tide of battle can be turned...if Noguchi can make a delivery to my location--here at the Killers' base...
...tell her we need a living Queen Bug.
I believe the tide of battle can be turned...if Noguchi can make a delivery to my location--here at the Killers' base...
...tell her we need a living Queen Bug.
!

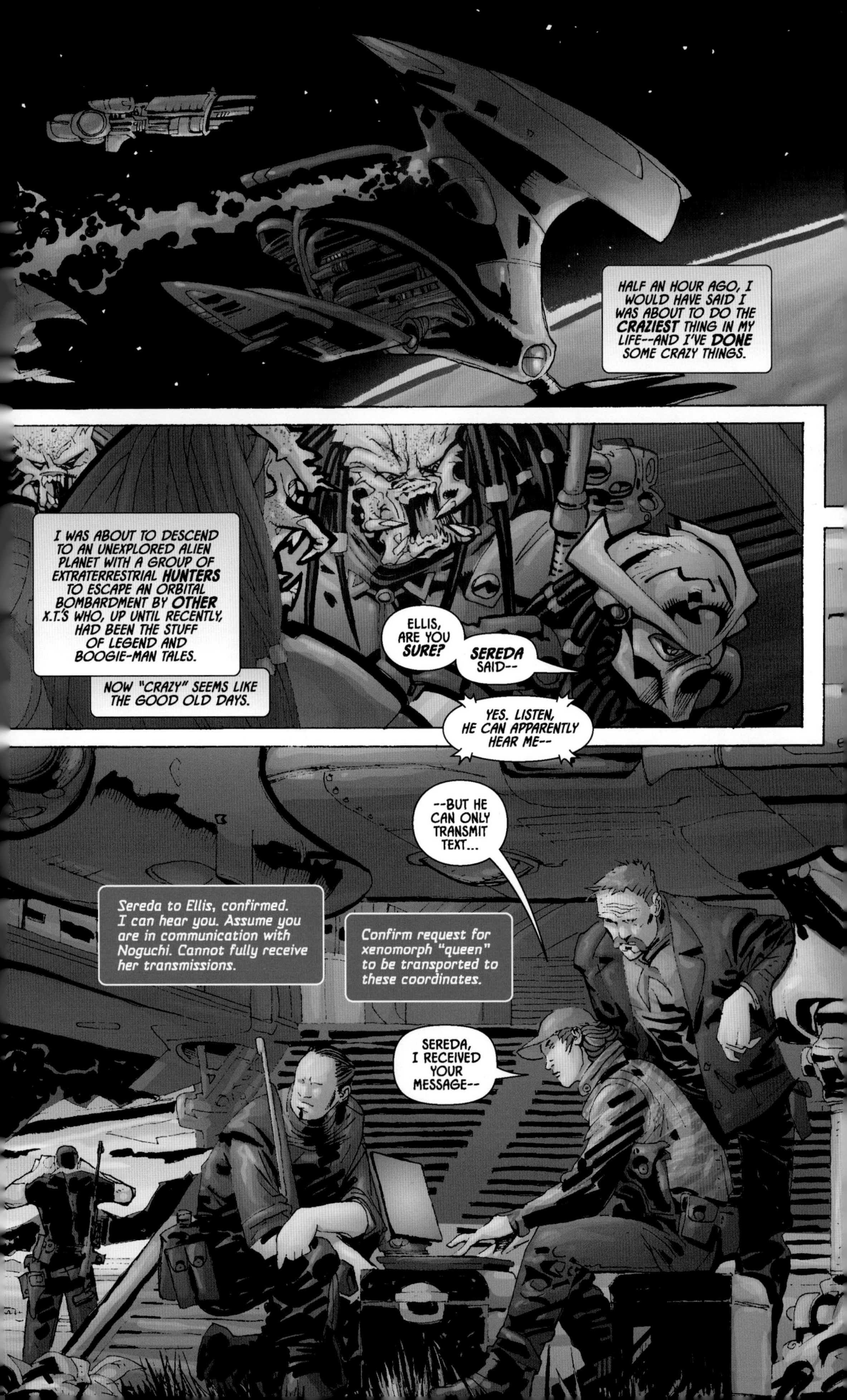

HALF AN HOUR AGO, I WOULD HAVE SAID I WAS ABOUT TO DO THE CRAZIEST THING IN MY LIFE--AND I'VE DONE SOME CRAZY THINGS.
I WAS ABOUT TO DESCEND TO AN UNEXPLORED ALIEN PLANET WITH A GROUP OF EXTRATERRESTRIAL HUNTERS TO ESCAPE AN ORBITAL BOMBARDMENT BY OTHER X.T.'S WHO, UP UNTIL RECENTLY, HAD BEEN THE STUFF OF LEGEND AND BOOGIE-MAN TALES.
NOW "CRAZY" SEEMS LIKE THE GOOD OLD DAYS.
ELLIS, ARE YOU SURE?
SEREDA SAID--
YES. LISTEN, HE CAN APPARENTLY HEAR ME--
--BUT HE CAN ONLY TRANSMIT TEXT...
Sereda to Ellis, confirmed. I can hear you. Assume you are in communication with Noguchi. Cannot fully receive her transmissions.
Confirm request for xenomorph "queen" to be transported to these coordinates.
SEREDA, I RECEIVED YOUR MESSAGE--

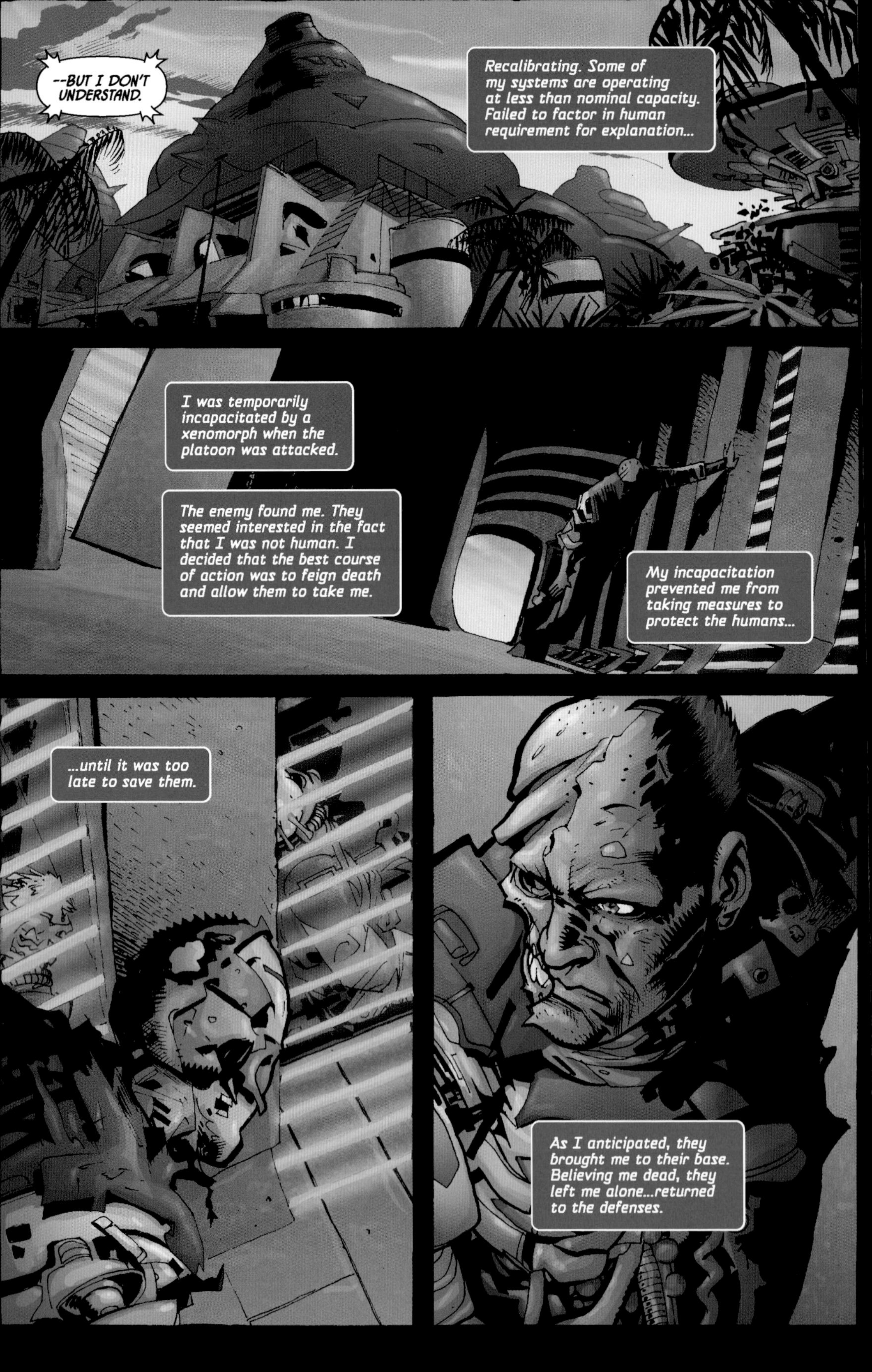
--BUT I DON'T UNDERSTAND.
Recalibrating. Some of my systems are operating at less than nominal capacity. Failed to factor in human requirement for explanation...
I was temporarily incapacitated by a xenomorph when the platoon was attacked.
The enemy found me. They seemed interested in the fact that I was not human. I decided that the best course of action was to feign death and allow them to take me.
My incapacitation prevented me from taking measures to protect the humans...
...until it was too late to save them.
As I anticipated, they brought me to their base. Believing me dead, they left me alone...returned to the defenses.

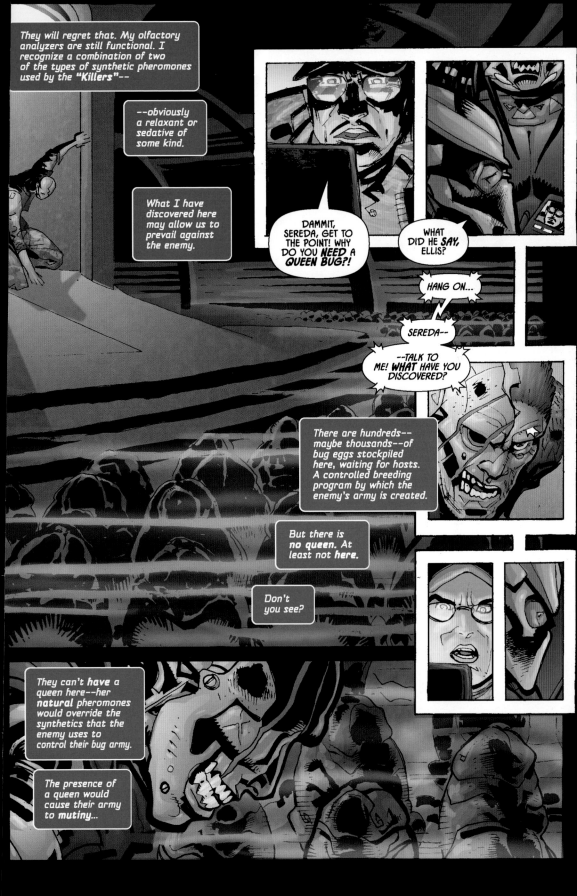

They will regret that. My olfactory analyzers are still functional. I recognize a combination of two of the types of synthetic pheromones used by the "Killers"--

--obviously a relaxant or sedative of some kind.

What I have discovered here may allow us to prevail against the enemy.

DAMMIT, SEREDA, GET TO THE POINT! WHY DO YOU *NEED* A QUEEN BUG?!

WHAT DID HE *SAY*, ELLIS?

HANG ON...

SEREDA--

--TALK TO ME! *WHAT* HAVE YOU DISCOVERED?

There are hundreds-- maybe thousands--of bug eggs stockpiled here, waiting for hosts. A controlled breeding program by which the enemy's army is created.

But there is *no queen*. At least not *here*.

Don't you see?

They can't *have* a queen here--her *natural* pheromones would override the synthetics that the enemy uses to control their bug army.

The presence of a queen would cause their army to *mutiny*...

117

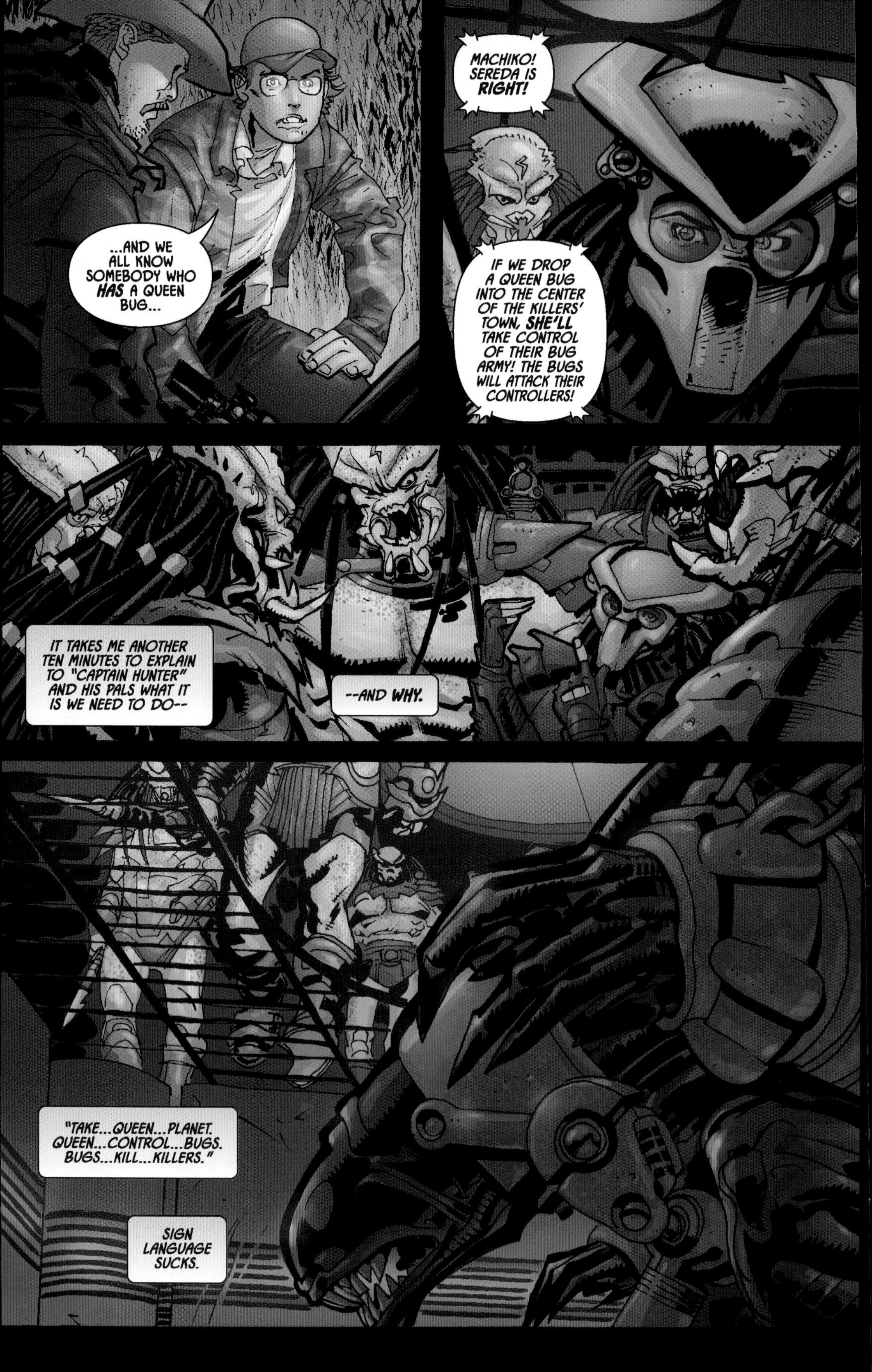
...AND WE ALL KNOW SOMEBODY WHO HAS A QUEEN BUG...
MACHIKO! SEREDA IS RIGHT!
IF WE DROP A QUEEN BUG INTO THE CENTER OF THE KILLERS' TOWN, SHE'LL TAKE CONTROL OF THEIR BUG ARMY! THE BUGS WILL ATTACK THEIR CONTROLLERS!
IT TAKES ME ANOTHER TEN MINUTES TO EXPLAIN TO "CAPTAIN HUNTER" AND HIS PALS WHAT IT IS WE NEED TO DO--
--AND WHY.
"TAKE...QUEEN...PLANET. QUEEN...CONTROL...BUGS. BUGS...KILL...KILLERS."
SIGN LANGUAGE SUCKS.

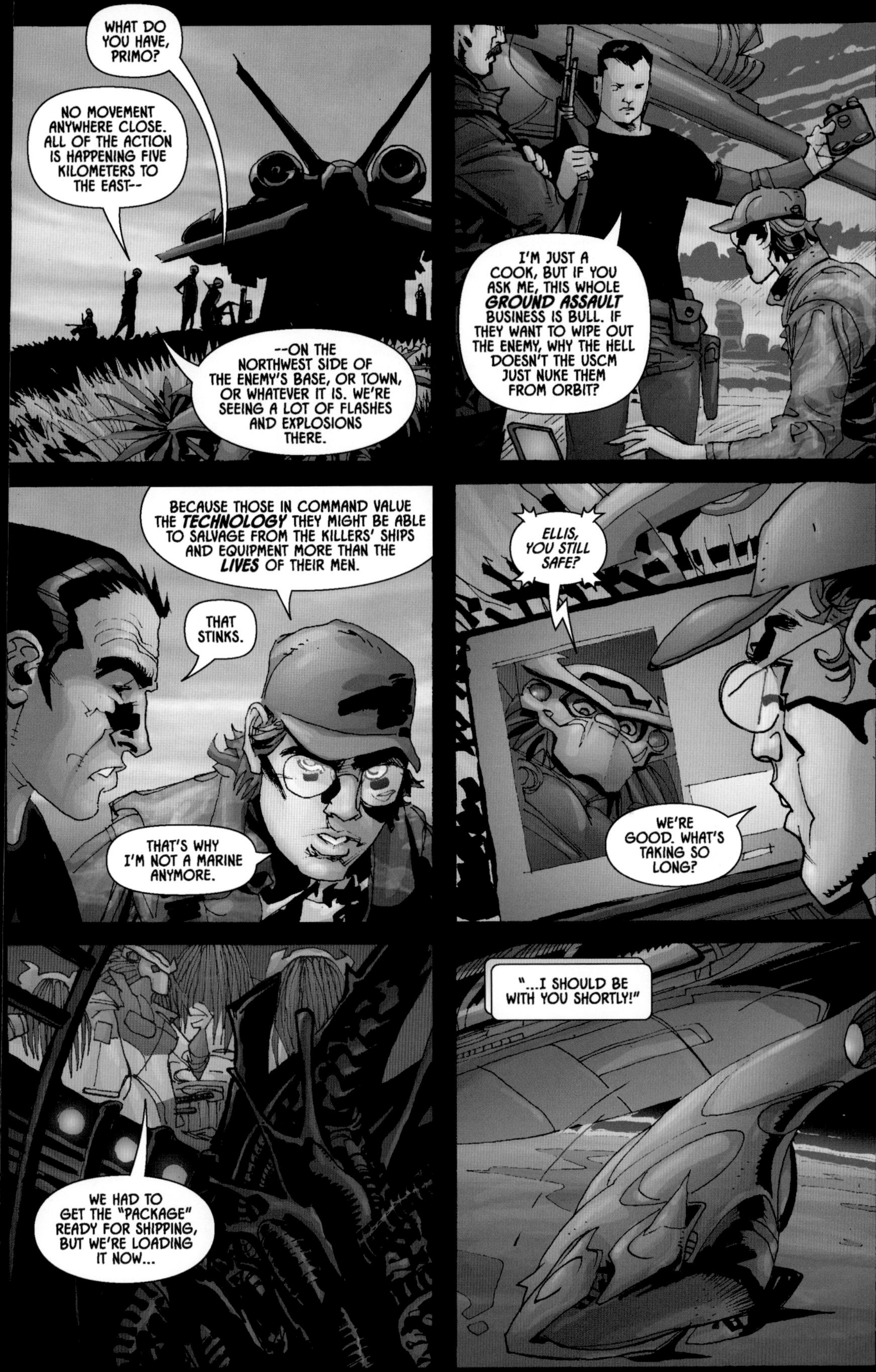
WHAT DO YOU HAVE, PRIMO?
NO MOVEMENT ANYWHERE CLOSE. ALL OF THE ACTION IS HAPPENING FIVE KILOMETERS TO THE EAST--
--ON THE NORTHWEST SIDE OF THE ENEMY'S BASE, OR TOWN, OR WHATEVER IT IS. WE'RE SEEING A LOT OF FLASHES AND EXPLOSIONS THERE.
I'M JUST A COOK, BUT IF YOU ASK ME, THIS WHOLE GROUND ASSAULT BUSINESS IS BULL. IF THEY WANT TO WIPE OUT THE ENEMY, WHY THE HELL DOESN'T THE USCM JUST NUKE THEM FROM ORBIT?
BECAUSE THOSE IN COMMAND VALUE THE TECHNOLOGY THEY MIGHT BE ABLE TO SALVAGE FROM THE KILLERS' SHIPS AND EQUIPMENT MORE THAN THE LIVES OF THEIR MEN.
THAT STINKS.
THAT'S WHY I'M NOT A MARINE ANYMORE.
ELLIS, YOU STILL SAFE?
WE'RE GOOD. WHAT'S TAKING SO LONG?
WE HAD TO GET THE "PACKAGE" READY FOR SHIPPING, BUT WE'RE LOADING IT NOW...
"...I SHOULD BE WITH YOU SHORTLY!"

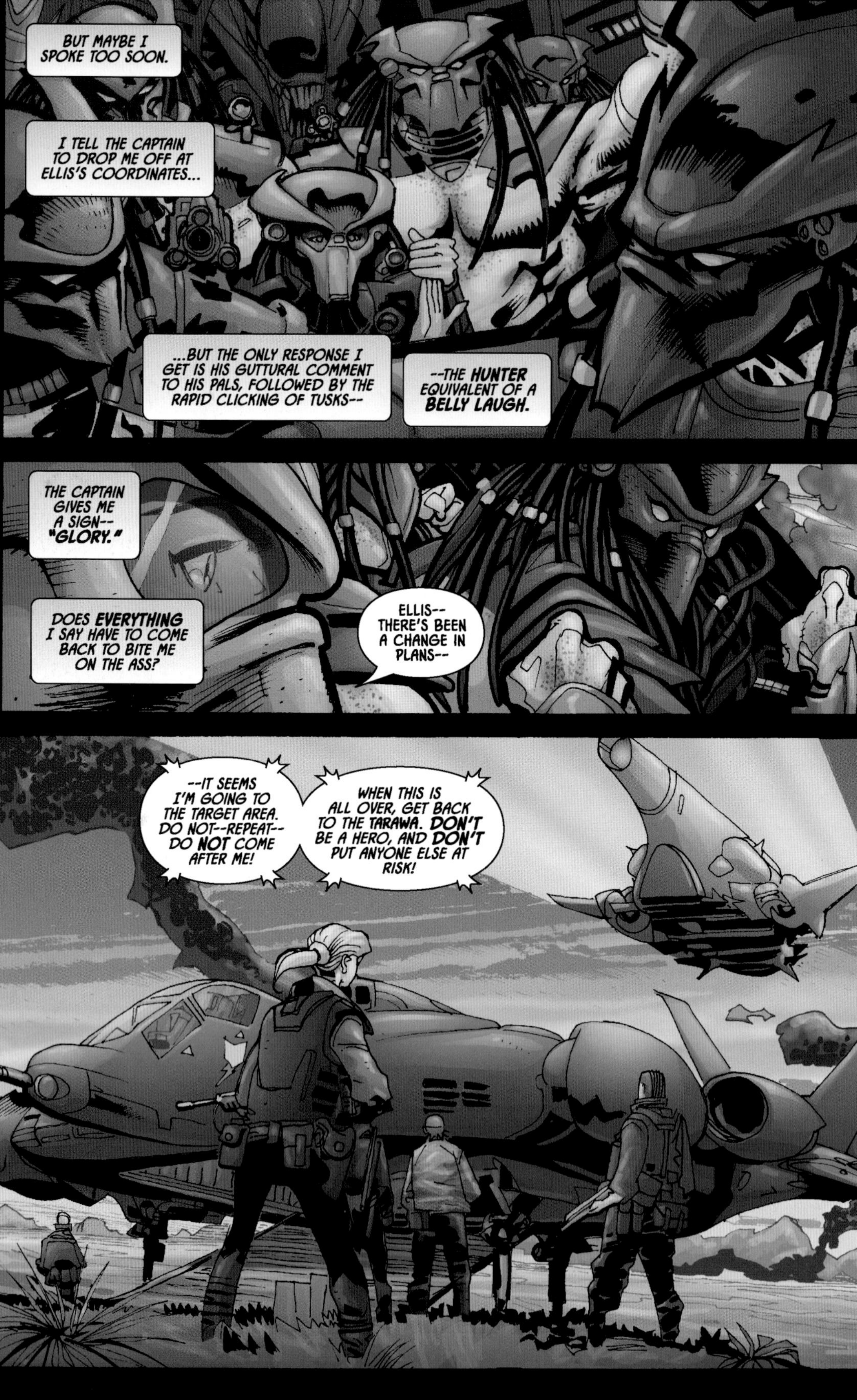

BUT MAYBE I SPOKE TOO SOON.
I TELL THE CAPTAIN TO DROP ME OFF AT ELLIS'S COORDINATES...
...BUT THE ONLY RESPONSE I GET IS HIS GUTTURAL COMMENT TO HIS PALS, FOLLOWED BY THE RAPID CLICKING OF TUSKS--
--THE HUNTER EQUIVALENT OF A BELLY LAUGH.
THE CAPTAIN GIVES ME A SIGN-- "GLORY."
DOES EVERYTHING I SAY HAVE TO COME BACK TO BITE ME ON THE ASS?
ELLIS-- THERE'S BEEN A CHANGE IN PLANS--
--IT SEEMS I'M GOING TO THE TARGET AREA. DO NOT--REPEAT-- DO NOT COME AFTER ME!
WHEN THIS IS ALL OVER, GET BACK TO THE TARAWA. DON'T BE A HERO, AND DON'T PUT ANYONE ELSE AT RISK!

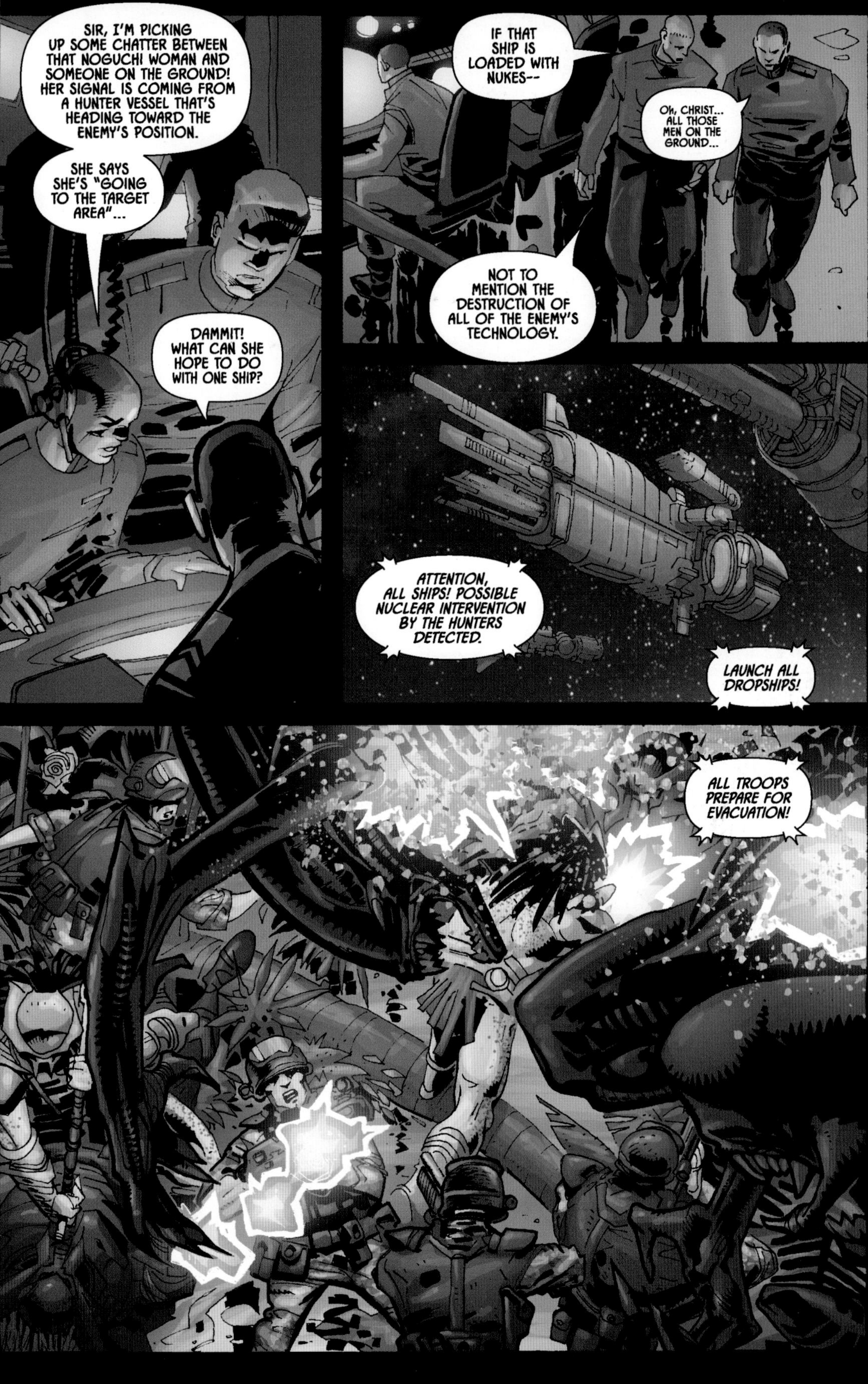
SIR, I'M PICKING UP SOME CHATTER BETWEEN THAT NOGUCHI WOMAN AND SOMEONE ON THE GROUND! HER SIGNAL IS COMING FROM A HUNTER VESSEL THAT'S HEADING TOWARD THE ENEMY'S POSITION.
SHE SAYS SHE'S "GOING TO THE TARGET AREA"...
DAMMIT! WHAT CAN SHE HOPE TO DO WITH ONE SHIP?
IF THAT SHIP IS LOADED WITH NUKES--
Oh, CHRIST... ALL THOSE MEN ON THE GROUND...
NOT TO MENTION THE DESTRUCTION OF ALL OF THE ENEMY'S TECHNOLOGY.
ATTENTION, ALL SHIPS! POSSIBLE NUCLEAR INTERVENTION BY THE HUNTERS DETECTED.
LAUNCH ALL DROPSHIPS!
ALL TROOPS PREPARE FOR EVACUATION!

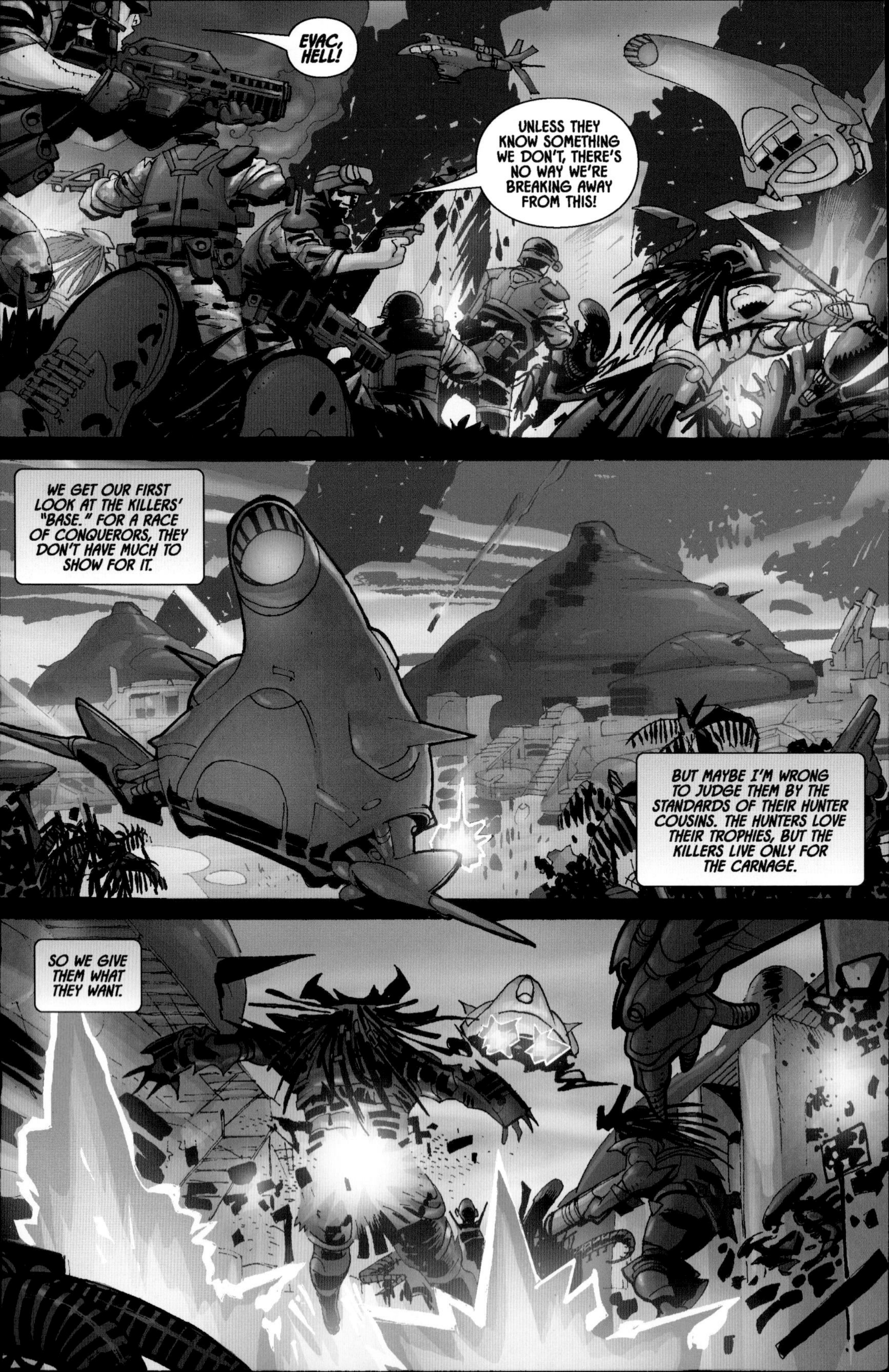
EVAC, HELL!
UNLESS THEY KNOW SOMETHING WE DON'T, THERE'S NO WAY WE'RE BREAKING AWAY FROM THIS!
WE GET OUR FIRST LOOK AT THE KILLERS' "BASE." FOR A RACE OF CONQUERORS, THEY DON'T HAVE MUCH TO SHOW FOR IT.
BUT MAYBE I'M WRONG TO JUDGE THEM BY THE STANDARDS OF THEIR HUNTER COUSINS. THE HUNTERS LOVE THEIR TROPHIES, BUT THE KILLERS LIVE ONLY FOR THE CARNAGE.
SO WE GIVE THEM WHAT THEY WANT.

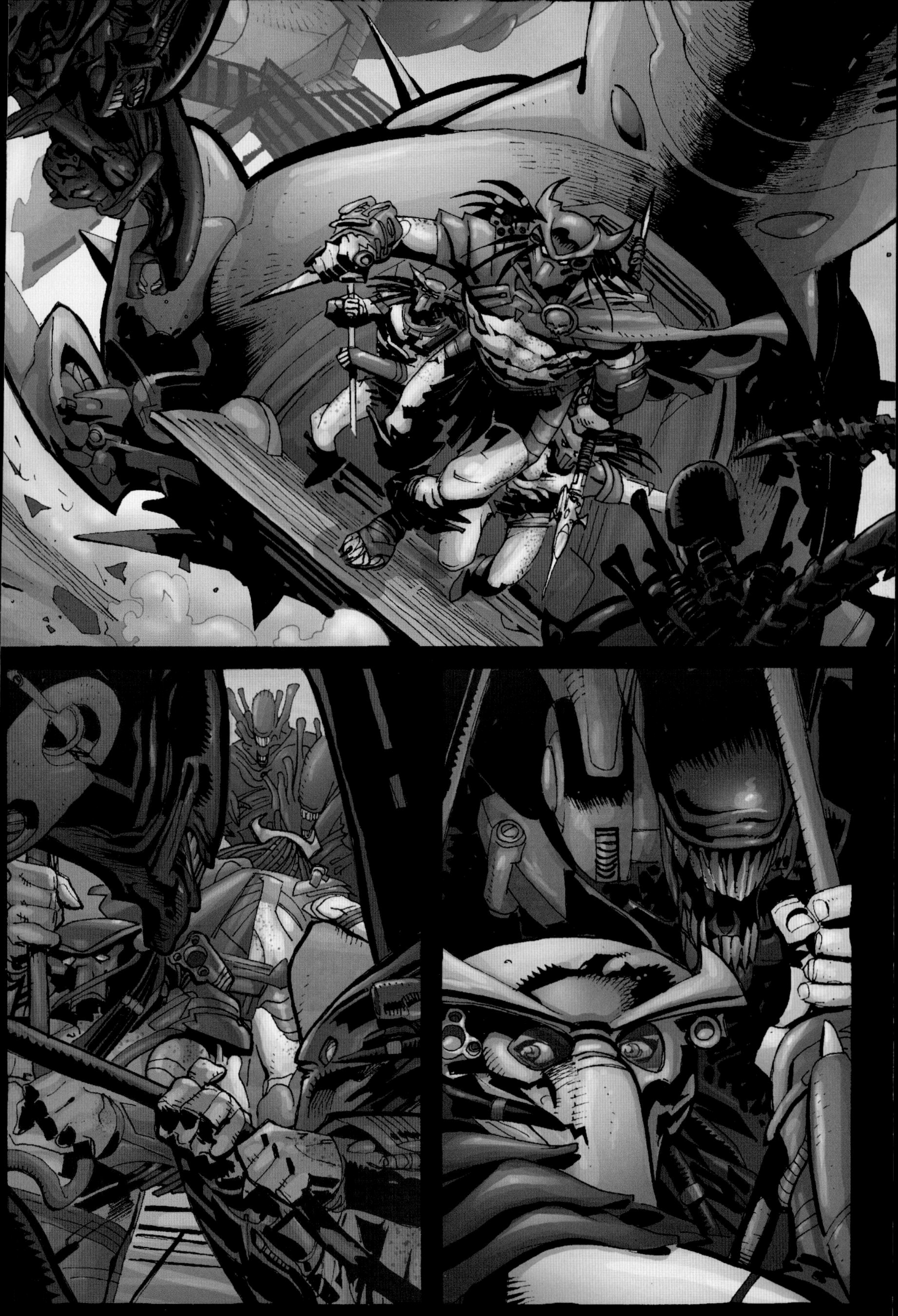

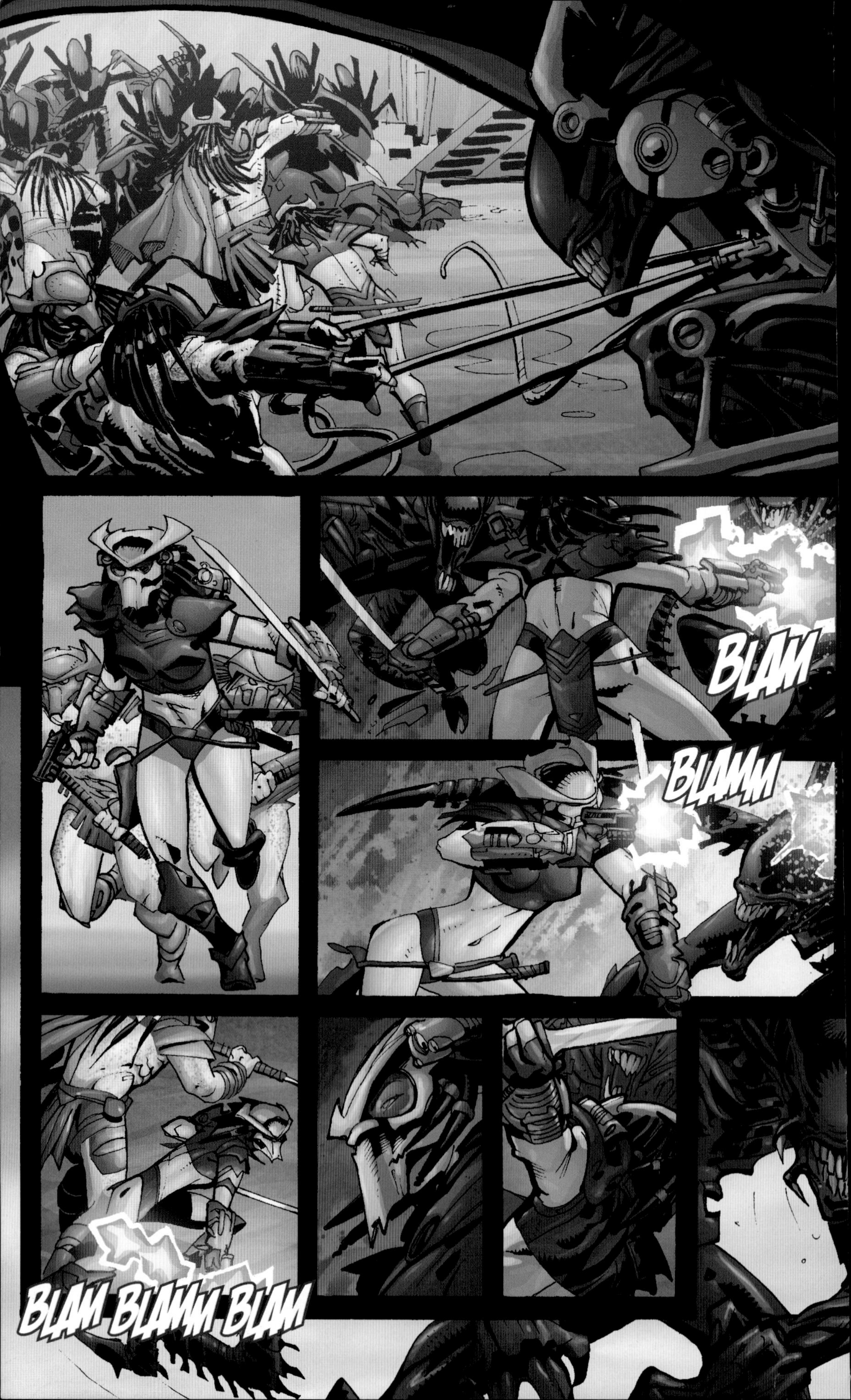
BLAM
BLAMM
BLAM BLAMM BLAM

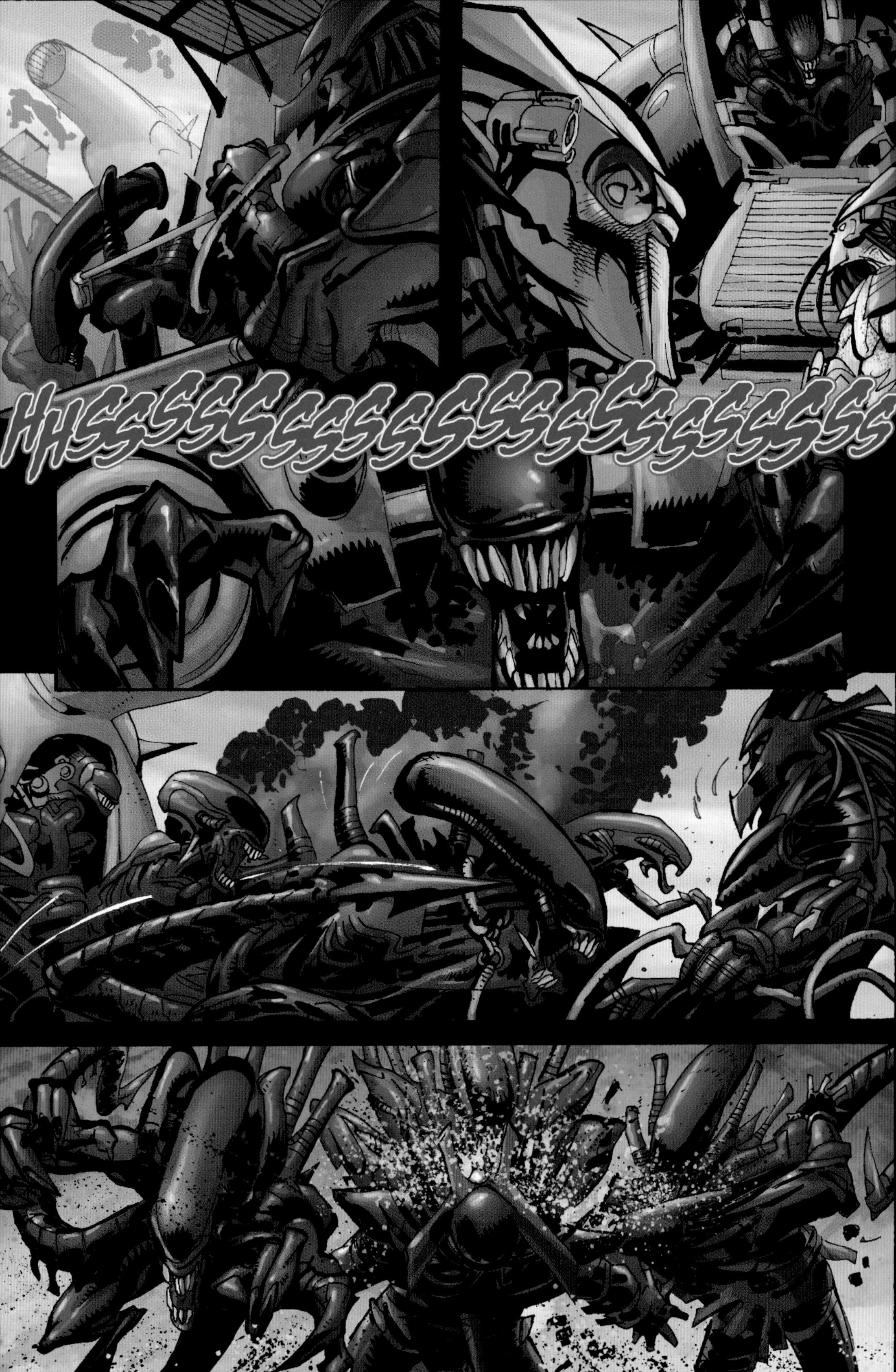
HHSSSSSSSSSSSSSSSSSSSS

SO, WHAT'S IT GONNA BE, ELLIS?

YOU HEARD MACHIKO, PRIMO. SHE SAID DON'T COME AFTER HER-- DON'T PUT ANYONE AT RISK.

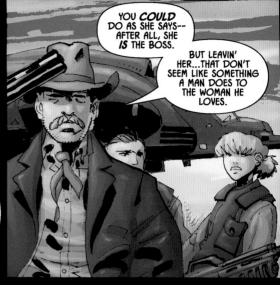

YOU *COULD* DO AS SHE SAYS-- AFTER ALL, SHE *IS* THE BOSS.

BUT LEAVIN' HER...THAT DON'T SEEM LIKE SOMETHING A MAN DOES TO THE WOMAN HE LOVES.

ROWDY'S RIGHT. IT SHOULD BE EASY. ALL YOU HAVE TO DO IS DECIDE WHO YOU CARE ABOUT MORE--

--HER, OR US.

MOUNT UP. WE'RE GOING IN.

ATTA BOY.

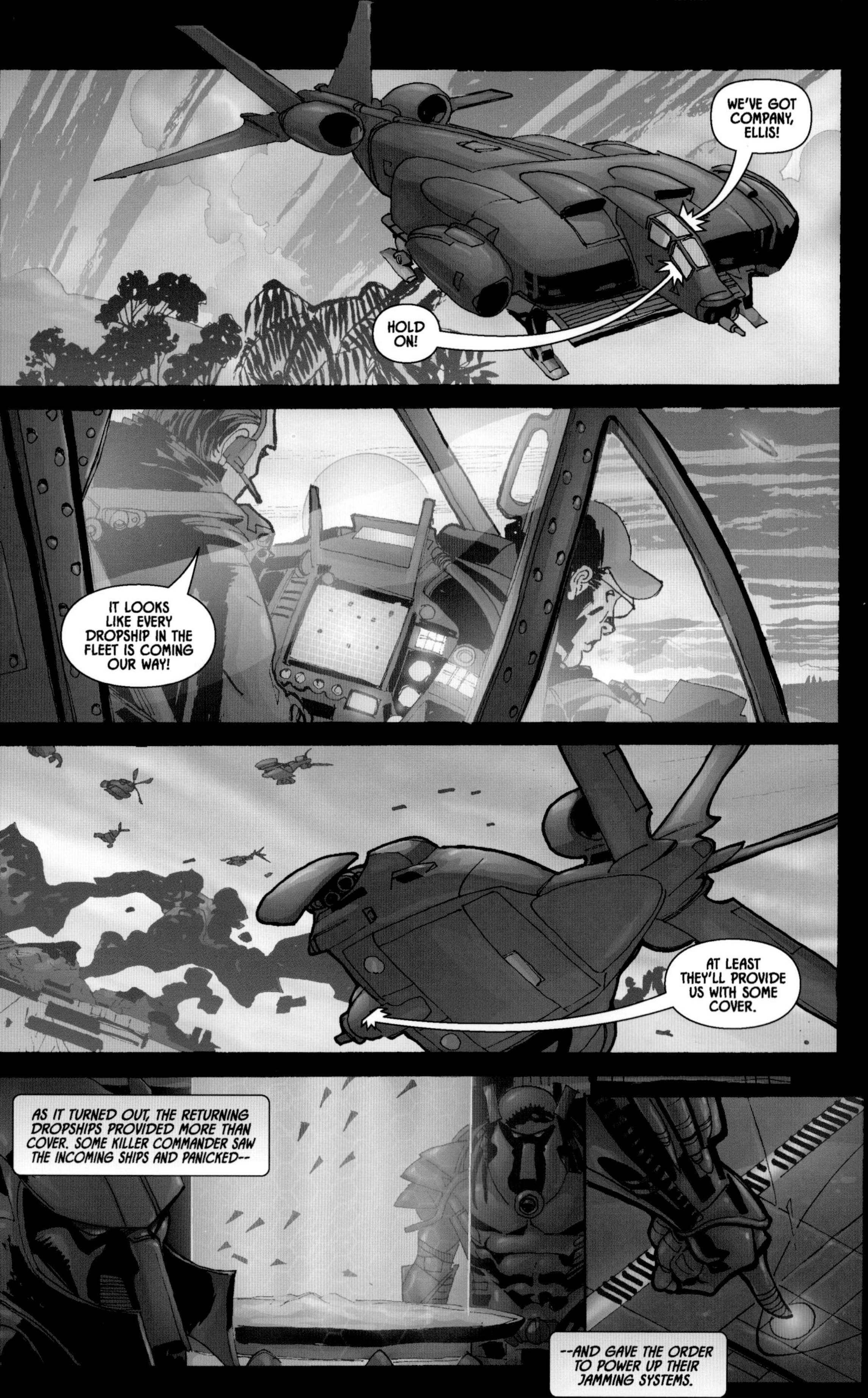
WE'VE GOT COMPANY, ELLIS!
HOLD ON!
IT LOOKS LIKE EVERY DROPSHIP IN THE FLEET IS COMING OUR WAY!
AT LEAST THEY'LL PROVIDE US WITH SOME COVER.
AS IT TURNED OUT, THE RETURNING DROPSHIPS PROVIDED MORE THAN COVER. SOME KILLER COMMANDER SAW THE INCOMING SHIPS AND PANICKED--
--AND GAVE THE ORDER TO POWER UP THEIR JAMMING SYSTEMS.

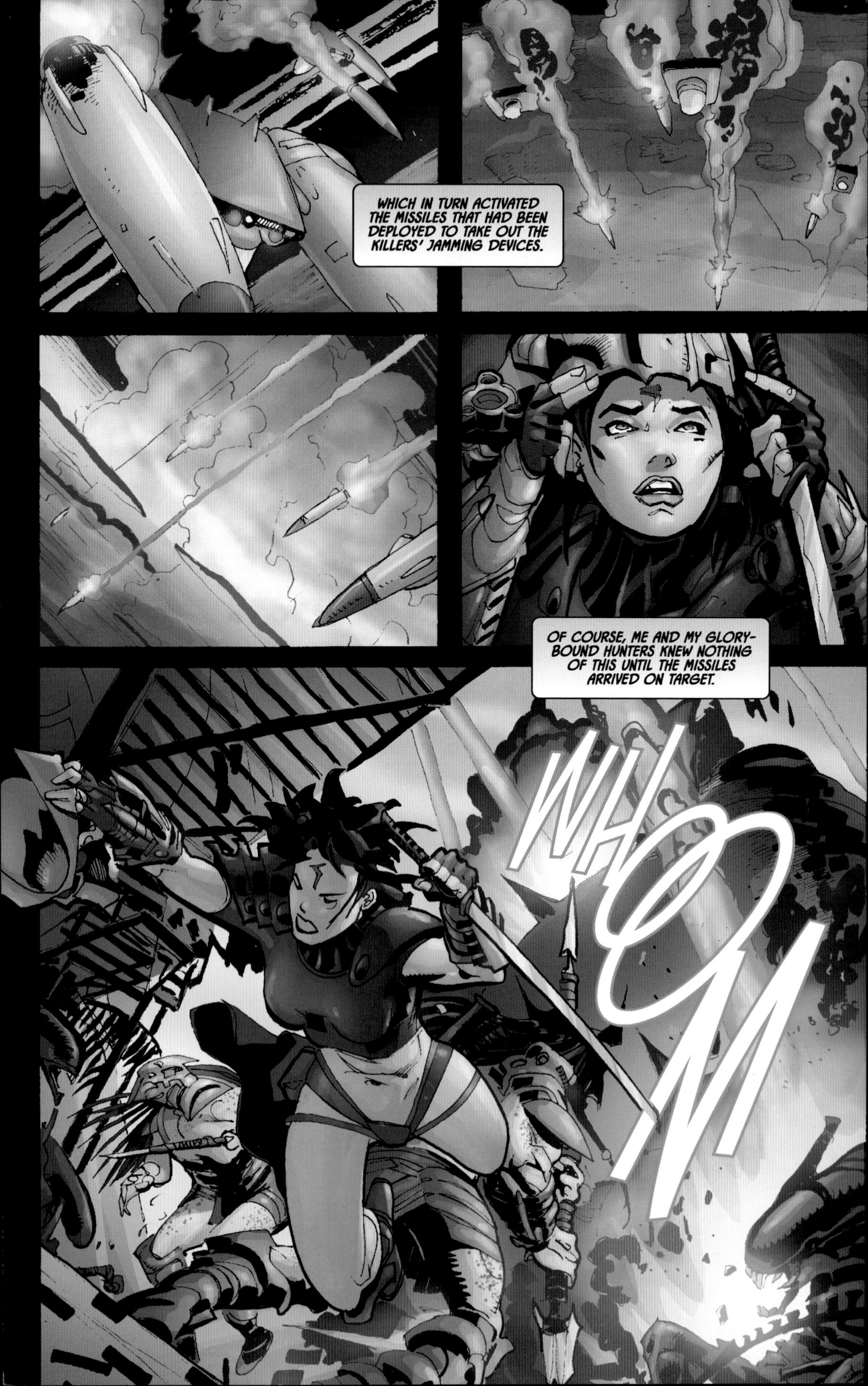
WHICH IN TURN ACTIVATED THE MISSILES THAT HAD BEEN DEPLOYED TO TAKE OUT THE KILLERS' JAMMING DEVICES.
OF COURSE, ME AND MY GLORY-BOUND HUNTERS KNEW NOTHING OF THIS UNTIL THE MISSILES ARRIVED ON TARGET.
WHOOM

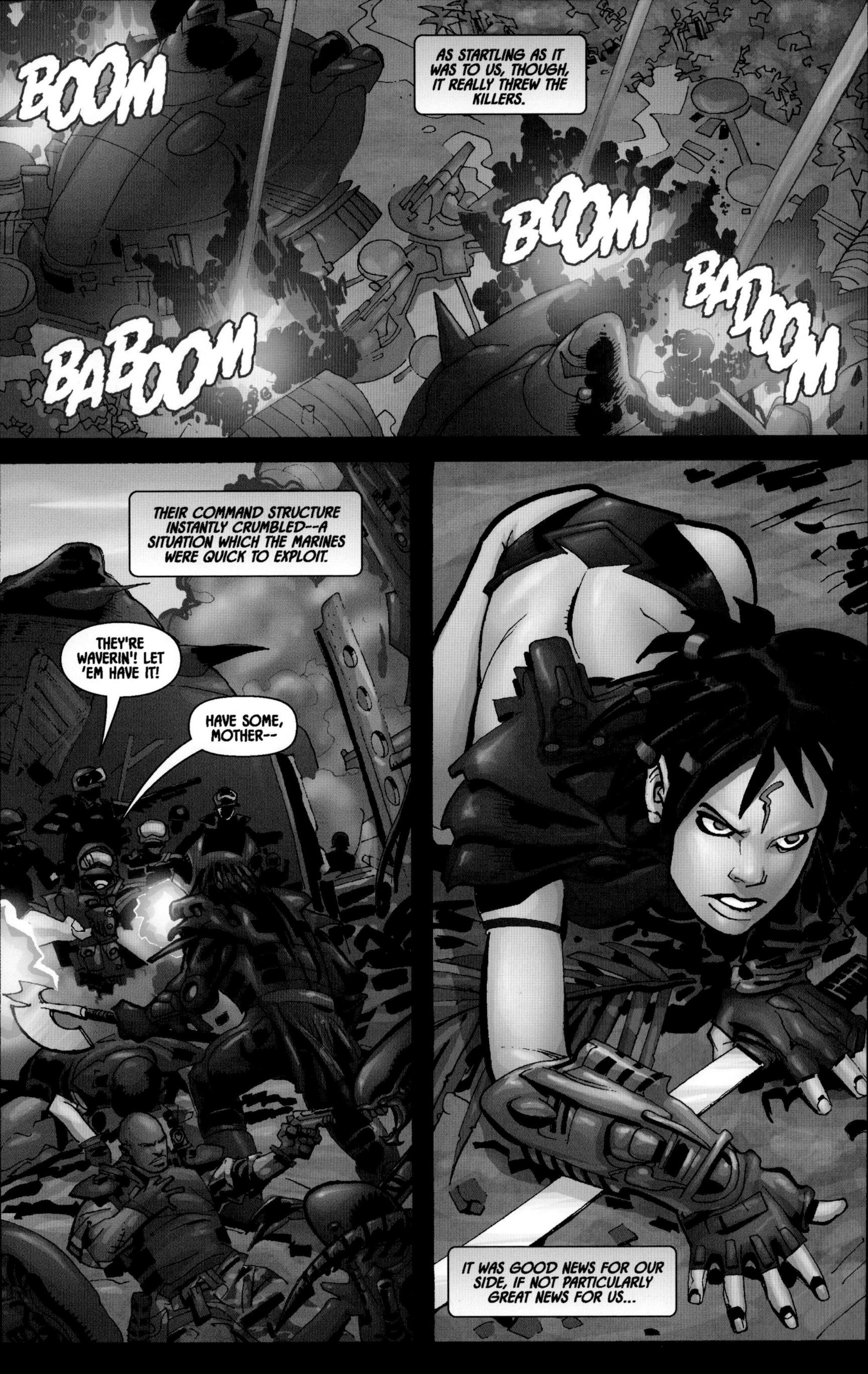
BOOM
AS STARTLING AS IT WAS TO US, THOUGH, IT REALLY THREW THE KILLERS.
BOOM
BADOOM
BABOOM
THEIR COMMAND STRUCTURE INSTANTLY CRUMBLED--A SITUATION WHICH THE MARINES WERE QUICK TO EXPLOIT.
THEY'RE WAVERIN'! LET 'EM HAVE IT!
HAVE SOME, MOTHER--
IT WAS GOOD NEWS FOR OUR SIDE, IF NOT PARTICULARLY GREAT NEWS FOR US...

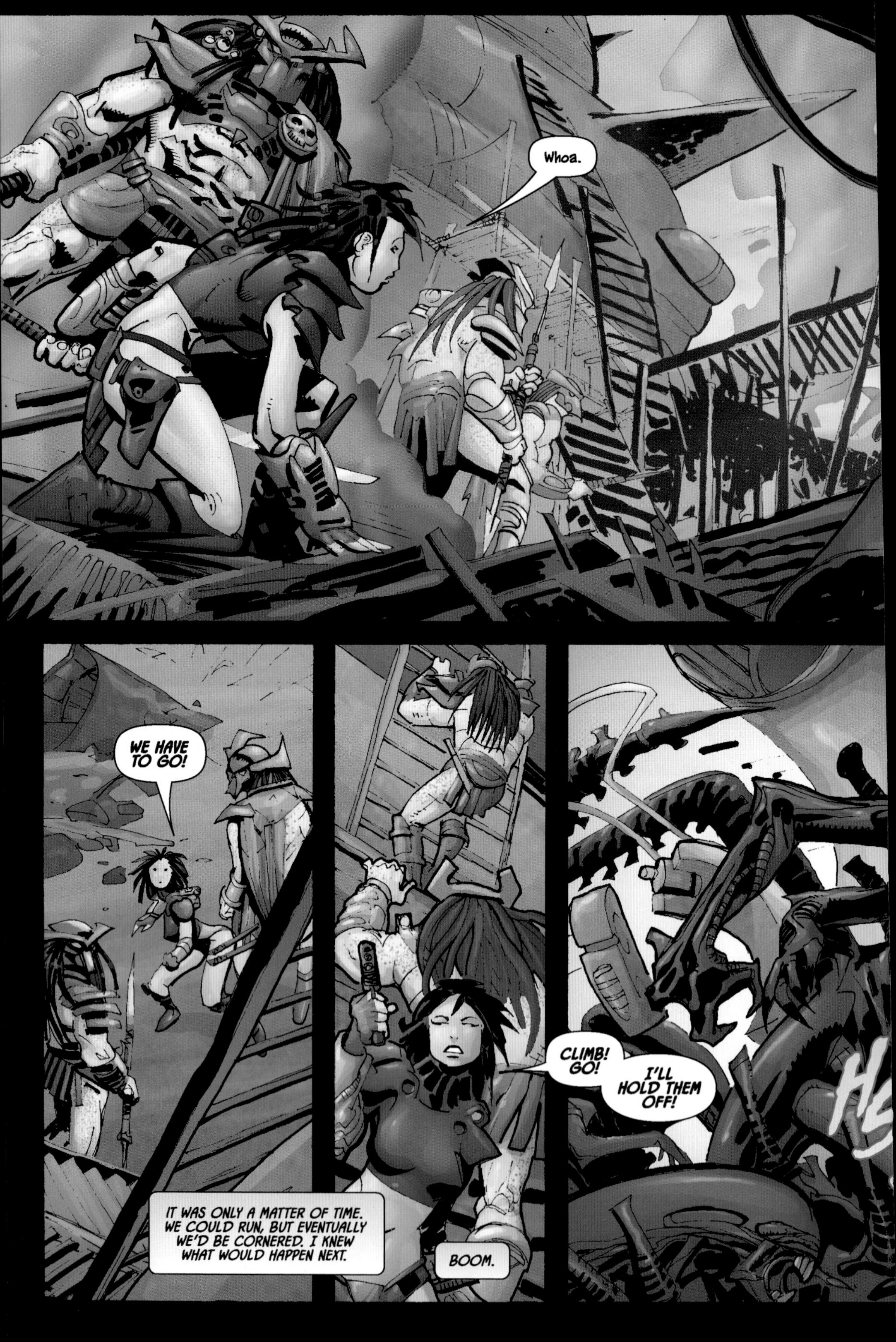
Whoa.
WE HAVE TO GO!
IT WAS ONLY A MATTER OF TIME. WE COULD RUN, BUT EVENTUALLY WE'D BE CORNERED. I KNEW WHAT WOULD HAPPEN NEXT.
CLIMB! GO!
I'LL HOLD THEM OFF!
BOOM.

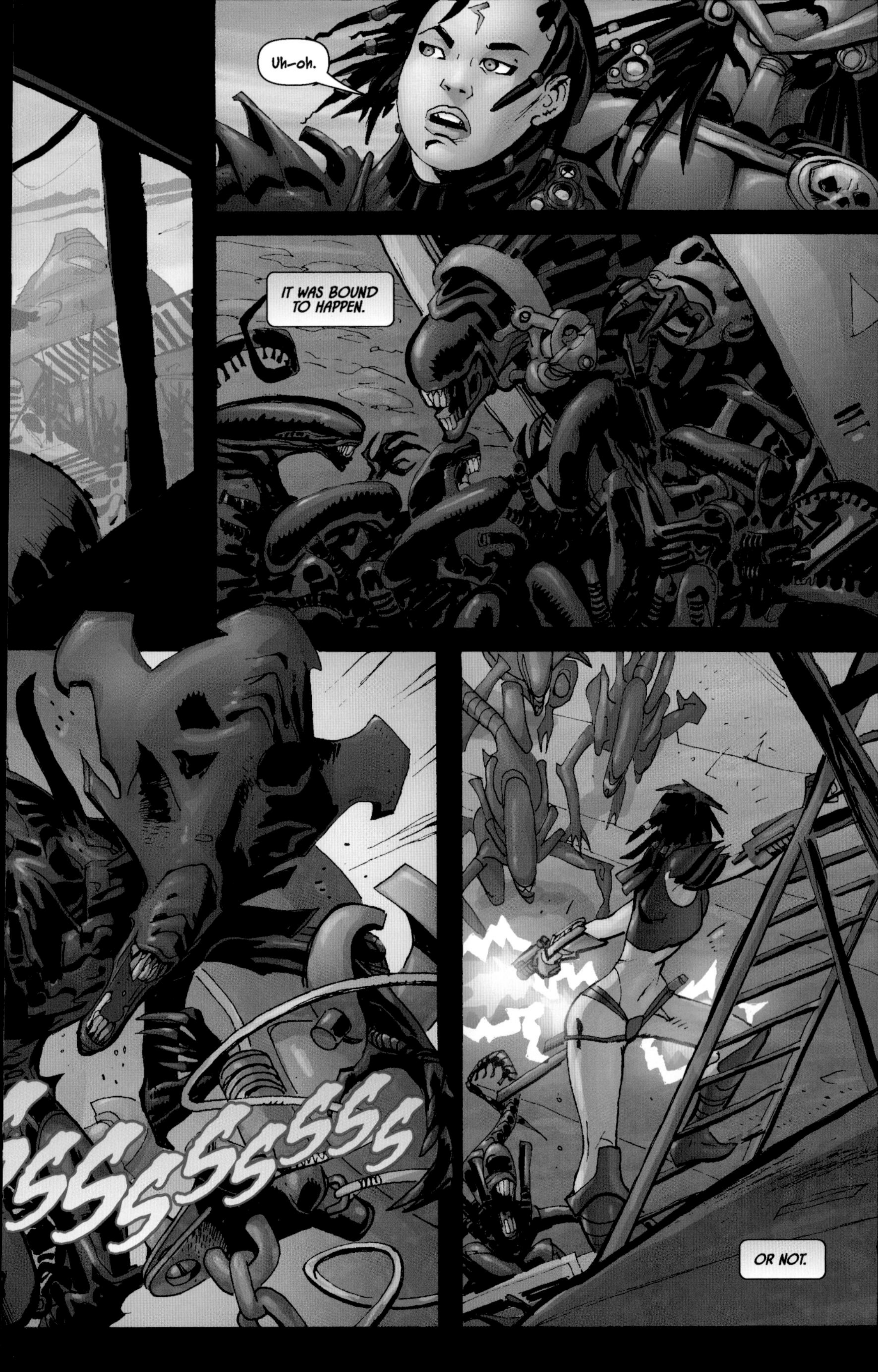
Uh-oh.
IT WAS BOUND TO HAPPEN.
SSSSSSSSS
OR NOT.

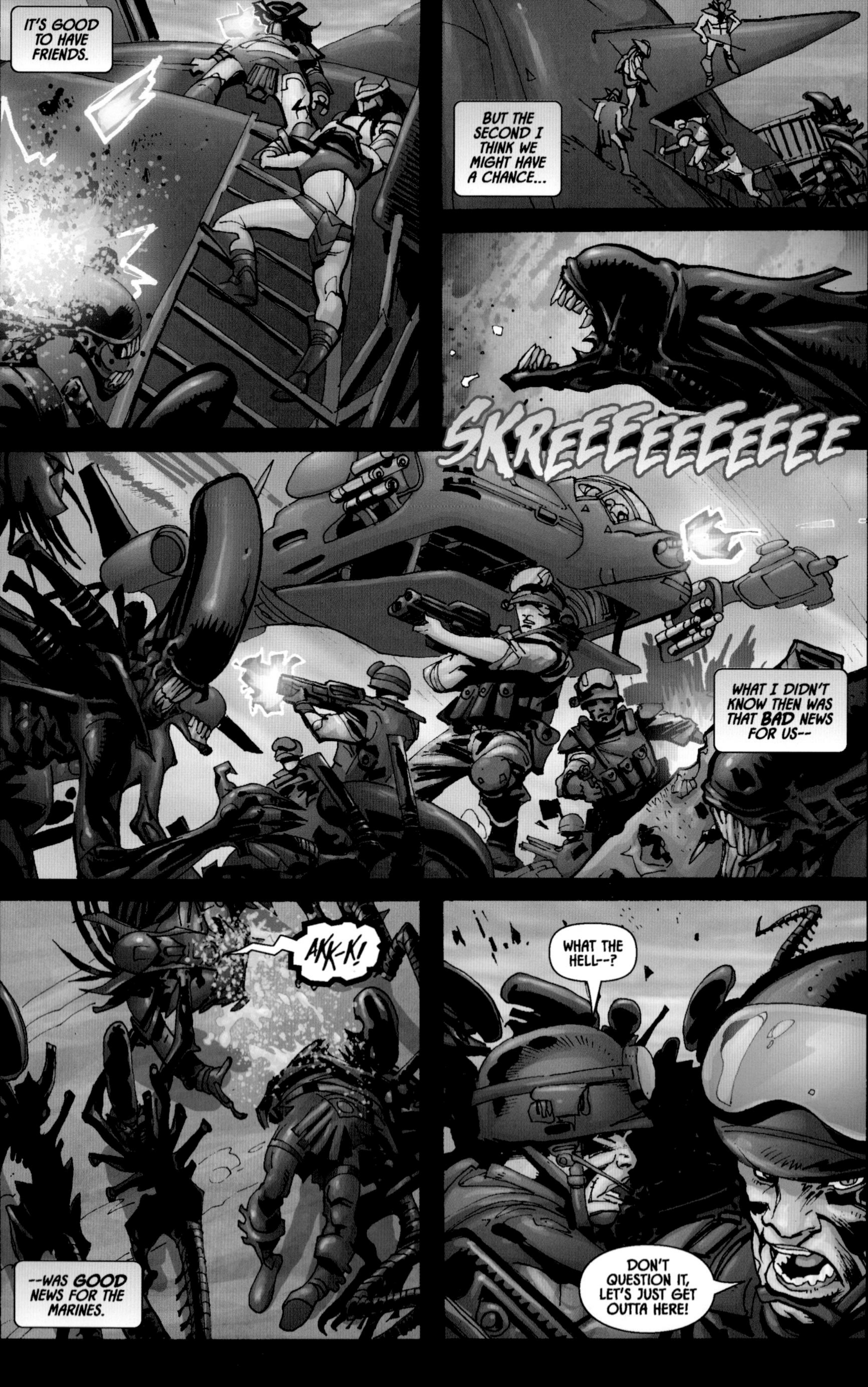
IT'S GOOD TO HAVE FRIENDS.
BUT THE SECOND I THINK WE MIGHT HAVE A CHANCE...
SKREEEEEEEEEEE
WHAT I DIDN'T KNOW THEN WAS THAT BAD NEWS FOR US--
AKK-K!
--WAS GOOD NEWS FOR THE MARINES.
WHAT THE HELL--?
DON'T QUESTION IT, LET'S JUST GET OUTTA HERE!

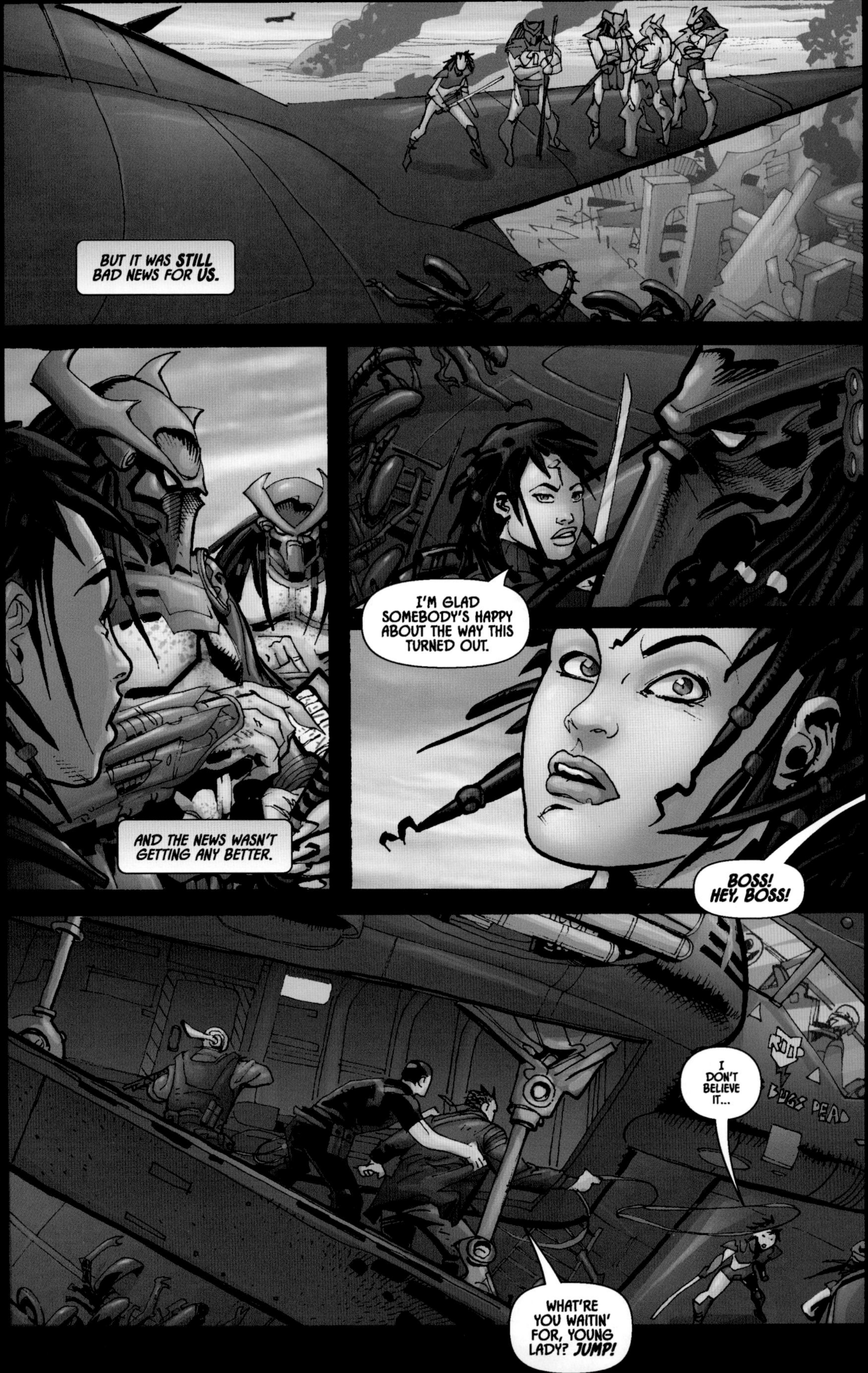
BUT IT WAS STILL BAD NEWS FOR US.
AND THE NEWS WASN'T GETTING ANY BETTER.
I'M GLAD SOMEBODY'S HAPPY ABOUT THE WAY THIS TURNED OUT.
BOSS! HEY, BOSS!
I DON'T BELIEVE IT...
WHAT'RE YOU WAITIN' FOR, YOUNG LADY? JUMP!

I'M READY TO GO, BUT I DON'T MOVE.

LEAVING WOULD BE THE ULTIMATE BETRAYAL--THE **DENIAL** OF GLORY.

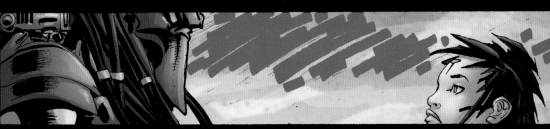

IS HE GOING TO USE MY OWN SWORD ON ME? MAYBE I **DESERVE** IT, BUT...

SLISH

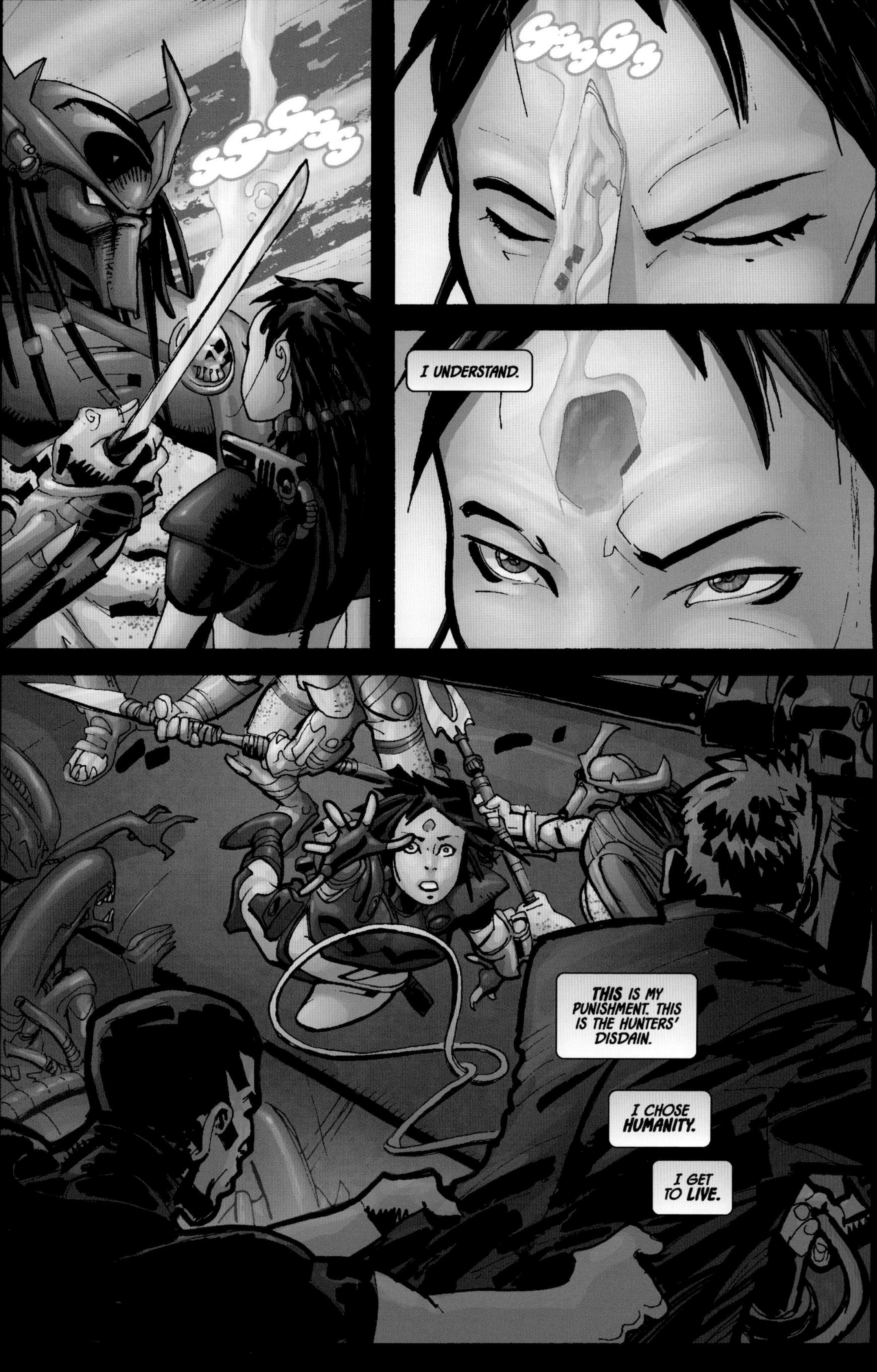
SSSSSS
SSSSS
I UNDERSTAND.
THIS IS MY PUNISHMENT. THIS IS THE HUNTERS' DISDAIN.
I CHOSE HUMANITY.
I GET TO LIVE.

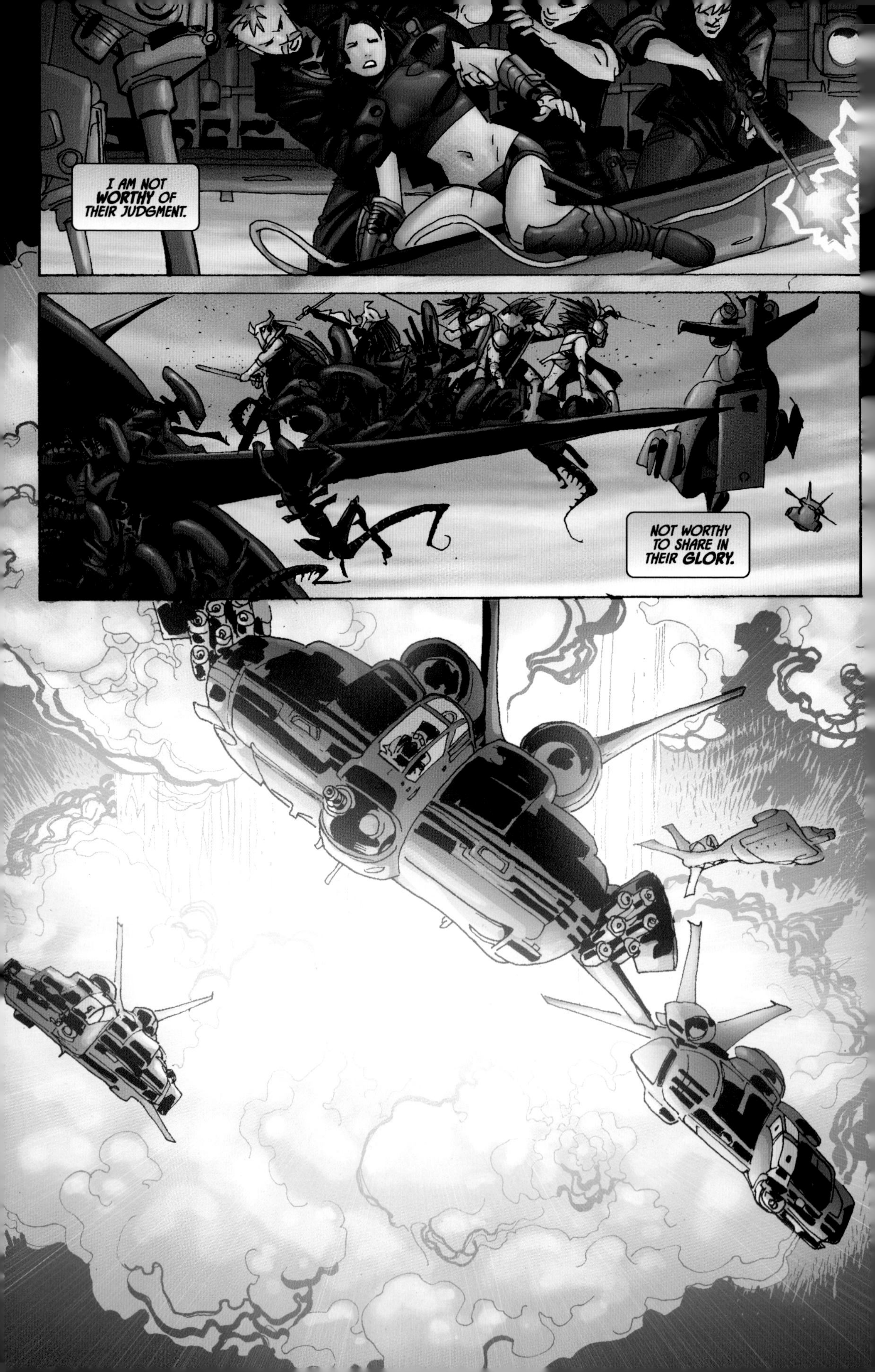
I AM NOT WORTHY OF THEIR JUDGMENT.
NOT WORTHY TO SHARE IN THEIR GLORY.

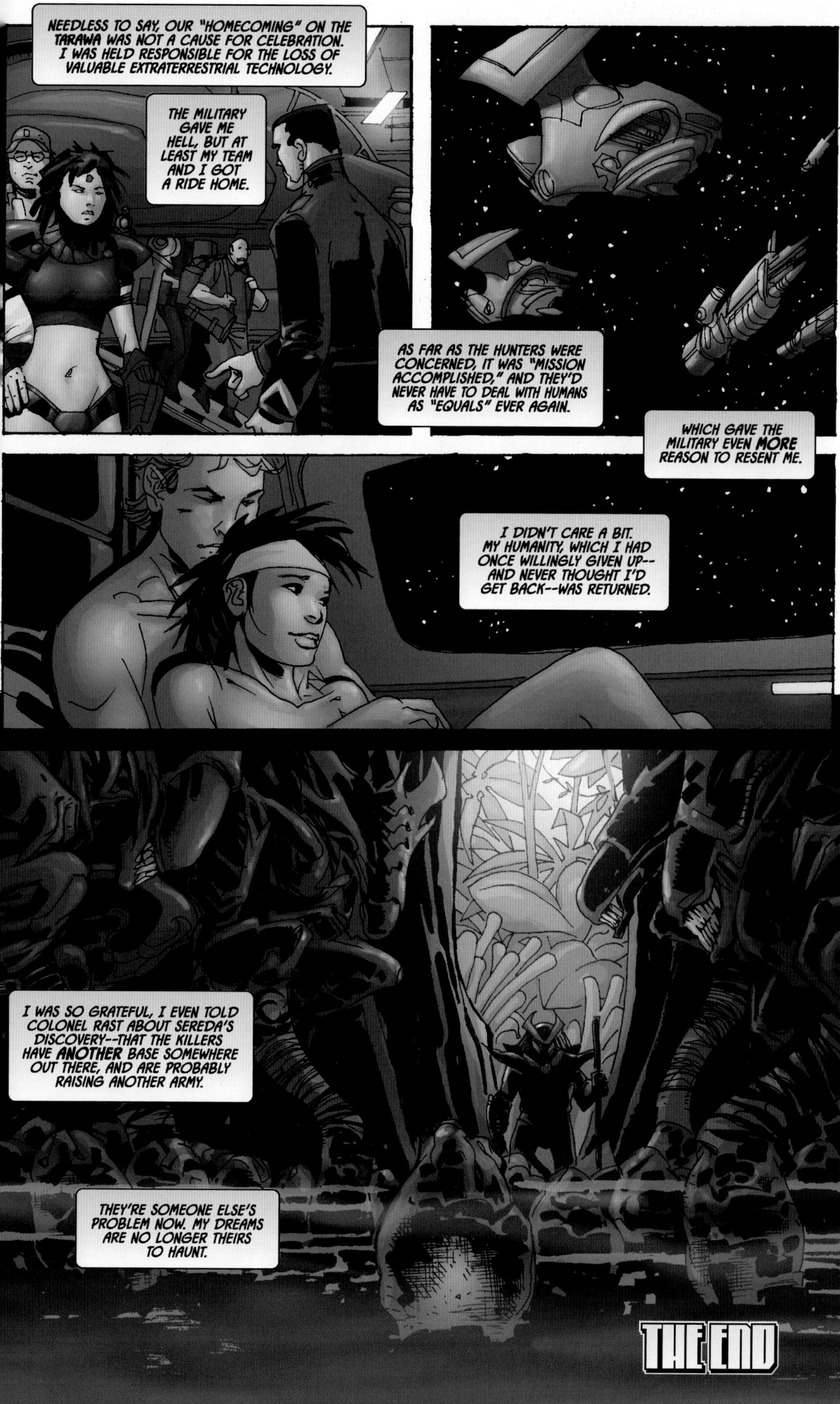
NEEDLESS TO SAY, OUR "HOMECOMING" ON THE TARAWA WAS NOT A CAUSE FOR CELEBRATION. I WAS HELD RESPONSIBLE FOR THE LOSS OF VALUABLE EXTRATERRESTRIAL TECHNOLOGY.
THE MILITARY GAVE ME HELL, BUT AT LEAST MY TEAM AND I GOT A RIDE HOME.
AS FAR AS THE HUNTERS WERE CONCERNED, IT WAS "MISSION ACCOMPLISHED," AND THEY'D NEVER HAVE TO DEAL WITH HUMANS AS "EQUALS" EVER AGAIN.
WHICH GAVE THE MILITARY EVEN MORE REASON TO RESENT ME.
I DIDN'T CARE A BIT. MY HUMANITY, WHICH I HAD ONCE WILLINGLY GIVEN UP--AND NEVER THOUGHT I'D GET BACK--WAS RETURNED.
I WAS SO GRATEFUL, I EVEN TOLD COLONEL RAST ABOUT SEREDA'S DISCOVERY--THAT THE KILLERS HAVE ANOTHER BASE SOMEWHERE OUT THERE, AND ARE PROBABLY RAISING ANOTHER ARMY.
THEY'RE SOMEONE ELSE'S PROBLEM NOW. MY DREAMS ARE NO LONGER THEIRS TO HAUNT.
THE END

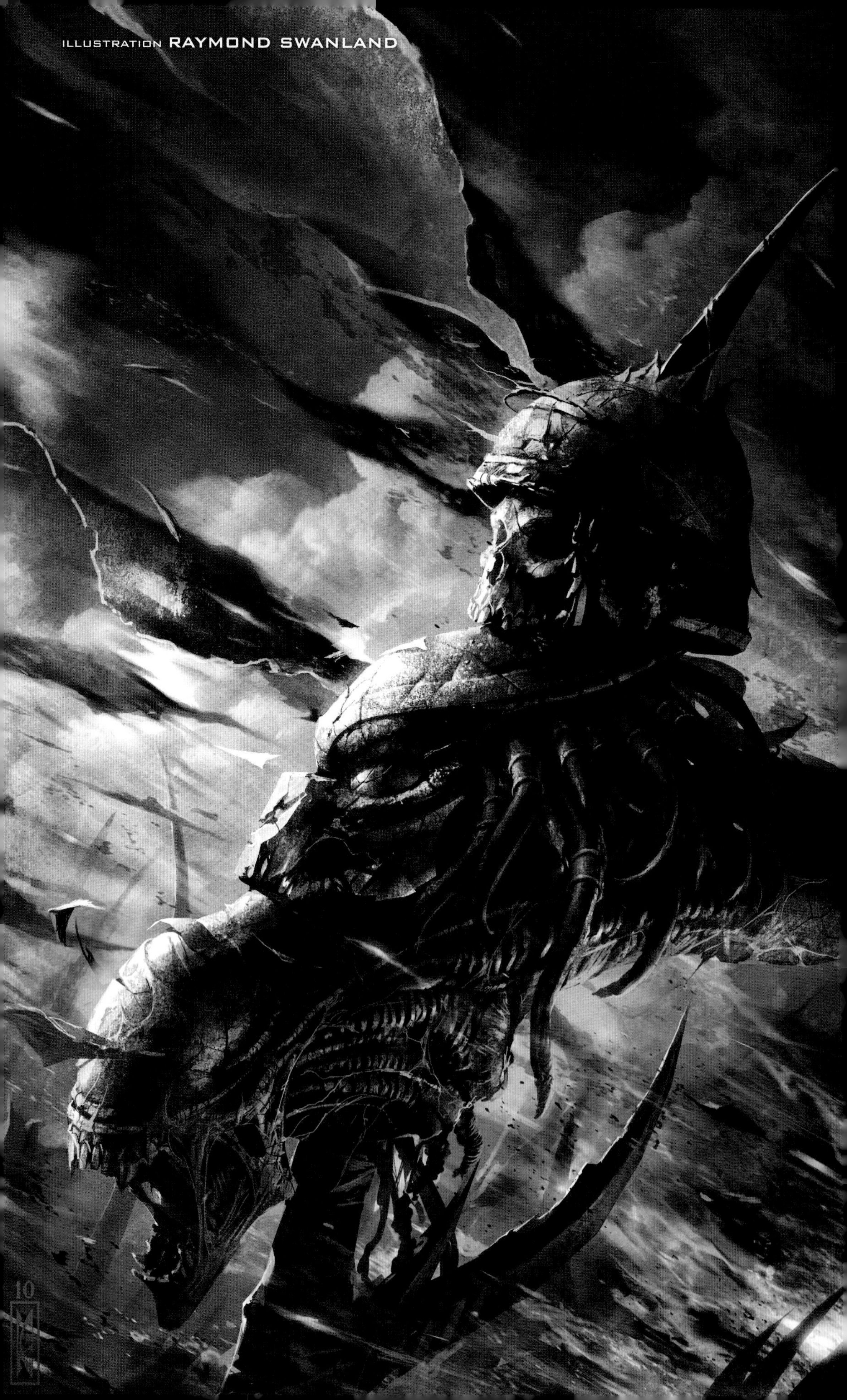
10

ILLUSTRATION RAYMOND SWANLAND

CREATOR BIOS

RANDY STRADLEY MAY BE BEST KNOWN AS COFOUNDER AND VICE PRESIDENT OF PUBLISHING OF DARK HORSE COMICS AND LEAD EDITOR OF DARK HORSE'S *STAR WARS* LINE, BUT HIS WRITING CREDITS ARE NO LESS IMPRESSIVE. RANDY PENNED THE VERY FIRST *ALIENS VS. PREDATOR* SERIES IN 1990, THE MOST SUCCESSFUL INDEPENDENT COMICS SERIES OF ITS TIME, AND THE SECOND ACT IN THE MACHIKO NOGUCHI *AVP* TRILOGY, *WAR*. RANDY HAS GONE ON TO WRITE MANY COMICS, INCLUDING A VARIETY OF POPULAR *STAR WARS* TITLES, AND EVEN SCRIPTED AN EPISODE OF *THE CLONE WARS*, "THE INNOCENTS OF RYLOTH."

RICK LEONARDI HAS BEEN AMONG THE MOST DISTINCTIVE COMICS PENCILERS SINCE BREAKING INTO THE PROFESSIONAL RANKS AT MARVEL IN THE 1980S. OVER HIS QUARTER-CENTURY CAREER RICK HAS ILLUSTRATED SOME OF THE INDUSTRY'S HEAVIEST-HITTING TITLES, INCLUDING *UNCANNY X-MEN*, *NEW MUTANTS*, *BATGIRL*, *NIGHTWING*, *SPIDER-MAN 2099*, AND *STAR WARS*. HIS FIRST FORAY INTO THE *AVP* UNIVERSE WAS IN 2000'S BLOCK-BUSTER *GREEN LANTERN VS. ALIENS* CROSSOVER SERIES. RICK RECENTLY RETURNED TO THE *STAR WARS* UNIVERSE, ILLUSTRATING *DARTH VADER AND THE LOST COMMAND*.

MARK PENNINGTON HAS BEEN WORKING IN THE COMICS AND COMMERCIAL-ART FIELDS SINCE GRADUATING FROM THE JOE KUBERT SCHOOL OF CARTOON AND GRAPHIC ART IN 1985. AS AN INKER, HE HAS WORKED EXTENSIVELY FOR A WIDE RANGE OF PUBLISHERS ON SUCH TITLES AS *X-FORCE*, *DAREDEVIL*, *FANTASTIC FOUR*, *STAR WARS*, AND *SHADE: THE CHANGING MAN*. MARK HAS ALSO DESIGNED TOYS FOR HASBRO AND MATTEL ON THE G.I. JOE AND TRANSFORMERS LINES AND HAS CONTRIBUTED NUMEROUS PAINTINGS TO TRADING-CARD GAMES SUCH AS LEGEND OF THE FIVE RINGS AND HACKMASTER.

WES DZIOBA HAS BROUGHT DAZZLING COLOR TO COMICS FOR OVER A DECADE, GETTING HIS START AT COMICS-COLORING STUDIOS DIGITAL CHAMELEON AND SNO CONE STUDIOS, AND MOVING ON AS AN INDEPENDENT COLORIST ON SUCH PROJECTS AS *EXILES*, *FORGOTTEN REALMS*, *STAR WARS*, *G.I. JOE VS. THE TRANSFORMERS: BLACK HORIZON*, AND *STAR WARS*. WES BROUGHT HIS DIGITAL PALETTE TO *ALIENS: MORE THAN HUMAN* AND *PREDATOR: PREY TO THE HEAVENS* PRIOR TO HIS SPECTACULAR WORK ON *THREE WORLD WAR*.

NATE PIEKOS, AKA BLAMBOT®, HAS CREATED SOME OF THE INDUSTRY'S MOST POPU-LAR FONTS AND USED THEM TO LETTER COMICS FOR DOZENS OF PUBLISHERS SINCE SETTING UP SHOP IN 1999, INCLUDING *ALIENS: MORE THAN HUMAN* AND *PREDATOR: PREY TO THE HEAVENS*, THE LEAD-IN STORIES TO *THREE WORLD WAR*. HIS TYPE DESIGNS HAVE APPEARED IN VIDEO GAMES, TELEVISION, AND FEATURE FILMS AND BEEN LICENSED BY COMPANIES LIKE MICROSOFT, SIX FLAGS AMUSEMENT PARKS, *THE NEW YORKER*, AND THE GAP.

RAYMOND SWANLAND'S STUNNING DIGITAL PAINTINGS HAVE GRACED NOVELS, COMIC BOOKS, ALBUMS, VIDEO GAMES, FEATURE FILMS, AND TRADING CARDS, HIS CLIENTS INCLUDING TOR BOOKS, NIGHT SHADE BOOKS, ODDWORLD INHABITANTS, ABRAMS BOOKS, AND WIZARDS OF THE COAST. WITH DARK HORSE'S RECENT *ALIENS: MORE THAN HUMAN*, *PREDATOR: PREY TO THE HEAVENS*, AND *ALIENS VS. PREDATOR: THREE WORLD WAR*, AND THE DARK HORSE RELAUNCHES OF *MAGNUS, ROBOT FIGHTER*; *TUROK, SON OF STONE*; AND *MIGHTY SAMSON*, SWANLAND HAS ESTABLISHED HIMSELF AS ONE OF FINEST COVER ILLUSTRATORS IN THE COMICS INDUSTRY.

ALIENS™

Mankind has fought for survival over countless millennia, but nothing has threatened humanity's existence like the murderous Alien scourge. While some have tried to use the creatures deadly abilities to serve their own selfish ends, no one can dance with the devil, and ultimately only one species must prevail. To that end, men have turned their own lethal instincts and cold intellect against the monsters, creating engineered plagues, cybernetic fighting suits, and even bogus android aliens; however survival rides not on technology, but on the primacy of the most deeprooted, feral instincts.

Dark Horse Comics' critically acclaimed *Aliens* series set the bar for how the universe of a popular film could be expanded through graphic fiction. The *Aliens Omnibus* collection presents these exciting series in value-priced, quality-format volumes, featuring the work of Mark Verheiden, Mike Mignola, Chris Claremont, John Arcudi, Doug Mahnke and more!

Aliens Omnibus Volume 1
ISBN 978-1-59307-727-3

Aliens Omnibus Volume 2
ISBN 978-1-59307-828-7

Aliens Omnibus Volume 3
ISBN 978-1-59307-872-0

Aliens Omnibus Volume 4
ISBN 978-1-59307-926-0

Aliens Omnibus Volume 5
ISBN 978-1-59307-991-8

Aliens Omnibus Volume 6
ISBN 978-1-59582-214-7

**Aliens vs. Predator Omnibus
Volume 1**
ISBN 978-1-59307-735-8

**Aliens vs. Predator Omnibus
Volume 2**
ISBN 978-1-59307-829-4

$24.99 each!

DARK HORSE BOOKS
darkhorse.com

AVAILABLE AT YOUR LOCAL COMICS SHOP OR BOOKSTORE!
To find a comics shop in your area, call 1-888-266-4226.
For more information or to order direct: • On the web: darkhorse.com • E-mail: mailorder@darkhorse.com • Phone: 1-800-862-0052 Mon.–Fri. 9 AM to 5 PM Pacific Time

PREDATOR™

Trophy hunters from another world, hiding in plain sight, drawn to heat and conflict. A historical scourge, lethal specters, powerful, savage, merciless. Utilizing their feral instincts and otherworldly technology in the sole pursuit of the most dangerous game . . . Man. Whether haunting the blazing deserts of the Southwest, stalking the claustrophobic woods of the Pine Barrens, or infiltrating a maximum security prison, the Predators take no prisoners and leave only death in their grisly wake. But even these bestial killing machines can meet their match when men swallow their fear and channel their own primal rage . . . and the hunter becomes the hunted!

These fantastic omnibus editions collect classic *Predator* comics in massive, value-packed editions, featuring work by top comics creators, including Mark Verheiden, Ron Randall, Mark Schultz, and Gene Colan.

Predator Omnibus

Volume 1
ISBN 978-1-59307-732-7

Volume 2
ISBN 978-1-59307-733-4

Volume 3
ISBN 978-1-59307-925-3

Volume 4
ISBN 978-1-59307-990-1

Aliens vs. Predator Omnibus

Volume 1
ISBN 978-1-59307-735-8

Volume 2
ISBN 978-1-59307-829-4

$24.99 each!

DARK HORSE BOOKS®
darkhorse.com

AVAILABLE AT YOUR LOCAL COMICS SHOP OR BOOKSTORE!
To find a comics shop in your area, call 1-888-266-4226.
For more information or to order direct: • On the web: darkhorse.com • E-mail: mailorder@darkhorse.com • Phone: 1-800-862-0052 Mon.–Fri. 9 AM to 5 PM Pacific Time

A L I E N S™

ALIENS: FAST TRACK TO HEAVEN
Script and art by Liam Sharp

Beneath the ice of Jupiter's moon, life teems in lightless oceans. But more spectacular discoveries elsewhere in the cosmos have left Europa's research facilities underfunded and ignored, a lonely wayside with an orbital station and a decaying space elevator. When one of the elevators stops midway, the rescue team discovers a deadly cargo that threatens life on Europa and on Earth.

ISBN 978-1-59582-495-0
$10.99

ALIENS: INHUMAN CONDITION
Written by John Layman
Art by Sam Kieth

On a distant, frozen world, "artificial persons" are manufactured in discreet seclusion. With formidable new security synthetics coming online, how better to test their mettle than against a hive of deadly xenomorphs? But as Socialization Specialist Jean DuPaul sees her ever-more-human android charges sent to their destruction, she learns that the most savage species in the universe is man.

ISBN 978-1-59582-618-3
$10.99

 TO FIND A COMICS SHOP IN YOUR AREA, CALL 1-888-266-4226. For more information or to order direct:
On the web: DarkHorse.com / E-mail: mailorder@darkhorse.com / Phone: 1-800-862-0052 Mon.–Fri. 9 AM to 5 PM Pacific Time.
Aliens™ & © 1986, 2005, 2006, 2007, 2013 Twentieth Century Fox Film Corporation. All rights reserved. Dark Horse Books® and the Dark Horse logo are registered trademarks of Dark Horse Comics, Inc. (BL 5099)

ALIENS VS. PREDATOR

MANKIND'S TWO ULTIMATE NIGHTMARES COME TOGETHER IN MORTAL COMBAT, AND WHOEVER WINS—WE LOSE!

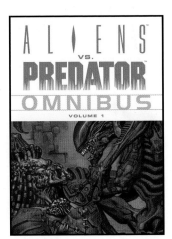

ALIENS VS. PREDATOR OMNIBUS VOLUME 1

On the remote planet Ryushi, a small community becomes an unwilling participant in a deadly ritual: extraterrestrial Predators have seeded Ryushi with Alien eggs in order to create the ultimate hunt. But what the Predators don't know is that an Alien queen egg is amongst those they've sent as potential hunting stock, and when the Predators arrive, the hunters become the hunted amidst a monumental swarm of Aliens, and they may need to turn to the very same humans they regard as little more than potential trophies to give them any hope of survival.

Aliens vs. Predator Omnibus Volume 1 packs over 400 pages of excitement and terror into one package, offering the original smash-hit *AVP* comics series that launched the franchise, plus the exciting continuation of the storyline previously published as *AVP: War*.
ISBN 978-1-59307-735-8

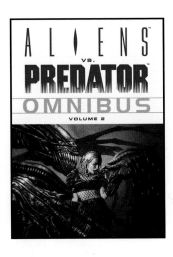

ALIENS VS. PREDATOR OMNIBUS VOLUME 2

In a skyliner high above the Alien-contaminated earth, Caryn Delacroix can't sleep. Terrifying images of pursuit, disfigurement, and bloody death have invaded her peaceful dreams in her safe and privileged world. But they're only nightmares . . . or are they? The beautiful trophy consort of corporate magnate Lucien Delacroix soon discovers that nightmares *do* come true and there are fates worse than death—when a Predator comes to call.

Featuring the smash-hit *AVP* epic *Deadliest of the Species*, written by Chris Claremont, plus other exciting *AVP* tales by a host of top comics creators.
ISBN 978-1-59307-829-4

$24.99 EACH

 DARK HORSE BOOKS®
darkhorse.com

AVAILABLE AT YOUR LOCAL COMICS SHOP OR BOOKSTORE!
To find a comics shop in your area, call 1-888-266-4226.
For more information or to order direct: • On the web: darkhorse.com • E-mail: mailorder@darkhorse.com • Phone: 1-800-862-0052 Mon.–Fri. 9 AM to 5 PM Pacific Time
Aliens vs. Predator Omnibus © 2011 Twentieth Century Fox Film Corporation. All rights reserved. TM indicates a trademark of Twentieth Century Fox Film Corporation. (BL5104)

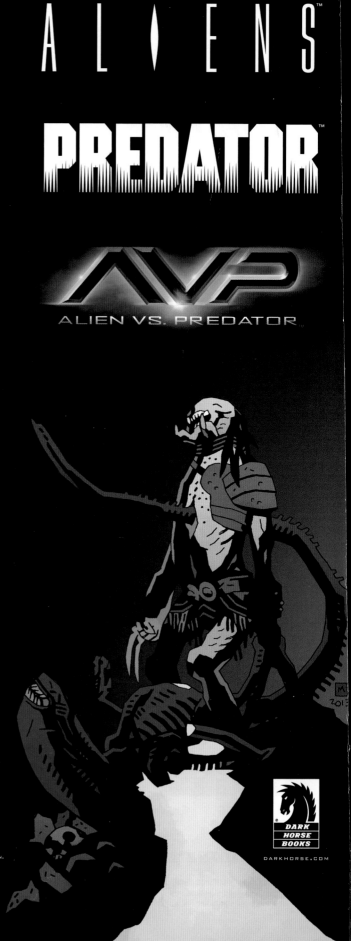

ALIENS OMNIBUS VOLUME 1
ISBN 978-1-59307-727-3
$24.99

ALIENS OMNIBUS VOLUME 2
ISBN 978-1-59307-828-7
$24.99

ALIENS OMNIBUS VOLUME 3
ISBN 978-1-59307-872-0
$24.99

ALIENS OMNIBUS VOLUME 4
ISBN 978-1-59307-926-0
$24.99

ALIENS: INHUMAN CONDITION
ISBN 978-1-59582-618-3
$10.99

ALIENS: MORE THAN HUMAN
ISBN 978-1-59582-490-5
$15.99

ALIENS: FAST TRACK TO HEAVEN
ISBN 978-1-59582-495-0
$10.99

ALIENS vs. PREDATOR OMNIBUS
VOLUME 1
ISBN 978-1-59307-735-8
$24.99

ALIENS vs. PREDATOR OMNIBUS
VOLUME 2
ISBN 978-1-59307-829-4
$24.99

ALIENS VS. PREDATOR:
THREE WORLD WAR
ISBN 978-1-59582-702-9
$19.99

ALIENS/PREDATOR:
PANEL TO PANEL
ISBN 978-1-59307-479-1
$19.99

PREDATOR OMNIBUS VOLUME 1
ISBN 978-1-59307-732-7
$24.99

PREDATOR OMNIBUS VOLUME 2
ISBN 978-1-59307-733-4
$24.99

PREDATOR OMNIBUS VOLUME 3
ISBN 978-1-59307-925-3
$24.99

PREDATOR OMNIBUS VOLUME 4
ISBN 978-1-59307-990-1
$24.99

PREDATOR: PREY TO THE HEAVENS
ISBN 978-1-59582-492-9
$15.99

PROMETHEUS: FIRE AND STONE
ISBN 978-1-61655-650-1
$14.99

ALIENS: FIRE AND STONE
ISBN 978-1-61655-655-6
$14.99

ALIEN vs. PREDATOR: FIRE AND STONE
ISBN 978-1-61655-691-4
$14.99

PREDATOR: FIRE AND STONE
ISBN 978-1-61655-695-2
$14.99

AVAILABLE AT YOUR LOCAL COMICS SHOP OR BOOKSTORE. TO FIND A COMICS SHOP IN YOUR AREA, CALL 1-888-266-4226. FOR MORE INFORMATION OR TO ORDER DIRECT: ON THE WEB: DARKHORSE.COM, E-MAIL: MAILORDER@DARKHORSE.COM, PHONE: 1-800-862-0052 MON.-FRI. 9 A.M. TO 5 P.M PACIFIC TIME.

ALIENS™

PREDATOR™

AVP
ALIEN VS. PREDATOR

DARK HORSE BOOKS
DARKHORSE.COM